PUERTO RICO: AN INTERPRETIVE HISTORY FROM PRE-COLUMBIAN TIMES TO 1900

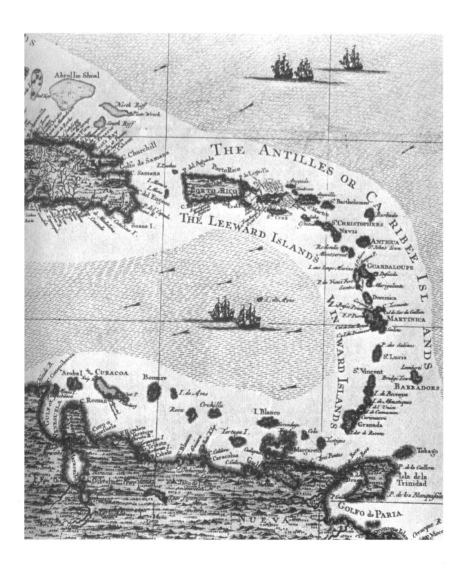

To Kal, and our children, David and María

Puerto Rico:
An Interpretive History
from Pre-Columbian Times
to 1900

OLGA JIMÉNEZ DE WAGENHEIM

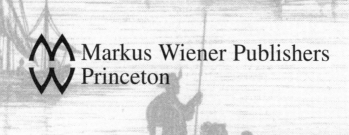

Markus Wiener Publishers
Princeton

COPYRIGHT © 1998 BY OLGA JIMÉNEZ DE WAGENHEIM.

FOR INFORMATION WRITE TO: MARKUS WIENER PUBLISHERS
231 NASSAU STREET, PRINCETON, NJ 08542

EDITED BY LEON KING

BOOK DESIGN BY CHERYL MIRKIN

THIS BOOK HAS BEEN COMPOSED IN TIMES ROMAN
BY CMF GRAPHIC DESIGN

PHOTOS COURTESY OF KAL WAGENHEIM ARCHIVES

LIBRARY OF CONGRESS CATALOGING-IN-PUBLICATION DATA

WAGENHEIM, OLGA JIMÉNEZ DE.
PUERTO RICO: AN INTERPRETIVE HISTORY FROM PRE-COLUMBIAN TIMES TO 1900/
BY OLGA JIMÉNEZ DE WAGENHEIM.
INCLUDES BIBLIOGRAPHICAL REFERENCES AND INDEX.
ISBN 1-55876-121-7 (HC: ALK. PAPER)
ISBN 1-55876-122-5 (PB: ALK. PAPER)
1. PUERTO RICO—HISTORY—TO 1898.
2. PUERTO RICO—HISTORY—1898-1952.   I. TITLE
F1973.W33   1997
972.95—DC21 B   97-36076   CIP

PRINTED IN THE UNITED STATES OF AMERICA ON ACID-FREE PAPER.

Contents

One of the earliest known maps of Puerto Rico

Preface

This book was written out of a desire to present the history of Puerto Rico as part of the history of the Caribbean, Latin America and Europe. Much too often the island is presented in isolation, except for the obligatory references to the colonizing metropolis.

To place the island's history in a broader context, I reread many of the chronicles and documents of the pre-twentieth century period and revisited many of the topics already studied by other scholars. I reviewed also the latest original research on a variety of topics, including my own extensive research on the nineteenth century society, and Lares' economy and uprising. This approach has yielded a much less insular history, which uncovers new meanings, raises new questions, adds new findings, and provides new leads for further research.

For example, in this work, I challenge the commonly accepted notion that the Tainos simply gave up at the first sign of provocation by the Spaniards. Instead, I highlight the fact (supported by literature of the period) that they not only fought the Spaniards, but continued to resist them for more than sixty years after the battle of Yagüecas.

Aware that many of the documents about Puerto Rico were written by the colonizer, I have purposely written this book from the viewpoint of the colonized. From that vantage point, I have chosen to highlight the struggle of the Puerto Ricans who have sought to take control of the island's destiny. But since the colonial society was itself divided along economic, racial, and ideological lines, I have also highlighted the internal tensions.

I provide a profile of Africa prior to the European conquest of America, and discuss the fate and roles of the Africans, who as slaves, or as free persons, became instrumental in Puerto Rico's social and economic development.

I also make it a point to include and depict women as active social agents, even though the documentary evidence I found for this group was at best fragmentary. In many instances, I had to piece together bits of data gleaned from official reports on education and the population, notarial records, works of fiction, and many other sources.

Finally, this volume was written out of necessity. For years, I, and many of my colleagues who teach Puerto Rican Studies, have struggled with the reality that there are so few materials in print in English that we can assign to our students. To date, there is only one general history of Puerto Rico in English still available for classroom use, and this is already 14 years old. There are, of course, numerous monographs in English, but their specialized nature, and often exorbitant costs, makes these hard to use other than as occasional supplementary readings. There are many excellent works and several general histories of Puerto Rico in Spanish, but these can not be assigned to the English-only reader.

The aim of this volume is to bridge part of this gap by making available in English a historical account of a large portion of Puerto Rico's development. Intended for the college student and the general reader, the book is organized thematically, within a chronological framework, and written in a jargon-free style. The present volume covers Puerto Rico's history until the year 1900. A second volume, covering the twentieth century, will be written separately.

Acknowledgements

Over the last twenty years, I have taught, lectured, and written on topics related to Puerto Rico. This book reflects my long acquaintance with the subject. It reflects also my debt to others in the field.

I am particularly indebted to the old master historian Salvador Brau, for showing us the way of national history; to Lidio Cruz-Monclova, Aida Caro-Costas, Loida Figueroa, Germán Delgado-Pasapera, and Arturo Morales-Carrión, for keeping alive the tradition started by Brau. I owe also a debt of thanks to many of my contemporaries and several younger scholars whose works have helped to enrich my own. Among the latter, I especially wish to recognize the generosity of María Barceló-Miller, Gladys Jiménez-Muñoz, and Felix Matos-Rodríguez for sending me copies of their dissertations and/or papers.

This work has also benefited from the critical advice and encouragement of my editor, Léon King, who patiently read and commented on every page of this work. He, of course, is not responsible for the shortcomings of this book.

I owe a debt of thanks to my colleagues Asela Rodríguez de Laguna and Virginia Sánchez-Korrol, and to my husband, Kal Wagenheim, for their comments and suggestions on earlier versions of some chapters. Lastly, I want to thank my family, friends, and students who listened patiently to my long-winded accounts about the project. Their encouragement and support helped me to continue.

Taino Indian ceremonial ballfield site

CHAPTER ONE

The Land and the Amerindians

The island of Puerto Rico lies on the northeast periphery of the Caribbean Sea and forms part of a cluster of 7,000 islands of various shapes and sizes. The area occupied by these islands is known as the West Indies, the Antilles and the Caribbean.[1]

The terms Antilles and West Indies were presumably derived from references Christopher Columbus made about the lands he sighted or explored during the 1490s. Bound for the Asian land of the fabled Kublai Khan, he thought he was in the vicinity of Asia when he landed in Cubanacán (Cuba). By his third voyage (1498), as the fabled city continued to elude him, Columbus conceded that he might have instead reached "Antilia", a land mass reported to exist between Europe and Asia by fifteenth century cartographers. At the very least, he reasoned, these islands were not very far from India. Thus, the terms Indians and Antilles were subsequently applied to the inhabitants and the region.

The term Caribbean, applied to the region later by other Europeans, was derived from the name Carib, one of the Indo-American groups that for centuries had inhabited parts of northern South America and many of the islands south of Puerto Rico.

The Islands and the Sea

The West Indies form a 2,500 mile arc in the Caribbean Sea, which begins at the southern tip of Florida and ends at the north-east coast of Venezuela.[2] The islands are generally subdivided into three main groups: the Bahamas, the Greater Antilles, and the Lesser Antilles. The Bahamas,

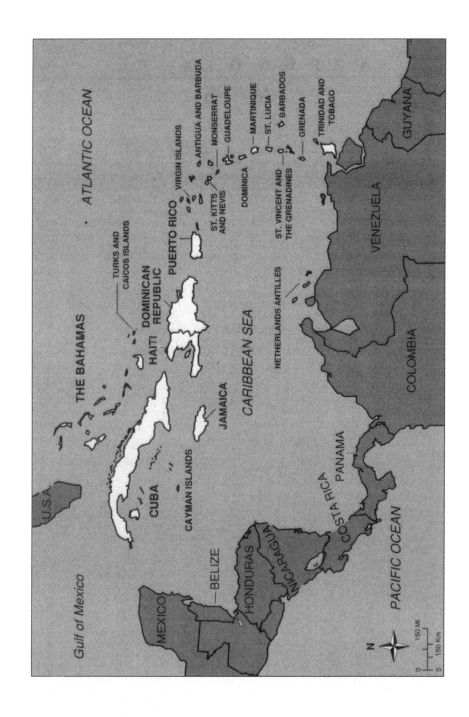

a group of approximately 700 small islands and islets which comprise an area of 4,403 square miles, lay in the Atlantic Ocean, north of where it meets with the Caribbean. The Greater Antilles form the greater land mass and include Cuba, Hispaniola (shared by Haiti and the Dominican Republic), Jamaica, and Puerto Rico. The Lesser Antilles, which curve southeast from Puerto Rico to the northeast coast of Venezuela, are themselves subdivided into two groups, known as the Leeward and the Windward Islands.

The Caribbean Sea, one of the larger branches of the Atlantic Ocean, stretches 1,800 miles east-west and 900 miles north-south. It covers a total area of 750,000 square miles, but only one-eighth of the Caribbean region (approximately 87,000 miles) is dry land.[3]

The Caribbean basin rests on a large rocky bottom of valleys and submerged mountains that rise gradually to the surface. The islands are the exposed tops of these mountains. The channels that link the Caribbean to the Atlantic are formed by great precipices between the mountains.

Geographical Similarity

Most Caribbean islands share a similar topography, climate, flora and fauna.[4] All of the Greater Antilles, except Cuba are traversed by an east-west mountain range. The highest peak, measuring 10,200 feet, is found in the Dominican Republic.

Rainfall is generally high, except in some of the southernmost territories. Most islands have short, fast flowing rivers, which are navigable by small vessels and only along brief stretches. The longest rivers, measuring about 250 miles, are the Cauto in Cuba and the Yaque del Norte in the Dominican Republic. Some of the islands of the Lesser Antilles have no rivers at all, depending on streams, waterfalls, and springs as sources of fresh water.

The Caribbean Islands are volcanic in origin, but have only three active volcanoes. Mont Pelée in Martinique, Soufrière in St. Vincent and Soufrière Hills in Monserrat, which last erupted in 1997.[5]

Puerto Rico and Its Island Territories

Puerto Rico is the smallest and easternmost island of the Greater Antilles. Its territory is composed of Puerto Rico, the largest island, the

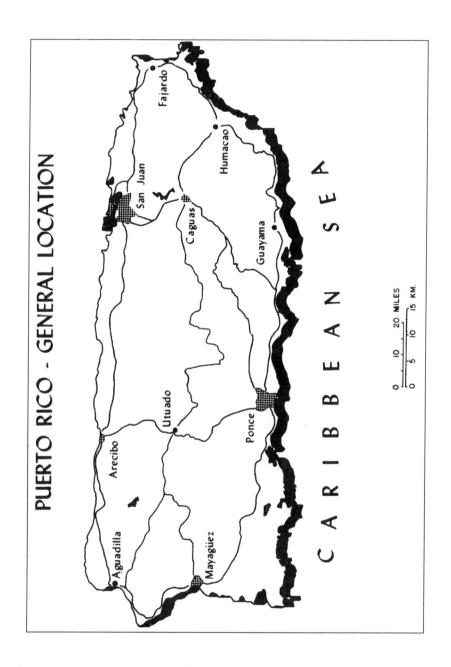

islet of San Juan, to the north, the isles of Mona, Monito, and Desecheo, to the west, Caja de Muerto, to the south, and Vieques and Culebra, to the east.[6]

Puerto Rico is shaped like a parallelogram and measures one hundred miles east-west by thirty-six miles north-south. Its total land area, including its offshore islands, is 3,435 square miles. Puerto Rico is one thirteenth as large as Cuba and one-sixth the size of the Dominican Republic.

Puerto Rico's north coast faces the Atlantic Ocean, while its eastern and southern shores face the Caribbean Sea. The island is separated from the Dominican Republic, to the west, by the Mona Channel. It is centrally located between North and South America, from which Havana, Cuba is merely 480 miles west, Caracas, Venezuela 550 miles south, Miami, Florida 1050 miles north-west, and New York 1,662 miles north-east.

Origin, Ecology and Topography

Puerto Rico is the exposed crest of a large underwater mountain which was volcanic in origin.[7] Two miles from its north coast, the sea floor drops 600 feet from the surface, while forty-five miles further north, the sea floor drops about 28,000 feet, creating the Milwaukee Deep, one of the largest chasms in the world.

Three quarters of Puerto Rico's terrain is hilly or mountainous, giving the island much variety in its landscape and geological formations. In a day's journey one can observe physical differences ranging from the coastal plains to the Cordillera Central, the interior mountain range that traverses the island from east to west; from the limestone "haystacks" and "sinkholes" near the north coast to desert terrain in the south. The highest peak on the island is Cerro de Punta (4,398 feet high), near the municipality of Jayuya. Yet, the best known Puerto Rican peak is El Yunque ("The Anvil"), located in the Luquillo Mountain Range, which measures 3,483 feet above sea level.

Puerto Rico has several topographical regions, ranging from the rich, well-watered, five-mile northern strip to the east coast valley, stretching from Fajardo to Cape Pascua, to the semiarid south coast.

Lakes, Rivers, and Climate

Puerto Rico has two natural lakes: Joyuda and Tortuguero. Its best-known lakes are Dos Bocas, Loíza, and Guajataca, three of the sixteen artificial lakes that were built during this century. Puerto Rico has over 1,000 watercourses, of which barely fifty are large enough to be called rivers. Of these, the largest ones (although none are navigable with large ships) are found in the northern strip of the island that faces the Atlantic Ocean. The strongest rivers flow down from the Cordillera, or central mountain range, to the north coast. Among these, the best known is the Loíza, which flows into the Atlantic just east of San Juan. The longest is the Río de la Plata, about forty-six miles, which meanders northward from Cayey to Dorado along the Atlantic shore.

The rivers of the island's southern region are short, fast-flowing bodies of water which empty into the Caribbean Sea. Of these, the best known are the Río Loco of Yauco, the Coamo, and the Río Grande of Patillas. The Río Grande of Añasco, the second longest river on the island, flows through the western lands, along with the Culebrinas and the Guanajibo.

Puerto Rico is in the torrid zone, but its distance from the Equator and the steady trade winds that blow from the northeast make for a pleasant climate. The average temperature in the summer months is about eighty-five degrees Fahrenheit and a cooler seventy degrees in the winter.

Areas near the shore and closer to the mountains in the interior are much cooler than those in the flatlands far from the shore. Every 500 feet of altitude means a drop of one degree in temperature. Thus, mountain towns such as Aibonito and Lares are generally between five and ten degrees cooler than coastal towns.

Although the island has experienced severe droughts over the centuries, it receives some 3,600 million gallons of rain a year. Rain falls more regularly in the highlands, about 108 inches, than in the southern plains, which average under forty inches a year. The El Yunque Rain Forest in the eastern region of the island is sprinkled daily by brief showers, averaging somewhere between 150 and 180 inches of rain a year. Declared a National Rain Forest during this century, El Yunque contains over 200 tree species, orchids, ferns, and a variety of birds.

The wet season in Puerto Rico generally lasts from May to November, and from December to April the weather turns dry. At times the rainfall turns erratic, flooding parts of the island, only to be followed by severe droughts.

Puerto Rico, like other Caribbean islands, lays in the path of tropical storms and hurricanes. The word "hurricane" is itself taken from the Arawak language. Until recently it was believed that the word stood for the deeds of a god the Tainos called "Juracán", but Professor Jalil Sued-Badillo contends that the Tainos believed that these were unleashed by the goddess Guabancex when angered.[8] Hurricane tales of destruction, poems, and popular songs have been woven into the folk tradition of the Puerto Rican people.

The hurricane season in the Caribbean generally spans from July to November.[9] Since 1508, when the Spaniards began to keep written records, Puerto Rico has been hit by seventy-three hurricanes. Such activity has been sporadic, with the eighteenth century registering as little as two and the nineteenth century as many as thirty-three. At least three hurricanes have hit Puerto Rico on August 16th and thus were named San Roque, in keeping with the calendar of the Catholic church. Since 1898 Puerto Rico has experienced the destructive forces of San Ciriaco (1898), San Felipe (1928), San Ciprián (1932) and Hugo (1989). The first three left many dead and extensive homelessness in their wake, while all four caused millions of dollars of damages to crops and property.

On several occasions Puerto Rico has suffered damage from river flooding, coastal waves, and earthquake shocks.[10] The most recent destructive earthquake in modern times occurred in October 1918. The tremor, which rocked the Mona Channel and the northwest corner of Puerto Rico, provoked tidal waves that took over one hundred lives and caused four million dollars in damages. While there is evidence that tiny shocks occur every year, only a few cause any tremor. In the past century, the island experienced repeated tremors from November 1867 to January 1868.

Flora and Fauna

In the sixteenth century Puerto Rico was densely forested, but by the beginning of the last century deforestation was a serious enough problem to lead the Spanish government to order the planting of trees along the river basins and in 1876 to place certain forest areas under its protection. During this century, the U.S. government has placed nearly 34,000 acres under its protection, including the 28,000 acre Luquillo Rain Forest. In recent years it has added another 55,000 acres to the list of protected lands.[11]

Despite the state's protective measures, trees such as nutmeg, satin-wood, Spanish elm, Spanish cedar, and candletree once plentiful in Puerto Rico are now rare. Almost extinct is the "ausubo" tree, a type of termite-resistant ironwood used as beams in construction throughout the island until the past century.[12] Although flowering trees, such as the "flam-boyán", are still plentiful along the coastal plains and mountains, only one per cent of the island's surface has survived in a virgin state.

The removal of trees and centuries of poor crop rotation practices have contributed to impoverishing much of the soil. At present, only one-third of the topsoil is considered good for agriculture although much of that land lies along the path of sprawling urban developments.

Despite the widespread deforestation, there are still over 200 species of bird life, of which the best known are the orioles, hummingbirds, gros-beaks, doves, owls, and pigeons. Three very popular species with the islanders are the *reinita* (little queen), the *pitirre* (Tyrannus dominicensis) and a flock of very rare parrots, which has survived in the El Yunque Rain Forest.

The tropical climate is ideal for the proliferation of frogs, and insects as well. Among the former is found the *coquí* (Eleutherodactylis portori-censis), a free-fingered amphibious frog, which delights the inhabitants with its high-pitched song, "ko-kee! ko-kee!"

Insects also thrive in the warm humid climate. Mosquitoes are a con-stant nuisance to the inhabitants in the low, damp lands, while tiny sand flies, or "mimes" drive bathers off the beaches after sundown. But poiso-nous spiders, such as the black widow, are extremely rare in Puerto Rico.

Crocodiles are not indigenous to Puerto Rico. Those found in the island's lakes and rivers in recent decades are believed to have been thrown clandestinely into the waterways by disinterested pet owners.

Puerto Rico's shores are teeming with colorful marine life that includes a huge variety of tropical fish, coral reefs, sea horses, sea cucumbers, crabs, and starfish. The most threatening of the sea creatures that thrive in the surrounding seas are the jellyfish and the sharks.

Natural Resources

Gold, the incentive that led the Spaniards to colonize Puerto Rico in the sixteenth century, gave out within forty years, just as the native population disappeared. Although no other metal has been exploited since then, the island is known to have deposits of copper, iron, manganese, cobalt, nickel, and titanium. [13] Of these, the copper deposits found in the mountainous towns of Adjuntas, Lares and Utuado, in the northwest, are large enough to be mined commercially. But fear of contamination of the island's environment, and a lingering controversy over royalties, immobilized the mining projects. Similarly, the large deposits of iron (mixed with nickel and cobalt) found in the vicinity of Mayagüez, are costly to mine because of the highly urbanized nature of the region.

Recent geological studies underscore the possibility that petroleum and natural gas deposits are present along the north and south coasts.

The most used natural resources in the island's economy are common minerals, such as sand, gravel, clay and limestone, which have become important to the cement and construction industries. The extraction of sand, however, has led to the erosion of some northern beaches.

Other common minerals utilized by local industry are silicate for making glass, marble for tiles, and blue limestone for the construction of local highways. Salt, a mineral used for table and industrial consumption, is collected on flat evaporation beds along the southern coastal shore.

Puerto Rico's Offshore Islands

Puerto Rico also has jurisdiction over several smaller offshore islands.[14] The largest of these is Vieques, called "bieque" by the Taino Indians. It measures 51.5 square miles and lies only nine miles off the eastern coast of Puerto Rico.

Its main and only city, Isabel Segunda, was founded in 1843. More than 70 per cent of the land on Vieques is at present held by the U.S. Navy, which uses it to conduct military maneuvers. Its protected harbor led the U.S. to build a long pier, to shelter the British fleet in the event that England fell to Germany during World War II.

Constant military operations have threatened the safety of local fishermen and discouraged the development of agriculture and tourism.

Viequenses unable to make a living, or dissatisfied with the quality of life on the island, tend to migrate to Puerto Rico, St. Croix, in the neighboring U.S. Virgin Islands and to the United States.

Culebra, another island possession, with an area of twenty-four square miles, lies twenty-two miles east of Fajardo, Puerto Rico. Its main urban settlement Dewey was founded in 1898. Like its neighbor Vieques, Culebra has been primarily used by the U.S. Navy for aerial and naval target practice. Unlike Vieques, Culebra has neither mountains nor rivers, and is very dry and warm most of the year.

To the southwest of Puerto Rico lies Mona Island, a tiny territory of 19.5 square miles. It is a hot, flat, uninhabited land just forty-two miles off the southwestern shore. It is good for hunting wild birds, goats, and pigs. Early in the eighteenth century, European pirates used it as a home base.

Other tiny islands belonging to Puerto Rico, and used mainly by boating enthusiasts for recreational purposes, are Desecheo ("Castaway"), Isla de Cabras ("Goat Island"), and Caja de Muertos ("Dead Man's Chest").

The Pre-Columbian Inhabitants

Knowledge of the earliest inhabitants of Puerto Rico is at best sketchy. The Taino Indians encountered by the Spaniards in Puerto Rico (then called Boriquén) were the latest of many Amerindian groups to settle the island. None of the groups had a written language. Thus what is known about them comes primarily from the chronicles of Spanish explorers, archaeological excavations, and recent studies of settlement sites, ceremonial parks, and burial grounds.

From these sources emerges the thesis that, at least three, and possibly four, distinct peoples had settled on the island before the Spaniards arrived. These have been identified as the Archaic, the Igneri, the Ostionoid, and the Taino.[15]

The Archaics

The earliest archaeological remains of human life in Puerto Rico were found by Professor Ricardo Alegría, at Cueva María de la Cruz, a limestone cave, close to San Juan's northeast coast. Artifacts unearthed by his excavations there point to the existence of a preceramic culture some time around the first century A.D.[16]

According to archaeological information derived from artifacts found at three other sites, this culture had no developed agriculture or pottery. Its members were seminomadic hunter-gatherers, who supplemented their diet by fishing. They settled near the shore and mangrove areas, used caves as homes and burial places. They made their principal artifacts from shells or stones.

Since their artifacts resembled those of some of the earliest inhabitants of Florida, some scholars have proposed the theory that the Archaics may have migrated from there to Cuba and from Cuba to other West Indian islands. Remnants of this culture were also found on the island of Vieques, east of Puerto Rico, leading still other archaeologists to propose an alternate theory that the Archaics were originally from South America, and used the chain of islands in the West Indies as resting places until they reached Puerto Rico.[17] The place of origin of this group is still unknown.

The Igneri or Saladoid

The Igneri, the second group to settle Puerto Rico, are believed to have migrated to the Antilles from South America.[18] They presumably sailed from the Orinoco River basin to the islands adjacent to Venezuela and from there to other Caribbean islands until they reached Puerto Rico. Studies of their remains, found at the Loíza River basin, in the northeast, date their arrival to 120 A.D.

The Igneri or Saladoid culture developed during the Stone Age and was apparently more advanced technologically than that of the Archaics. Besides fishing, hunting and gathering skills, they developed a technique for making fine ceramic pottery. They produced polished vases and pots, decorated with red and white designs.

They shaped tools out of stones and were adept at using the petaloid or rectangular hammer stones. They founded their settlements near the coast and used the sea as a source of food. Apparently, they survived on the island until the sixth century A.D. What became of them after that date has led to at least two theories. One holds that they evolved into the more sophisticated Ostionoid culture, which appeared later in the interior of Puerto Rico. The other proposes that they were conquered by other migratory groups from South America, which reached the island after the sixth century.[19] Until evidence is found to corroborate one of these, or some other theory, the only thing we can claim with some degree of certainty is that this group excelled in the art of making fine pottery.

The Ostionoid

The Ostionoid, who apparently reached Puerto Rico around the sixth century A.D., founded their settlements farther away from the shore and devoted more time to making highly polished stone artifacts.[20] With the Ostionoids the art of making pottery apparently declined, since the vases and other utensils they made were coarse and utilitarian. They made well-polished stone axes and grinders as well as amulets.

Archaeological excavations have uncovered a variety of sacred objects from this period, including the three-pointed stone idol, or *cemí*. The sites of early ceremonial courts on the island are also attributed to this culture. The courts were used to play an early ball game and to conduct tribal ceremonial rites, known as *areytos*. This evidence, in turn, has led some scholars to conclude that the religious beliefs later attributed to the Tainos were part of the Ostionoid culture. They are similarly credited with having developed a complex social organization by the eleventh century, which was later adopted by the Tainos.

The Tainos

The Tainos were the most culturally advanced of the Arawak group to settle in what is now Puerto Rico.[21] Although they spread throughout the Greater Antilles, they reached the height of their culture in Hispaniola (present-day Haiti and the Dominican Republic) and Puerto Rico in the thirteenth and fifteenth centuries. They were part of the Stone Age, but they made extensive use of pottery and had a sophisticated knowledge of agriculture. They shared a common language with other groups in the Caribbean, with whom they also engaged in commercial and war activities. They founded their settlements around villages and organized their chiefdoms, or *cacigazgos*, into a confederation.

Their social organization was two-tiered with a class called *nitainos* at the top and one called *naborias* at the bottom. Tribal groups settled in villages under a chieftain, known as *cacique*, or *cacica* if the ruler was a woman. Ricardo Alegría explains that many of the women the Spaniards called cacicas were not always rulers in their own right, but were mistakenly recognized as such because they were the wives of caciques. Chiefs were chosen from the nitainos and generally obtained their power from the maternal line. This meant that a male ruler was more likely to be succeeded by his sister's children than his own, unless their mother's lineage allowed them to succeed in their own right. At the time of the Spanish arrival in Boriquén the island had twenty chiefdoms organized into a confederation.

The chiefs had both temporal and spiritual functions. They were expected to ensure the welfare of the tribe and to protect it from harm from both natural and supernatural forces. In the mundane matters of assigning and supervising communal work, planting and harvesting crops, and keeping peace among the village's inhabitants, they were assisted by advisors they selected from among the nitainos.[22]

For the more difficult task of negotiating with angry or indifferent gods, they enlisted the services of medicine men, or women, known as *behiques*. As the accepted lords of the spiritual world, the behiques were expected to communicate with the gods, to soothe them when they were angry, and to intercede on the tribe's behalf. It was their duty to cure the sick, heal the wounded, and interpret the will of the gods in ways that would satisfy the expectations of the tribe. Before carrying out these functions, the behiques performed certain cleansing and purifying rituals, such as fasting for several days and inhaling sacred tobacco snuff.

Not curing the sick could be dangerous for the behiques. According to Ramón Pané, the friar commissioned by Columbus to study Taino culture, the dead person's relatives "beat him [the behique] with clubs till they break his legs, his arms, and his head", leaving him for dead. But, at night "many snakes of different kinds lick the face and body of the behique and restore him back to life". They believed that behiques did not die, "unless their testicles [we]re destroyed."[23]

Taino religion was highly complex with a well-developed account of the origin of humans and a cosmology that included a long list of supernatural deities, each of which was credited with ruling a certain aspect of their lives and of the world around them.[24]

The highest deity was an immortal, invisible Supreme Maker, called *Yocajú Bagua Maorocoti*. But above all, they worshiped a female deity with five names, believed to be the mother of Yocajú. Known by most historical sources as *Atabey*, she was also called *Yermar Guacar Apito* and *Zuimaco*, according to Pané. Each of these names, his informants told him, symbolized a distinct realm of power and action.

The longer list of names used to describe the goddess Atabey, and a statement found in Pané's work, which traces the "origin of the matrilineal tradition among the Tainos" to this female deity, has led Professor Jalil Sued-Badillo to conclude that the mother goddess was more important than her son Yocajú. Sued-Badillo suspects that the good friar elevated the son Yocajú over the mother to fit with his own beliefs.[25]

In addition to Yocajú and Atabey, the Tainos worshiped a series of lesser gods, as well as the spirits of dead ancestors, especially those of their chieftains. These were generally represented through idols, or cemíes, they carved out of wood or stone. Their belief in life after death led them to bury their dead with food, tools, and weapons, to make their journey more comfortable. In the case of a cacique, his favorite wife was presumably buried with him as well.[26]

The Tainos also believed that the dead walked among the living. Those who had been kind and wise in their lifetime returned as spiritual guides for the tribe, while the less enlightened spirits roamed around at night and frightened those who ventured outdoors after dark.[27]

Taino villages, known as *yucayeques*, were founded near rivers and other sources of water, some distance from the shore. In the villages, they built two kinds of houses: the *caney*, a rectangular abode for the chief, and the round-shaped *bohío*, where the rest of the population lived. All houses were built with reeds and thatch and converged on a center clearing or square, called *batey*. In the villages closest to the shore they also built observation towers. Not far from the village they built a fairly large ceremonial court.

The ceremonial courts were locales for various traditional and recreational activities such as *areytos*, or dances, and ball games. Areytos were important tribal celebrations during which the elders taught the young and reinforced their own memories of Taino myths, traditions, and history. Music for these dances was provided by drums made from hollow tree trunks, *maracas* (rattles), and *güiros*, made from gourdes. The ball games were played with a large rubber ball, by competing teams of ten to thirty men and women. Players could hit the ball with many parts of their bodies (head, shoulders, elbows, hips) or with a heavy ceremonial belt made of stone, but never with their hands.[28]

According to Spanish chroniclers, the Tainos were friendly, sedentary people, who believed they inhabited the Land of the Noble Lord. They were short and strong with copper-colored skin, straight black hair and prominent cheekbones. A back-sloping forehead was considered a sign of beauty, and to achieve it, they wrapped the heads of their infants with tight-fitting cotton bands at birth.

Except for a *nagua* (half-slip) worn by married women, the Tainos went about naked, though they painted their bodies with red vegetable dyes and wore jewelry fashioned from bones, clay, and shells. The chief wore a *guanín*, or gold disc, around his neck. It is unknown whether women chiefs enjoyed such a privilege.

By the time the Tainos came into contact with the Spaniards, they also had a well developed system of farming, based on commonly cultivated fields. They planted crops by digging holes in the ground with a stick, they called *coa*. They surrounded the seedlings with mounds of soil, to provide nourishment and prevent erosion. The rather advanced technique of cultivation in beds was also used.

Among the plants most in demand by the Tainos were yucca (manioc), corn, tobacco, yams, and sweet potatoes. The variety of yucca they cultivated was poisonous, but they devised a system to extract the poison by grating and draining the root. The grated meal was then used to make an unleavened bread, called *casabe*. They also planted corn, sweet potatoes yams, peanuts, ajíes (chili peppers), tobacco and cotton. Also used to supplement their diet were a variety of native fruits, including guavas, guanábanas (custard apples), jobos (hogplums) papayas, pineapples quenepas (Spanish lime, also known as limoncillo in Cuba) and tamarind. Tobacco was cultivated for religious and medicinal purposes. The cotton they grew was used to make hammocks, fishing nets, and other products. Bananas,plantains, coffee, coconuts, sugar cane and the citric family of lemons, oranges and grapefruits, so common in Puerto Rico, are not native to the island, but were introduced by Spanish settlers.

For meat, the Tainos hunted iguanas, *jutías* (a large rodent still found in some of the Greater Antilles), *coríes* (small guinea pigs), and raised mute dogs, now extinct. From the sea, they took oysters, clams, turtles, and fish. The domesticated chickens, turkeys, pigs, goats, cows, horses, mules, cats and dogs were also introduced by the Spaniards.[29]

Women played many important roles in the Taino economy. They generally planted and harvested the fields, presumably because they represented the fertility goddess. They also ground the yucca and the corn, prepared the food, cared for the children, made the pottery (clay pots and dishes much coarser than those of the Igneri), and processed the raw cotton and other plants into fibers from which they made a variety of products.[30] Taino men engaged in hunting, fishing, building canoes, and protecting the territory from intruders. Although basically a peaceful people, they had apparently been devoting more and more time to perfecting weapons and defensive tactics, possibly out of fear of the Carib, who had been raiding the larger islands from the Lesser Antilles for decades before the Spaniards arrived.

By the 1490s, the Tainos had perfected a few weapons, namely the bow and arrow, the *macana* (wooden club), and the stone ax. They also used a deadly poison extracted from the yucca against their enemies. Hence some scholars speculate that the decline in ceramics among the Tainos and their growing preoccupation with weapons were signs that they might have been under siege from the Carib when the Europeans arrived. In support of this argument,they also point to the development of the island-wide confederation in which otherwise autonomous chiefdoms opted to unite for defense. Christopher Columbus claimed that the Carib[31] were feared by all the inhabitants of the Greater Antilles because they abducted women of the enemy and cannibalized the males.

In the 1508, when Juan Ponce de León began the colonization of Boriquén, the recognized leader of the Taino island-wide confederation was the elderly chieftain Agüeybana, the cacique of *Guainía*, a chiefdom near the southern shore.

The Tainos and their culture were annihilated by the onslaught of the European conquest and colonization rather than by the Carib. Of their world we retain some fragmented accounts of their history and spiritual beliefs, some of the items they used in their daily lives and a few dozen words that were incorporated into Spanish and other languages. Among the words still used to represent foods or items borrowed from them by the new society, are *hamaca* (hammock), *yucca* (manioc) *canoa* (canoe), *casabe*,and *maraca* (rattle).

Suggested Readings

Alegría, Ricardo E. "El juego de pelota entre los aborígenes antillanos", *Revista Mexicana de Estudios Antropológicos*, vol. 12 (1951).

———, "Apuntes para el estudio de los caciques de Puerto Rico," Separata de la *Revista del Instituto de Cultura Puertorriqueña*, No. 85 (Dec. 1979).

———, "La población aborigen antillana y su relación con otras areas de America". In: Aida Caro-Costas. *Antología de lecturas de historia de Puerto Rico* (San Juan, Puerto Rico: 1971).

———, *Discovery, Conquest and Colonization of Puerto Rico, 1493-1599* (San Juan: Colección de Estudios Puertorriqueños, 1971).

Biaggi, Virgilio, *Las Aves de Puerto Rico* (Río Piedras: Editorial Universidad de Puerto Rico, 1970).

"Columbus' Journal". In John Cummins. *The Voyage of Christopher Columbus: Columbus' Own Journal of Discovery Newly Restored and Translated* (U.S. Edition, 1992).

Descartes, Sol Luis. *Puerto Rico: Trasfondo de su Economía* (Hato Rey, Puerto Rico: Inter American University Press, 1973).

Fewkes, Walter J. *The Aborigines of Porto Rico and Neighboring Islands* (25th Report of the Bureau of American Ethnology, 1903-04) (Wash. D.C: Government Printing Office, 1970).

Gómez, Labor and Manuel Ballesteros. *Culturas indígenas de Puerto Rico* (Río Piedras, Puerto Rico: 1978).

Little, Elbert L., Jr., Frank H. Wadsworth, and José Marrero, *Árboles Comunes de Puerto Rico y las Islas Vírgenes* (Río Piedras: Editorial Universidad de Puerto Rico, 1967).

Meyerhoff, H.A., *Geology of Puerto Rico* (Río Piedras: Editorial Universidad de Puerto Rico, 1933).

Olsen, Fred. *On the Trail of the Arawaks*. Reprint of 1891 Edition (Norman: University of Oklahoma Press, 1974).

Pané, Ramón. "The Indian Way of Life" in *The Puerto Ricans: A Documentary History*. Edited by Kal Wagenheim and Olga Jiménez de

Wagenheim (Princeton: Markus Wiener Publishers, 1993).

Picó, Rafael, *Nueva Geografía de Puerto Rico* (Río Piedras: Editorial Universidad de Puerto Rico, 1975).

Rogozinski, Jan. *A Brief History of the Caribbean: From the Arawak and Carib to the Present* (New York: Meridian Books, 1992).

Stevens-Arroyo, Antonio. *Cave of the Jagua: The Mythological World of the Tainos* (Albuquerque: U. of New Mexico Press, 1988).

Sued-Badillo, Jalil. *La mujer indígena y su sociedad* (Río Piedras: Editorial Antillana, 1979).

———. *Los caribes: realidad o fábula: ensayo de rectificación histórica* (Río Piedras, Puerto Rico: Editorial Cultural, 1978).

Watts, David. *The West Indies: Patterns of Development, Culture and Environmental Change Since 1492* (Cambridge and New York: Cambridge University Press, 1987).

West, Robert and Augellis, John. *Middle America: Its Lands and Peoples.* Third Edition (Englewood Cliffs, NJ: Prentice Hall, 1989)

Ruins of the house of Ponce de León in Caparra (1508–1521)

CHAPTER TWO

The Newcomers to Boriquén

Puerto Rico's relationship with Spain began in 1493, when a group of explorers, under the command of Christopher Columbus, landed briefly on the island. Spain's subsequent occupation of the island fifteen years later stems in part from the economic and political changes that Europe and the Mediterranean world had been undergoing for some time.

Iberian and European Background

Until the beginning of the fifteenth century, Europe's lucrative commerce with Asia had been conducted over land through the territories of Alexandria and Constantinople. But when Constantinople fell to the Turks in 1453, the land route to Asia became much too costly and the European merchants began to look for an alternative commercial route.

Turkish control of the Middle East and growing Turkish presence along the Mediterranean sea lanes mounted obstacles for the experienced merchants of the Italian city-states and posed threats to the Portuguese and Spanish traders.[1]

By the time Columbus set out in search of a western sea route to Asia, the Iberian territory was politically dominated by the states of Spain and Portugal. Both had achieved independence from Moorish rule, the latest of the many groups to colonize the peninsula, after centuries of intermittent resistance.

The Iberian land had first been settled by prehistoric tribes, some of which left paintings later found in the caves of Altamira. Before 1000 B.C. other groups, namely the Iberians, from northern Africa and the Celts, from central Europe, had settled parts of the area. These were, in turn, conquered and absorbed by the Phoenicians, the Greeks, and the Carthaginians.

War between Rome and Carthage, at the beginning of the third century before the Christian era, placed the Iberian peninsula under Roman sovereignty for the next 600 years, from B.C. 201–400 A.D. The Romans changed the name of the territory to Hispania and imposed their laws, their political and economic systems, their beliefs, values, and the Latin language on the Iberian inhabitants.

To discourage the Iberians from revolting, the conquerors established military garrisons and exiled potential troublemakers to other parts of the empire. Iberian towns were placed under control of Roman officials, who in addition to their administrative duties were expected to promote and regulate all commerce and trade.[2]

The imprint of the Roman colonization is still visible on the Iberian land in the ruins of impressive public buildings and the famous aqueducts still standing in the peninsula. Many of their laws provided the basis for portions of the Iberian legal codes, while Latin became the foundation for the Spanish and Portuguese languages. But of all the Roman institutions the one that most notably changed the culture of the Iberians forever was the Catholic church.

At the beginning of the fifth century, when Rome's imperial power began to wane, new waves of Germanic tribes (the Goths), from central Europe, invaded Hispania. For the next 200 years they kept the territory politically divided, as family dynasties struggled to maintain control over certain Christian kingdoms.

Political fragmentation made it difficult to resist the much more powerful Arabic-speaking, Islamic invaders pushing in from north Africa at the beginning of the eighth century. By 711 A.D. much of the Iberian peninsula, except for the north and northwest corner of present-day Spain, was occupied by the Islamic people, known to the Christians as the Moors.

In the area now occupied by Spain, Moorish rule and cultural influence became entrenched along the eastern seaboard and the southern region of Andalusía, where the conquerors established seats of government and trade. The northern and northwestern regions of Spain, separated by long distances from the conquerors' seat of power, remained *de facto* Christian enclaves.

The Moors, or Moslems, as they were also called, ruled much of the peninsula for the next 700 years and left a substantial legacy. In general, they introduced important changes in the economy, education, architecture and the arts. They improved agriculture by crop rotation and irrigation, founded impressive libraries and universities, disseminated the scientific, and philosophical knowledge they had gleaned from the Hellenist world, and beautified southern Spain with impressive buildings, fountains and gardens.[3]

But the Moors, unlike the Roman colonizers, did not impose their language, customs, values or religion on the vanquished. Moslem Spain preached and practiced religious tolerance, and thus allowed Christians and Jews alike to worship in peace. All that was required of all non-Islamic worshipers was that they obey the law and pay a poll tax. As a result, the Moors ruled in relative peace until the middle of the tenth century, when internal strife and tribal feuds began to threaten their power.

Complacency, corruption, and internal strife among the Moslem rulers of southern Iberia split the Califate of Córdoba in 1050 A.D. The rift, in turn, weakened their hold over the rest of the land at a time when Berbers of North Africa (recent converts to Islam) were preparing to invade the peninsula and some Christians had begun to revolt.

Christian Reconquest and Expansion

The cracks in the edifice of Moslem power encouraged many Christian lords in the north and western portions of the peninsula (present-day Portugal and Spain) to make the Catholic Faith a rallying cause for a war of independence against the Moors. This armed resistance was later known as the Reconquest.[4]

The Portuguese (Lusitanians) were the first to evict the Moors in 1270 A.D. Freedom from Moslem rule, however, did not bring them the independence they sought until a century later, in part because they had to contend with periodic threats of invasion from their eastern neighbor, the kingdom of Castile. That problem, however, was finally laid to rest in 1385, when John of Avis beat the Castilian contender to the throne of Portugal, and established *de facto* independence from Castile. Once in power, King John surrounded himself with administrators who, like himself, shared the dream of expanding Portugal's territory and economy.

Blocked on the east by the powerful kingdom of Castile, the

Indians washing gold in the rivers

Portuguese, under the direction of King John, sought alternate trading outlets in Africa and a western sea route to Asia. Subsidized by large grants from King Henry (the Navigator), the maritime interests of Portugal spent much of the fifteenth century exploring the northern and western coasts of Africa. In their path, they took possession of three groups of islands: the Azores, Madeira, and Cape Verde.[5]

By 1415, they had seized the fortress of Ceuta, on the northern coast of Africa, and by 1481 had penetrated the African continent as far as present-day Ghana. Portuguese merchants in search of gold, ivory, slaves, and grains followed the explorers, establishing trading posts in the new lands, as was the practice in the Mediterranean world at the time. Yet, the Portuguese *feitorias* differed from the traditional trading posts in that they also served as military garrisons. In this way, the Portuguese were guaranteed to remain a commercial presence in heavily populated areas such as Africa, without having to engage initially in costly wars of occupation. This apparent reluctance to colonize foreign lands, however, was overcome years later when the state, strengthened by the economic rewards of such ventures, agreed to offer military aid to the expansionists. In 1486, an expedition led by Bartolomeu Dias enabled the Portuguese to be the first Europeans to reach the Indian Ocean, by rounding the Cape of Good

Hope, at the southern tip of Africa. Twelve years later, they were again the first to find the coveted sea route to Asia.[6]

Spanish resistance against the Moors began soon after occupation, but independence from their rule was not achieved until 1492, when the kingdom of Granada, a bone of contention since the mid-thirteenth century, was finally seized by the Christians. The struggle to reclaim their land began in the north and was gradually advanced by Christian lords through the plains of Castile as far south as Andalusía, and eastward into the major port cities of Valencia and Barcelona. Yet it took the joint royal armies of Aragón and Castile to evict the Moors from Granada in 1492.

After centuries of intermittent fighting the territory was finally returned to the Christians, but the effects of the war brought about some changes in the economy and the society. The constant demand for warriors, for instance, contributed to the creation of a military culture that rewarded and elevated those who lived by the sword to positions of importance in the society. Many of the Christian lords who led the military charges found also that war offered new avenues to wealth and power. For example, members of the landed gentry, hermandades, or religious military orders were regularly compensated for their services with vast estates from the land liberated from the Moslems.[7] Although granting the Moorish estates to the Christians was a way of removing their control over the territory, it became also a mechanism for the consolidation of land into a few hands while hundred of thousands of peasants remained landless. In time, such acquisitions gave the lords, as well as the Catholic church, added sources of economic power with which to resist the reforms envisioned by the emerging state.

Over time, the society came to define its actions by many religious and military values. Military values such as courage, endurance, and honor, for instance, were often confounded with the Christian principles of compassion, caring, and generosity as the ideals to which warriors and civilians aspired. Displays of these in the battlefield could bring any warrior rewards ranging from pensions to well-paid jobs, to land, or other possessions.

Another effect of the long war was the displacement of large sectors of the population. From central Castile to the south large tracts of land were abandoned by peasants fleeing from the advancing armies. The land they vacated, in turn, was utilized by sheep farmers from the north to graze their stocks during the winter months. As demand and prices for Castilian wool rose in the European market, the sheep barons organized a powerful association (the Mesta) to protect their claim to the land they held and in the process contributed to the ongoing trend of land consolidation.[8]

As the opportunities for wealth and glory that had lured many to the battlefields waned, as the war ended, many veterans migrated to the southern cities and ports within Andalusía. As the cities also failed to meet their expectations, some of the veterans joined local and foreign armies and others signed on as mariners with merchant ships bound for outer ports or with promising exploratory expeditions.

One institutional legacy of the Reconquest that made its way to Spanish America was the *municipio*, or frontier town. The municipio was a settlement established in areas contested by the Moors that received a variety of incentives from the Crown in order to attract Christian settlers. Generally, the Crown offered the founding settlers charters of incorporation, called *fueros* which permitted them to organize a *cabildo* (town council), to select the cabildo members, the *regidores*, elect the mayor, and appoint the court's magistrates. The town's officers were also entitled to fix the municipal budget, to distribute land, and to tax the inhabitants. From these revenues, howeveer, they were expected to pay royal taxes in order to be represented in the Royal Council.

In exchange for these privileges, the municipal government was expected to protect the Crown's interests from its enemies and challengers, such as the ambitious Christian lords eager to encroach on the royal lands. Hence, the fuero (charter of incorporation) gave the town jurisdiction over the surrounding countryside and empowered it to form a militia.

Although by the time the Spaniards reached America the frontier town of medieval Spain had lost many of its earlier powers, the tradition that gave rise to them lived on, invoked time and again by the conquerors. Far from the royal seat of power and often surrounded by hostile forces, the Spanish conquerors and settlers built frontier towns in America and appropriated the powers conferred by the tradition of the Reconquest.[9]

Aragón and Castile Unite

Even before the Moors were evicted, the kingdoms of Aragón and Castile had sought to consolidate their hold over the greater part of the peninsula by ruling under one monarchy. The marriage of Ferdinand of Aragón and Isabella of Castile in 1469 not only accomplished this goal, but finished the liberation campaign by ousting the Moors from Granada.

Castile, the largest of the two kingdoms had the least maritime experience. Lack of access to the Guadalquivir river, the region's largest waterway to the Mediterranean sea, until its first major victory over the Moors in 1236, had reduced Castile's potential to explore beyond the Mediterranean world.

Aragón, meanwhile, with a firm grip over the eastern ports and the major cities of Barcelona and Valencia, had developed a commercial and political presence in the Mediterranean world. Its maritime explorations had brought it within sixty miles of Africa's west coast in 1330, a deed that led it to claim the Canary Islands for itself. Thus, by the time it joined with the crown of Castile, more than a century later, it could offer the emergent state a foothold in what was to become the new route to Asia. The Spanish monarchy's claim to the Canary Islands was eventually recognized by Portugal by the 1479 Treaty of Alcaçobas. In exchange Spain, too, recognized Portugal's claims over the islands of Azores, Cape Verde and Madeira, and its exclusive right to trade with Africa.[10]

Castile's control over the Guadalquivir River after 1236 led the monarchy to funnel all the kingdom's maritime commerce through the city of Seville even though Seville was miles inland from the sea. Its access to the river attracted foreign capital and traders to the city, which resulted in a thriving trade. Thus, by the time the Castilian kingdom joined Aragón, it had also its own commercial linkages and experienced merchants with which to engage in overseas commerce.

Commercial dealings with neighboring European markets had taught the merchants of Seville to pool their resources and to establish mercantile societies, called *compañías* (companies). When the society or company had two investors, as was often the case, the larger partner tended to remain in Seville, administering the company, while the smaller partner, the *aviador*, or salesman, went on the road. Before Spain conquered the New World the majority of these companies were small to medium-sized partnerships, owned by members of the same family or in conjunction with neighbors from the same town or region.[11]

Following the conquest of America, Seville's fortune rose substantially in part because it became the only authorized port in Spain's trade with its colonies. To protect this lucrative monopoly, the merchants of Seville organized themselves into a powerful *consulado* (guild) which, like some of the other Spanish monopolies, detracted from the Crown's power and ultimately hindered the economic development of both Spain and its colonies.

The Stipulations of Santa Fe

Victory over Granada offered the monarchs Isabella and Ferdinand the freedom to embark on their own exploratory projects. One that appealed to them, but which had been pending for six years, was Christopher Columbus' proposal to find a western sea route to Asia. As the exigences of war vanished, the monarchs summoned Columbus to Santa Fe, where they still camped after the war, and offered him a contract, known henceforth as the *Stipulations of Santa Fe*. According to the terms of the contract, the Crown would cover the cost of the expedition, estimated at 5,000 gold ducats, in exchange for which it demanded 20 percent of all the riches resulting from the venture.[12]

For his services, Christopher Columbus was entitled to be reimbursed for his investment and to receive one tenth of the riches he found during the expedition. Of the remaining funds, after expenses were deducted, he was to pay the members of his group. As commander of the expedition, he received the title of Admiral of the Ocean Sea and the right to a monopoly over all the commercial routes he discovered on his voyage. As representative of the Spanish monarchs, he was appointed Viceroy and Governor of any lands he claimed for the monarchy. These titles and the perquisites that stemmed from them were extensive to his descendants. The contract promised Columbus powers in the new lands that in Spain were only surpassed by those of the monarchs.

The Government

The ideal form of government envisioned by the Spanish rulers was a centralized monarchy, but reality disposed otherwise and they had to settle for a loosely-knit group of agencies with overlapping functions and conflicting interests.[13]

In general, the most important agency in the monarchy was the King's Council, composed of powerful lords and clergymen, whose jurisdiction extended over all the government agencies. Ideally, these were linked to the King's council by a well-delineated chain of command. Yet anyone of them could, and often did, bypass this chain to appeal to the King directly. That practice provided the King the opportunity to intervene whenever it suited his interests, or suspected that his counselors were acting in their own best interests rather than on behalf of the Crown.

Next in importance to the King's council were the courts of appeal, or *Audiencias*. These acted independently and ruled over administrative, legislative, and civil matters. But their decisions, like those of other agencies, could be challenged or ignored by the monarch.

The Catholic Church

With the eviction of the Moors, the Catholic Church of Spain became much more powerful than it had been.[14] The spiritual and military roles the clergy played in the armies of the Reconquest earned them prestige, vast expanses of land, and important positions in government.

From this vantage point, the Catholic church was able to spread its influence through its teachings, values, and rituals. With the cooperation with the Christian rulers, it became possible to unite the society under one God, one religion, and one monarchy. Those who obeyed its laws were promised happiness and eternity as their due rewards in the hereafter, while those who ignored or challenged its precepts were either deported or subjected to forceful conversion and the rigors of the Inquisition (as the cases of the Jews, 1492, and the Moors, 1502, attest). The Catholic church's unification strategies also served the monarchy well, for they not only brought cohesion among the Christians, but helped to neutralize any brewing opposition.

The Catholic clergy exerted much of its influence over the community by the many social services it provided. These ranged from health care (usually provided free of charge to the poor), to education and spiritual guidance. The church also kept the community's records of births, deaths, and marriages, administered the cemeteries, and provided safe havens for orphans, widows, and unmarried men and women. On many occasions, it even provided entertainment for the community in its effort to permeate every aspect of the Christians' lives and culture.

Yet, in its efforts to convert all the inhabitants to the Christian faith, it created a highly intolerant climate for non-Christians to practice their beliefs. Muslims and Jews, who accepted the offer to convert, rather than risk eviction, could never adequately prove the religious orthodoxy demanded of them. Nor could they escape the requirements of the insidious system that required suspicious Catholics to produce certificates of "purity of blood" (limpieza de sangre) as proof of descent from the "old Christians".[15]

Lack of such proof could deprive the converts of jobs and bar them from certain professions and social circles. Conversion, however, did not necessarily protect them from persecution, discrimination, and the horrors of the Inquisition which operated in Spain since 1478.

Yet for all its influence, the church, too, was from time to time reminded of its subjugation to the monarchy of Ferdinand and Isabella. For it was under their reign that Pope Sixtus IV agreed to place the Spanish church under the authority of the Spanish government, by the accord known to history as the *patronato real* (royal patronage). The accord authorized the monarchs both to appoint the top officers of the Spanish church and to share its wealth. In exchange for the power and privileges conferred, they were obligated to spread the Christian faith and to finance the church's expansion and activities.

The Catholic church of Spain, like the government itself, was organized in hierarchical fashion in which the top tier of the pyramid was occupied by the high-ranking members of the clergy. The bottom tier was reserved for the minor clergy, part of which was made up by the mendicant orders.[16] Since the mendicant friars prided themselves in being able to spread the teachings of Christ, without pomp or ceremony, it was to them that Ferdinand and Isabella turned when they wished to challenge the authority of the higher clergy or to carry out some proselytizing work. Hence, it should not come as a surprise that while members of the secular church accompanied and often helped to finance many of the Spanish expeditions to the New World, it was the friars who did the work of converting the natives. But as long as the expansion of the kingdom was justified in religious terms, the top clergy of the church would find a way to demand a share of the spoils.

The Iberian Society

At the end of the fifteenth century Iberian society was organized in hierarchical fashion, along rather complex dividing lines. Each social group was further subdivided by gradations into smaller groups, each of which was defined by a combination of factors. Thus, one's place in the social ladder was determined by such factors as one's profession or function, life-style, lineage, religious beliefs, and ethnic background.[17]

At the top of the social hierarchy were the landed nobility and the aristocracy. Their place at the top was insured not only by their wealth, but by their affluent life-style, education, membership in the Christian community, and the pious deeds they performed on behalf of the church.

Below them were the professionals, a social group whose learning and titles enabled them to rise socially by the services they performed for the royal court and powerful aristocrats. In some cases they improved their social status by marrying into the nobility.

Third from the top were the merchants. This group was also subdivided into two categories: the wholesale merchants, the most important of the group, and the retailers. The social status of merchants was significantly improved if they were educated and owned land or other property. Having money alone did not guarantee social acceptance.

Below the merchants were the public servants, military officers, artists, and the numerous individuals employed by the royal court and the nobility. The number of servants and retainers employed and supported by a lord was generally considered an indication of his power and generosity. In an effort to curtail the power of the aristocrats and limit their influence over the court, the monarchs sought to replace them with professionals.

At the bottom of the rural society were the peasant farmers, field workers and herdsmen, while in the cities the groups at the bottom were the marginal workers, the unemployed, and the slaves. Slavery in fifteenth century Spain, however, was neither chattel nor confined only to Africans. It included individuals of all racial types, ethnic origins, and religious persuasions, even though the Catholic church had for some time been arguing against the enslavement of Christians.

In the Iberian society, the family was the basic organizational unit around which all its members revolved. The family, like the society itself, was organized in hierarchical fashion, with a senior figure, generally the father, in the role of ruler or patriarch.

The family included not only its immediate members: mother, father, and children, but grand-parents, uncles, aunts, and other distant relatives as well. If the patriarch was sufficiently wealthy, he was expected to provide for the less fortunate members of society, such as orphans, widows and loyal servants. It was also not unusual for illegitimate children fathered by the patriarch to form part of his household.[18]

Women's roles in the Iberian family depended on the places they occupied in the home and on their relationship to the patriarch. The wife of the patriarch, as the mother of his legitimate heirs, had power over other women, especially servants, in the estate, unless her post was already being occupied by her mother-in-law. The wife and all other immediate female members of the family were entrusted the family's honor. To help them in this task, they were closely guarded in the patriarch's home or in convents. In exchange for their loyalty and devotion to the family, they were supported by their husbands, fathers, and other male relatives and protected by local laws and customs. In Spain, for instance, women were also entitled by law to own and to inherit property and could administer family estates, as well as buy and sell properties. That legal tradition served Spanish women well during the conquest of America, as it permitted many of them to carry on the work initiated by their husbands.[19]

Yet the ideal of the secluded, retiring woman persisted as part of the patriarchal legacy. Hence every action of this family was aimed at pressuring women to marry, in part to solidify the family fortune, by gaining access to dowries and inheritances, and partly to keep the males from straying from the community.

The Africans: A Profile

The Africans were among the earliest groups to arrive in Puerto Rico as a result of the Spanish conquest of the island. Africans and their descendants began to form part of the Puerto Rican society in the sixteenth century. As with all newcomers, their history begins elsewhere. But since they were brought in as slaves, it is important to provide some details about their historical development, in order to dispel the notion (unfortunately still upheld by some) that their enslavement was justified by their primitive conditions.

When the Portuguese (the first Europeans to do so) reached Africa at the beginning of the fifteenth century, they found a continent of great variety in geography and culture. An estimated 100 million inhabitants made their living from agriculture, cattle and sheep farming, and commerce. They had adjusted and thrived in all of Africa's ecological zones: from vast deserts to grasslands, and from great forests to woodlands.[20]

Some regions of the African landscape were naturally more conducive to the type of economic activities that resulted in greater social organization and overall development. The western coast, for example, with its good soil, abundant minerals, and adequate rainfall offered ideal conditions for the rapid development of several complex cultures. Long before the fifteenth century, Africans had developed sophisticated farming methods to allow them to feed the growing population. They had fashioned iron tools and implements and devised many labor-saving devices.

In politics, they were not so far behind the Europeans, as the slave captors later argued. In fact, by the time the Portuguese reached the west coast of Africa, the continent (three times larger than Europe), had a history of kingdoms and empires. The best known, due to its territorial expansion, was the Empire of Ghana, which reached its summit between the fifth and sixth centuries of the Christian Era. During this period its rule spanned the territory from the Sahara desert to the Gulf of Guinea and from the Niger River to the Atlantic Ocean. The area encompassed extensive urban settlements with advanced architecture, elaborate art, and highly complex social and political organizations.

But as in Europe, the empire of Ghana became the object of repeated attacks from the Islamic invaders from northern Africa during the eighth and ninth centuries. Once in control, the Moslems created a new empire, with its capital and seat of power at Timbuktu. During the Middle Ages, Timbuktu was known throughout the civilized world for its vast wealth, fine university, extensive library, and great scholars.

In addition to the empires, there were numerous smaller kingdoms, of which the Kongo and Benin were the best known for the skills of their inhabitants. They excelled in metallurgy, weaving, ceramics, architecture, and a variety of arts and crafts. Many cities in these kingdoms had been for centuries important centers of trade, just as their counterparts had been to the Europeans.[21]

Although the cities of west Africa came in contact with other civilizations after the seventh century and learned to profit from their access to the Arab world, those on the eastern coast took advantage of their contacts and access to the Asian civilizations facing the Indian Ocean.

Thus, when the Europeans reached the African continent in search of gold, grain, ivory and slaves, they were neither the first foreigners nor the most cultured groups the Africans had encountered. Nor were they much more advanced economically or socially. They were, however, a highly militarized people, with an arsenal of weapons, and the determination to use them in their quest for wealth, power, and glory, even if that meant enslaving millions of Africans.

The Slave Trade

Both Africa and Europe had traded in slaves for centuries before they were introduced into the New World. Slavery had been known in Europe, for example, since the days of the Roman empire. But slaves, as stated earlier, were not confined to any racial, religious, or ethnic group. Consequently, when the Portuguese began trading with Africa, slaves were just one of the purchases they made in addition to gold, ivory, spices and other items in demand in the European ports.[22]

In general, the slaves they imported were purchased by the upper classes as personal and domestic servants, by artisans in need of skilled workers, and by lords and others seeking to create private or government armies.

In both Africa and Europe slavery was considered a misfortune that was meant to be temporary. Typically, slaves were prisoners of war, persons too poor to pay their debts, criminals, and those declared "infidels" by opposing religious groups. Prior to the "discovery" of the New World, slavery neither carried the stigma we associate with it, nor did it deprive the enslaved of their human rights or the opportunity to redeem themselves. Slaves were permitted to marry free persons, to buy, sell, and inherit property, and obtain their freedom in various ways. Moreover, slavery was not hereditary.[23]

Following the conquest of the New World and the rapid decimation of its population, the Europeans began to look to Africa as a source of labor for the economic enterprises they envisioned. At first, African slaves were imported to work the mines, but as these were few in number, or quickly exhausted, the slaves were employed in the sugar, cotton, and tobacco plantations that soon sprouted in the Caribbean and the Americas.

As the plantations increased, the number of slaves multiplied, and their living conditions worsened. They were gradually stripped of the rights they had known in Europe and Africa and slavery itself was transformed into a permanent and hereditary condition from which most slaves were hard-pressed to escape.

The most conservative estimate places the number of persons taken from Africa somewhere between ten and fifteen million in the 400 years the trade lasted.[24] In this, as in all such human tragedies, Africans also played a part as willing partners in the trade. Motivated by ambitions of power and wealth, many African lords staged wars against their neighbors and then sold the prisoners of war to European traders. In exchange they took as payment a variety of European manufactures, guns and gunpowder with which to continue their wars. In time, some Europeans did away with the intermediary expense of the African middlemen and sent their own captors into the interior.

In Puerto Rico, a neglected Spanish colony for most of the first three centuries, the demand for slaves was minuscule until the end of the eighteenth century in part because the colonizing population remained tiny (about 6,000 in 1700 and 44,000 in 1765) and sugar plantations did not take hold until the first quarter of the nineteenth century.[25] Nonetheless, the fact remains that enslaved Africans fluctuated between 10 and 11 percent of Puerto Rico's population between the 1760s and the 1870s. In Puerto Rico, perhaps because of the belated and incipient nature of the plantation system, the African group that predominated were free blacks and mulattoes. That reality, in turn, may help to explain why racial relations in Puerto Rico's history have been relatively amicable.

Suggested Readings

Beirao, Caetano. *A Short History of Portugal* (Lisbon: Panorama, 1960).
Bertrand, Louis and Petrie, Sir Charles. *The History of Spain: From the*

Musulmans to Franco (New York: Collier Books, 1971).

Curtin, Philip. "Measuring the Atlantic Slave Trade," in *Race and Slavery in the Western Hemisphere: Quantitative Studies*. Edited by Stanley Engerman and Eugene D. Genovese (Princeton University Press, 1975).

Davison, Basil. *The African Slave Trade: Precolonial History, 1450–1850* (Boston: Little, Brown and Co., 1961).

Elliott, J.H. *Imperial Spain, 1469–1716* (New York: The New American Library, 1963).

Lavrin, Asunción (ed.). *Sexuality and Marriage in Colonial Latin America* (Lincoln: University of Nebraska Press, 1989).

Lockhart, James. "Spanish Women of the Second Generation in Peru" in *Spanish Peru* by James Lockhart (Madison: University of Wisconsin Press, 1968).

McAllister, Lyle N. *Spain and Portugal in the New World, 1492–1700* (Minneapolis: University of Minnesota Press, 1984).

Mellafe, Rolando. *A Brief History of Negro Slavery in Latin America* (Berkeley and Los Angeles: 1975).

Miller, Francesca. "Precursoras" in *Latin American Women and the Search for Social Justice*. Edited by Francesca Miller (Hanover, NH: University Press of New England, 1991).

Nash, Gary B. *Red, White, and Black* (Englewood Cliffs, New Jersey: 1974).

Nowell, Charles E. *Portugal: The Modern Nation in Historical Perspective* (Englewood Cliffs, NJ: Prentice-Hall, Inc., 1973).

Rout, Jr., Leslie. *The African Experience in Spanish America, 1502 to the present day* (Mass.: Cambridge University Press, 1976).

Russell-Wood, A.J.R. "Female and Famile in the Economy and Society of Brazil" in *Latin American Women: Historical Perspectives*. Edited by Asunción Lavrin (Westwood, Conn.: Greenwood Press, 1978).

Santiago-Marazzi, Rosa. "La Immigración de mujeres españolas a Puerto Rico en el período colonial español" in *Homines* Vol. 10, No. 2 (1986–87).

Sobrequés Vidal, S. *Hispania: Síntesis de Historia de España*. (Barcelona: Editorial Vicens-Vives, 1979).

CHAPTER THREE

"Discovery", Conquest and Colonization

For his first voyage Columbus recruited 105 men and outfitted three caravels: the Niña, the Pinta, and the Santa María. The expedition left Palos, a port near Cádiz, on August 3, 1492. Its destination was the Canary Islands, Spain's furthest domain, off the west coast of Africa.

After a brief rest there, the expedition ventured westward into the unknown ocean. Finally, on October 12, after two months of enormous hardships, Rodrigo de Triana, cried out from the Pinta, that land lay ahead. They had stumbled upon an island of the Bahamas group. Columbus named it San Salvador and claimed it for the Spanish monarchs.[1]

Suspecting that he was not far from Cathay (China), Columbus set out to explore the area in search of the passageway connecting the islands to the mainland. Instead he found the island of Cuba and later another the Indians called Haiti (present-day Haiti and Santo Domingo). He claimed both for the Spanish monarchy and renamed the latter island Hispaniola.

Off Haiti's northwest coast, he lost the Santa María to a hurricane and was forced to leave behind forty of his men. With the remains of the ship he had a fort, La Navidad, built for them, while he returned to Spain with the others, to notify the monarchs of his exploits. As samples of his discoveries, he took back some gold, an assortment of plants and birds, and a few inhabitants from the place.

Back in Spain in March 1493, Columbus was given a hero's welcome by the King and Queen, who were then in Barcelona. After one week of celebrations, the monarchs authorized him to begin preparations for a second voyage, while they sought the Pope's (the Spaniard Alexander VI) confirmation of their new possessions.

The Demarcation Line

The Pope's ruling on this matter was important, because, as Catholic nations, both Spain and Portugal had come to accept the Holy Father's role as mediator. It was also a necessary step because Portugal's king, John II, had begun to question Spain's rights to the new lands. He claimed that since the territories discovered by Columbus were not very far from the Azores, they really belonged to Portugal.

In 1493, the Pope resolved the problem in typical Solomonic fashion.[2] He issued three bulls, the first of which recognized Spain's claims over the lands explored and those about to be explored by Columbus. The second established that Spain's rights to the new lands entailed an obligation to Christianize the inhabitants. The third divided the world into two spheres, along an imaginary line, from north to south on the Atlantic Ocean, 100 leagues west of the islands of Azores and Cape Verde. The lands and sea west of the line he assigned to Spain, and those east of the line to Portugal.

Unhappy with the Pope's ruling, King John complained that the space between the line and the African coast was too narrow to allow Portugal much room to maneuver. He appealed directly to the Spanish Monarchs with the proposal that he would abandon all claims to the lands discovered by Columbus if they agreed to move the line another 270 leagues west.

The offer was accepted and the location of the new line was ratified in 1494 by the Treaty of Tordesillas. Neither party knew then that the new line would wind up dividing the South American continent, and allow Portugal to claim its eastern portion, Brazil.[3]

Columbus Discovers Boriquén

Columbus' second journey found none of the obstacles of the first. In a few months, he obtained the funds, provisions, and sailors needed to return to the Indies. He left Spain on September 25, 1493, with seventeen well-stocked ships and 1,500 persons ready for glory and adventure. Besides the standard provisions, weapons and munitions, the ships carried seeds, a variety of domestic animals, work tools, and utensils of all kinds.

On the ships also were dozens of skilled workers and artisans, seasoned warriors, clergymen, and a few hidalgos, or poor relations from the upper classes. To translate for them, Columbus brought back six of the Indians he had taken to Spain the previous year. In the group also was Juan Ponce de León, the man destined to become Puerto Rico's first Spanish governor.

Before the second expedition reached Hispaniola, Columbus stopped at the present-day island of Guadeloupe. There, he came upon some Taino women and children, who claimed to be captives of the Carib Indians and desirous of returning home. He claimed to have have allowed them to guide him through a multitude of tiny islands to a larger, beautiful island they called Boriquén. He renamed this island San Juan Bautista (St. John the Baptist) in honor of Don Juan, son of the King and Queen of Spain.[4]

Where Columbus landed on Boriquén has been a subject of speculation among local historians, in part because the Admiral's notes on this issue are imprecise. He merely notes that he spent two days exploring the west coast of this island, fishing, and replenishing his stores. This has led some historians to claim that he landed at Aguada, and others that the honor belongs to Aguadilla. The commonly accepted version, however, is that he disembarked in an unknown spot somewhere between these two places. Once claimed and recorded as Spanish property, Boriquén was forgotten for the next fifteen years.

When he finally reached Hispaniola in late November 1493, he found neither the men nor the fort he had left there the previous year. Using his viceregal powers, he established a new settlement, Isabela, in honor of the Queen of Castile, and placed his brother Bartolomé in charge of the government, while he went on to explore the area.

Settlers Revolt in Hispaniola

In 1498, while Columbus was in Spain, preparing for his third voyage, the Spanish settlers in Hispaniola revolted under the leadership of Francisco Roldán, the mayor of Isabela.[5] Dissatisfied with the meager prospects of wealth found in the colony, and what they called the "tyrannical rule of Bartolomé Columbus", the rebels took up arms against his government, established their own settlement in the southwestern region of the island, and appointed a new administration.

Upon his return from Spain in August, the Admiral chose to negotiate with the rebels, for fear that divisions in his ranks might encourage the Taino Indians to revolt. He acquiesced to some of the rebels' demands, provided they put down their arms. He then brought some into the government, granted access to the placer mines to others, and *encomiendas*, service grants, to all. Temporarily pacified, the majority accepted his terms, but a few returned to Spain to complain to the Crown.[6]

A royal appointee, Francisco de Bobadilla, commander of the Order of Calatrava, arrived in August of 1500 with powers to investigate, judge the case, and take over as "royal governor... of all the islands and mainland of the Indies". Shortly after his arrival, Bobadilla had the Columbus brothers arrested and shipped to Spain in chains. In Spain, the monarchs ordered their release and authorized the explorer to undertake another (the fourth) voyage on their behalf. They warned, however, that since there were still charges pending against him, Columbus was no longer welcomed in Hispaniola nor authorized to rule any of the lands he discovered.

Bobadilla died in 1502, and the monarchs sent Nicolás de Ovando, a friar and Knight Commander of Alcántara, to replace him. In addition to provisions, tools, and animals, the new governor brought with him 2,500 additional settlers, including the first women and children. Christopher Columbus died in Spain, in 1506, still deprived of his rights to govern or to return to Hispaniola. His widow and son sued the Crown, and the struggle between them had repercussions in Puerto Rico a few years later.[7]

The Encomienda and its Aftermath

The *repartimiento*, or distribution of Indians into encomiendas, initiated by Columbus, had devastating effects on the native populations of the Caribbean. Treated as part of the spoils, they were expected to pay tribute to the newcomers, in gold, food, or other products. But as the settlers' demands usually exceeded the available gold and products, the encomiendas were required to make up the balance in personal services and labor.[8]

The system, which rapidly turned into a disguised form of slavery, soon threatened to extinguish the native population. From the monarchs' perspective, such destruction was not only bad for the colonial economy, but could become a justification for any of her rivals to intervene in the Indies. The monarchs also worried that, since the encomenderos also controlled much of the colony's wealth, they might become powerful lords and begin to challenge their authority.

To arrest such potential problems, the monarchy sought to tighten its control over the colony by acting as mediator between the two populations. Thus, in 1503–1504, it issued a series of edicts by which it declared the Indians free persons, vassals of the Crown and thus entitled to royal protection. Part of that protection stipulated that the *encomenderos*, grantees, pay the natives cash wages for their labor, allow them free time to rest and plant their own fields, and instruct them in matters of Faith. For their part, the Indians were obliged to obey the laws of the kingdom, which demanded that they work for the colonists and convert to the Christian faith.[9]

The decrees were selectively enforced by the colonists and thus did little to lighten the burden of the natives. They were, however, of use to the monarchy, for they set a legal precedent in the struggle for power it was engaged in with the Columbus family. Having placed the native population under its control, the monarchy gained power over the encomienda, a tool it would also use in its struggle with the settlers.

The Church's Cry for Justice

Shortly after the monarchy interjected itself in the affairs of the colony, it authorized the Dominican friars to establish themselves in Hispaniola. The first friars arrived in 1510.

Among them was Antonio de Montesinos, the first member of that order to denounce the settlers' abuses against the natives. Over two consecutive Sundays in November 1511, he chastised his parishioners, accusing them of ignoring their Christian obligations, and warning them that they would die in sin, unless they abandoned their unjust ways.

Deeply offended by his words, many of them appealed to Diego Columbus (son and heir of the discoverer) to silence him. But since Columbus' powers did not extend to the members of the church, he reported the matter to the King. Not easily intimidated, Montesinos, too, sent a report to the King, detailing the many abuses the Indians endured at the hand of the Spaniards. Aware of the moral and legal obligations the colonial project entailed, he questioned by what rights were the Indians deprived of their natural freedom and despoiled of their lands and wealth.[10]

Caught between multiple obligations—to itself, the settlers, the natives, and the Pope—the monarchy appointed a commission of jurists and theologians to study the matter, taking into account the interests of these groups, and offer recommendations. The decrees that emerged from the Commission's suggestions, in 1512, became known as the Laws of Burgos (the place where the deliberations took place in Spain).

In principle, the Laws of Burgos[11] differed little from the 1503 decrees. Like them, they recognized the Indians' freedom, the Crown's necessity to protect them, and the settler's obligation to treat them humanely. The Indians were obliged to obey the laws of the kingdom, accept conversion to the Catholic faith, continue to work for the colonists, in exchange for cash wages, and donate part of their free time to building public and religious projects.

There were differences, however, between the two sets of laws. The 1512 laws restricted the encomienda to individuals and groups present in the colony. It was no longer hereditary or transferable. When an encomendero died, the natives under his charge regained their freedom and were not to be subjected to further captivity. The remaining encomenderos were advised to exempt married Indian women and children under fourteen years of age from hard labor, to provide healthcare for the sick, to ensure that all were baptized and that they married within the church. They were also expected to teach at least one of those under their charge to read and write.

To keep the emancipated Tainos from fleeing to the hills, where neither the clergy nor the colonists could reach them, the Burgos Laws called for the establishment of Indian villages, separate from the Spanish settlements. Protection and guidance for the village Indians was entrusted to a resident priest.[12] The Burgos Laws also failed to end the abuses against the Indians, in part because, in the struggle for control that ensued between the competing groups, the conquerors had the upper hand. Aware that without them the colonial enterprise could not continue, the Crown compromised on its commitments to the native population.

Concerned about the fate of the Indians, Bartolomé de Las Casas, another Dominican friar, took up their case, demanding that justice be done in the name of Christianity.[13] Provoked by such arguments, the great jurist Juan López Palacios Rubios replied that, if Spain's mission was to Christianize the "heathen", then the explorers had to be advised how and when were they to respect the natives' freedom and bring them to the Faith peacefully. He proposed that such privileges should be enjoyed by the natives who received the explorers without armed resistance, but that they did not apply to those who took up arms against them. He said these were enemies, subject to the terms of war, and when captured could be sold into slavery.[14]

In 1513 Palacios Rubios' ideas were incorporated into the *requerimiento*, requirement, a document to be read aloud by the explorers as they approached the Indian communities. The fact that the natives might not understand what was expected of them was apparently besides the point. The requirement was, after all, a legal justification for war against any Indian group that dared to challenge the conquerors. Although there isn't any evidence that this document was ever read by the colonizers of Boriquén, it is probable that its principles were known to Ponce de León and the other governors who organized periodic expeditions against the Tainos who fled from them.

Conquest and Settlement of Boriquén

In 1505, Vicente Yañez-Pinzón (captain of the Niña in Columbus' first voyage and later discoverer of Brazil) received authorization from the Crown to colonize San Juan Bautista (Boriquén). Distracted by other projects, Yañez sold his rights, in 1508, to Martín García de Salazar. But since Salazar also failed to undertake the project, the task fell to Juan Ponce de León.[15]

Ponce de León, an impoverished hidalgo, had distinguished himself in the wars against the Tainos of Hispaniola, and was at the time mayor of Salvaleón del Higüey (a settlement in Hispaniola). Apparently dissatisfied with his lot, he asked the governor, Nicolás de Ovando, to grant him permission to explore the island of San Juan. Ovando obliged, and on August 12, 1508, Ponce de León and forty-two companions landed near the port of Guánica, on Boriquén's southern shore.

They proceeded to the chiefdom of Guainía, where Agüeybana I, (also known as the Elder), received them in amicable fashion, sharing with them food and shelter. Assuring Agüeybana that they came in peace, he went on to exchange names with the Taino chief, as was their custom. The Tainos believed that in taking another man's name, one also acquired his virtues. At the conclusion of the ritual, Ponce de León received permission from Agüeybana to explore the island and establish a settlement.

After reconnoitering the north coast, including the bay of present-day San Juan, he named its port Puerto Rico, and ordered his men to build a settlement about a league inland, at the basin of the River Toa. With only one large house, and few dirt roads leading to the harbor, the settlement, which he called Caparra, was a modest place.

Pleased with his progress, Ponce de León ordered the natives to plant a few crops for the Spanish king, and after gathering a few gold samples returned to Hispaniola, to seek authorization from Governor Ovando to begin colonization of the island. If granted, the charter would permit him to relocate his family, to secure the settlers and resources needed to found and protect the colony.

Governor Ovando approved Ponce de León's plan and appointed him Lieutenant Governor of San Juan. The post recognized him as the maximum ruler on the island and afforded him sufficient flexibility to conduct the colonization as he wished. It empowered him to decide the fate of the island's inhabitants, and to demand loyalty and obedience from the settlers. He was also free to appeal to the King directly, to confirm his post and prerogatives.

By March 1509, Ponce de León had returned to Caparra, and by August had been confirmed in his post by the King.[16] Yet the ongoing legal battles between the Columbus family and the Crown made his governorship uncertain from the start. Just the previous year (1508) Columbus' heir, Diego, had won a favorable ruling from the Spanish courts, which forced the Crown to restore the family's rights to the Indies.

Publicly, the King abided by the legal judgment, permitting Diego Columbus to take charge of the Indies government. Privately, he sought to sabotage his government by insisting that Columbus honor all the appointments and arrangements made previously by the Crown or its appointees. Diego, for his part, did his best to ignore the King's demands, and began to replace the existing officers as soon as he reached

Hispaniola. Among these was Ponce de León, who in October 1509 was replaced by Juan Cerón.

Out of government, Ponce de León retreated to his farm, while Cerón took charge of the colonization. When it came to assigning encomiendas, Cerón apparently favored his own followers, and earned the enmity of Ponce de León's men. From then on his fate was sealed; all that was needed was a pretext to remove him.

That pretext was soon provided by the King himself, when he sent Cristóbal de Sotomayor to San Juan. Still trying to sabotage Columbus' government, the King instructed Cerón to grant Sotomayor permission to establish a settlement in the western region of the island and to assign him an encomienda. The governor approved the request and Sotomayor founded Villa Tavara, not far from Guainía, in present-day Guayanilla. The site was infested with mosquitoes and Sotomayor moved the settlement near the port of present-day Aguada. He renamed the relocated settlement Villa Sotomayor, in his own honor.

In March 1510, the King ordered Ponce de León to assume the governorship of San Juan once again. Unsure how to proceed, Ponce de León consulted Sotomayor, who advised him to depose Juan Cerón and ship him off to Spain in chains. Ponce de León heeded the advice, forcing Puerto Rico to experience a coup d'état less than two years after the first Europeans arrived. Ironically, in June 1510, the King rewarded Ponce de León for this usurpation of power with the titles of Captain of Land and Sea, and First Justice of the Island of San Juan.[17]

Despite the ongoing intrigues at the top, the natives remained calm and the colony prospered. New settlers continued to arrive from Hispaniola and Spain, laden with seeds, tools, and the determination to succeed. The promise of gold led to the establishment of a smelter and the impressive yield of approximately 100,000 pesos in gold in October 1510. One-fifth of this sum was sent to the King, two-fifths were assigned to cover the costs of colonization, including the expansion and fortification of the governor's house, and the remaining two-fifths were presumably kept by the miners.

As the thirst for gold and the demand for laborers increased, life became intolerable and the Tainos began to resist the invaders. The decision to revolt came out of the western region, where Sotomayor's methods were the cause of much discontent among the displaced Taino nobility.

The Tainos Revolt

In early 1510, Agüeybana the Brave, nephew of Agüeybana I, and heir to the chiefdom of Guainía, became part of the encomienda that was granted to Sotomayor.[18] His sister Guanina was also included in the lot. Disdainful of their positions as leaders, and intent on being obeyed, Sotomayor soon earned the hatred of Agüeybana and other chiefs in the region.

Deprived of their freedom and made to endure indignities and hard work, the Tainos waited for the day when they could avenge themselves. What delayed them was a disturbing myth that the Spaniards might be immortal. The notion was based on the Christian teachings propagated by the conquerors, which stressed that Christ was resurrected on the third day. In November 1510, Urayoán, the chief of Yagüecas (between present-day Añasco and Mayagüez) decided to test the myth. He selected for the experiment a young Spaniard named Diego Salcedo, who happened to be waiting for the chief's men to carry him across the Guaorabo River. Instead, the chief ordered his men to drown Salcedo, take his body ashore, and watch him for several days.[19]

The report of Salcedo's decaying corpse confirmed what he already suspected: the Spaniards were as mortal as themselves. Reassured, the other chiefs began to prepare for war, attending a meeting the following January, convened by Agüeybana the Brave. The purpose of that meeting, according to the spy Juan González, who claimed to have witnessed the event, in disguise, was to set the date and place for the attack. He reported also that Caguax, chief of Turabo, and don Alonso, a Christian convert from the area of Otoao, did not endorse the war plan. But given that Guarionex, Mabodomoca, Urayoán, Agüeybana and many others wanted war, the date was set for the following day. The targets were the Villa Sotomayor, the settlers and their haciendas, and then Caparra and its settlers.

News of the impending attack was conveyed by González to Sotomayor the next morning while he was still at his hacienda. Accompanied by his nephew and three others, Sotomayor attempted to

Chief Urayoán's men drown Salcedo
(16th century print)

return to the settlement. To do so, without alerting the enemy was difficult, so Sotomayor put up a brave front and notified Agüeybana to send
some of his men to carry his baggage and provisions. Feigning obedience,
Agüeybana sent the requested carriers, except that this time they had
orders to lead Sotomayor and his companions into an ambush by the
Coayuco River.[20]

The only one to survive the attack was the spy Juan González. Legend
has it that, although severely wounded, González crossed the Cordillera,
to alert his compatriots at Caparra. Meanwhile, at Villa Sotomayor, Chief
Guarionex and his troops killed 80 of its inhabitants and razed the settlement. News of the attack was reported to Ponce de León days later by
"fearless" Diego de Salazar and the survivors he escorted to Caparra.

Experienced in such wars, Ponce de León gathered and divided his
forces into three companies of thirty men each, and requested reinforcements from Hispaniola. One of the companies was left to protect Caparra,
and the others he took with him into enemy territory. They surprised a

group of Tainos at the Coayuco Valley, and after punishing them severely moved on to Yagüecas, the heart of the rebel territory. There, according
to official accounts, they ran into 11,000 armed men, under the command
of chiefs Agüeybana and Mobodomaca. Outnumbered, they would have
been massacred had it not been for a stroke of luck. As both sides waited
for orders to begin the attack, one of Ponce de León's harquebusiers mor-
tally wounded chief Agüeybana. The loss of their brave chief led the
rebels to retreat temporarily, granting the Spaniards a reprieve which they
used to return to Caparra, to regroup and to devise ways with which to
divide and punish the enemy.[21]

One tactic that proved valuable was Ponce de León's offer of amnesty
to any rebel group who laid down their arms. Chiefs Caguax and Don
Alonso, the two who had argued against war from the start, were said to
have accepted Ponce de León's offer immediately.

Disoriented by Agüeybana's death, the remaining chiefs and rebels followed different paths. Some took cover in the Luquillo Sierra and from
there launched sporadic attacks on the eastern settlements for many years.
Others fled to neighboring islands, joined the Caribs, and continued to
attack the coastal settlements for decades. Hundreds sought refuge in the
mountainous interior, and when caught were sold into slavery. Many
accepted defeat and resigned themselves to life in encomiendas, while
others, dispirited by the prospect of a life in slavery, killed themselves and
their children.

In the end, so many Tainos died or fled after the war that the governor
began to fear that soon there would be no one left to work the mines. Six
years of hard work, exposure to diseases war, and flight had reduced the
original population, from an estimated 60,000, in 1509, to 14,636, in
1515 (see Table 3.2). To arrest the decline, Ponce de León requested permission from the king to purchase a ship, to "bring back the fugitives"
from their hiding places in the Lesser Antilles. Once approved, the ship
also served to raid the islands of the Lesser Antilles, and carry off its
inhabitants into slavery. Ultimately, when these practices failed to satisfy
the settlers' demands for workers, the governor petitioned the King to let
the island import African slaves.

The Rocky Colonial Government

Shortly after the Spanish victory at Yagüecas, Ponce de León was once again deprived of his post.[22] This time it was the King who ordered that he return the government to his nemesis Juan Cerón, as the courts had again ruled on behalf of the Columbus family. The King suggested that Ponce de León explore other lands and visit him at the royal court.

Always the obedient servant, Ponce de León did what the King requested, and sailed north in search of gold, new lands to conquer, and a magic fountain of youth. In March 1513, he reached an area he called Florida and thus became the first European to lay claim to a portion of present-day North America. But finding neither gold nor the magic fountain, he returned to San Juan for a brief rest before going to meet the King. He remained in Madrid until May 1515, when he returned to his beloved Caparra.

Meanwhile, Governor Cerón continued his predecessor's work, distributing encomiendas, devising ways to keep the Tainos from fleeing, and establishing a western settlement. To block the flight of the Tainos, he had their canoes destroyed, and organized raids and punitive expeditions against the neighboring islands.

San Germán, a new settlement established in 1512, by order of Diego Columbus, was unsafe.[23] Intended to replace the Sotomayor settlement, destroyed the previous year, San Germán, became the target of repeated attacks by the natives. Determined to regain control of the placer mines and restore Spanish rule in the western region, Diego Columbus visited Puerto Rico in 1512 and appointed the experienced military figure Cristóbal Mendoza as the new governor. Mendoza led a harsh campaign against the rebels the following year, with disastrous results. Provoked, the Tainos not only destroyed San Germán, but rowed right into San Juan bay and set fire to Caparra. On their way out, they also attacked the northeastern village of Loíza, killing the cacica Luisa and her Spanish husband, Pedro Mejías.

Unsuccessful in San Germán, Governor Mendoza organized an expedition against a group of rebels that operated out of Vieques. He launched his attack at night and, in the uneven battle that ensued, more than one hundred Indians died, including the group's leader Yaureibo. The Vieques "victory" gave the Spaniards in Puerto Rico a brief respite, but by no means ended the Taino and Carib attacks against the settlements.

This time, the King intervened directly, ordering the San Germán settlers to rebuild, but to do so at a mid-way point between the mines and the shore, for easier access for the inbound ships to collect the gold. San Germán was rebuilt at the mouth of the Añasco river, where it would remain for another forty years, until frequent floods forced it to move to the southern port of Guayanilla.

Meanwhile, Ponce de León, who had returned to Caparra from Spain in 1515, with the titles of Captain of the Land and Sea of San Juan, Captain of the Armada Against the Caribs, Adelantado of Florida, Land Surveyor of San Juan, and Member For Life of the cabildo (town council) of Caparra, devoted himself to the mundane tasks of building a stone castle for himself, surveying the land, and helping to defend the place from Taino-Carib attacks.[24] He divided the island into two districts, using the Camuy River as the demarcation line. The north to south division left San Germán as the seat of government of the western district and Caparra as the one for the eastern, or Puerto Rico district.

A proposal to move Caparra from its humid, mosquito-infested site, at the basin of the river Toa, to the drier and cooler isle of San Juan split the settlers into two camps. Prospective merchants favored the move because they saw the bay and the adjacent natural port as ideal places from which to trade. In the other camp were Juan Ponce de León and those who argued that the existing site was convenient for the supervision of the mines and farms.

Bored with his life, and tired of the constant bickering about moving Caparra across the bay to present-day San Juan, Ponce de León left for Florida in 1521. There, he was wounded by a poisoned arrow, and died five months later of gangrene in Havana, Cuba. He was forty-seven years old. His remains were eventually transferred to San Juan; first to the San José Church and later to the nearby Cathedral. His statue still guards the plaza in front of the San José Church.

With his death, the arguments against relocating Caparra lost support and it was moved to the islet across the bay in 1521. In time, the name Caparra was replaced by San Juan, and the island adopted the name of the port, Puerto Rico.

Population and the New Society

By the 1520s, Puerto Rico's population consisted of three distinct racial groups: Spaniards, Indians, and Africans. It is not known with certainty when the first African slaves were brought to Puerto Rico, but it is suspected that they were there in 1513 because slaves had been present in nearby Hispaniola for some time. Although outnumbered by Indians and Africans, the Spaniards controlled the government and economy, and imposed their values on the emerging society. Enslaved, the Indians and Africans occupied the bottom rungs of the social ladder.

Despite their power, the Spaniards were not safe. Exposed to enemy attacks, epidemics, accidents, and natural forces, such as hurricanes, they witnessed a decimation in their ranks.[25] To stem the decline, the governor petitioned the Crown to send settlers. In theory, the King was expected to give preference to his Castilian vassals, but in practice, he extended residency permits ("cédulas de vecindad") to others willing to relocate to Puerto Rico. To farmers and artisans, the groups in greatest demand, the Crown provided free passage. In 1520, a total of 200 new settlers arrived in Puerto Rico, many of them from the Canary Islands. Although their arrival was welcomed, they could hardly be expected to replace the native workers lost to a small epidemic the year before. Other offers by the Crown went unclaimed and Puerto Rico's population stagnated.[26]

According to a 1530 census, the Spanish population on the island consisted of 426 *vecinos*, permanent residents, and 298 temporary residents. Of the permanent settlers, 369 were males, most of them single, and fifty-seven were females, all married.

The Indian population, according to the same census, consisted of less than 2,000 persons, compared to the 14,436 that were reported in 1515 (see Table 3.2). There has been some speculation in recent years that the figure reported by the census only reflected the Indians in the encomiendas and did not take into account those who lived freely in the interior of the island.

TABLE 3.1
Spanish Residents in Puerto Rico, 1530

Civil Status	Males	Females
Married	71	57
Single	298	—
Total	**369**	**57**

Sources: Data taken from Governor Lando's Report, Cited in: Blanca Silvestrini and María Dolores Luque, *Historia de Puerto Rico: Trayectoria de un pueblo* (San Juan: Cultural Puertorriqueña, Inc., 1987), p. 91.

TABLE 3.2
Indians in Slavery and Encomienda

Status	1515	1530
Encomienda Indians	9,100	497
Indian Slaves	—	1,040
Indian children	3,970	—
Elderly Persons	566	—
Totals	**14,436**	**1,537**

Sources: Data appears in Salvador Brau, *Historia de la Colonización de Puerto Rico* (San Juan: Instituto de Cultura Puertorriqueña, 1969) 389–390 and Governor Lando's Report, Silvestrini and Luque, op. cit., p. 91.

The African population reported by the 1530 census was larger than the native population (see Table 3.3). At first, the African royal policy for the Caribbean had insisted that it be limited to *ladinos*, Christianized, Spanish-speaking slaves. The reasoning behind the policy was that these were less likely to revolt or to ally themselves with the natives. When reality proved otherwise, the policy was abandoned in favor of another that permitted importation of *bozales*, slaves directly from Africa.

In either case, the supply of slaves to the colonies was part of a commercial venture that required royal approval and the active participation of the Seville merchants. Interested slave traders received permits and licenses from the Crown in exchange for payment of numerous fees and a commitment to route their shipments through the port of Seville.

One of the first to engage in this trade with the Caribbean was Lorenzo de Garrevod, who in 1518, introduced 1,000 slaves (500 ladinos and 500 bozales).[27] Whether Garrevod sold any from that shipment to Puerto Rico is hard to say. All that is known is that by 1530 the island had 2,264 African slaves, the majority of whom lived in the eastern district (see Table 3.3).

In the African group, as in the white population, males (1,783) out-numbered females (406). In the slave group, females represented 17.9 percent, while in the white group, females constituted 13.3 percent of the total. There were 55 slaves for whom information on gender is lacking (see Table 3.3).

Originally brought to mine gold, the African slaves were reassigned to other jobs when the placer mines ran out. The majority were absorbed by a nascent sugar industry. The rest were hired out as day laborers by their owners, placed in homes as domestics, and employed by the cattle growers.

TABLE 3.3

African Slaves in Puerto Rico, 1530, by Sex, by Region

Sex	San Juan	San Germán
Male	1,577	226
Female	354	52
Not Known	—	55
Totals	**1,931**	**333**

Source: Data taken from Aida R. Caro, "Esclavos y esclavistas en el primer tercio del siglo XVI (1530)," in *Revista del Museo de Antropología, Historia y Arte,* Vol. 1. no. 1 (1979), Universidad de Puerto Rico.

Settlement Patterns

In 1530, San Juan, the capital and major settlement on the island, had 120 houses, some of them built in stone. It had a central plaza, a cathe-dral, and a Dominican convent under construction. It served also as a launching site for other settlements.[28] From San Juan, the more adventur-ous settlers following the course of the Dagüao and Loíza rivers explored the eastern shoreline, and settled the area of present-day Luquillo. This settlement, however, was destroyed in October 1530, by a group of Carib Indians, who, in addition to killing the Spaniards, set fire to the place and took the twenty-five African and Taino slaves as captives. Exposed to repeated attacks from the Carib and Taino Indians, the eastern corner of the island was neglected for most of the sixteenth century.

Others sailed northwest along the Toa and Cibuco rivers and in 1556 established the nucleus of present-day Arecibo. There, without much contact with San Juan, but protected from enemy attacks by the rough waters of the Atlantic Ocean, the original families grew in number from thirty to eighty by 1617, and earned their living by raising cattle.[29]

San Germán, the new seat of the western district, was less fortunate than Arecibo, as it was sacked and burned by French corsairs numerous times. The attacks began in 1528, when sixty Frenchmen, seeking gold, set fire to the settlement.[30] The settlers saved their own lives by hiding in nearby farms. The settlement was rebuilt, but the inhabitants no longer felt confident they could survive without government protection.

Because the region's gold was nearly exhausted, they had little leverage with the government and were not able to command the attention of earlier years. After a few more French attacks, the settlers of San Germaán decided to move the settlement inland.

Perched on the Hills of Santa Marta (its present location since 1573), San Germán began a slow economic recovery as its residents turned to farming and cattle raising. Short of gold, San Germán also lost favor with the Seville merchants. Abandoned by all, the western settlers became involved in contraband trade with Spain's rivals. Their cooperation, in turn, reduced the rivals' attacks and permitted the economy to prosper. The number of families increased from fifty in the 1530s to one hundred at the end of the century. In 1606, the Dominican friars began constructing the Porta Coeli convent.

From the new site, some cattle ranchers moved their herds eastward along the Coamo river, and by 1579 had established San Blas de Illescas (present-day Coamo). Another group explored the northwest as far as the port of Aguada, where they laid the foundations for present-day San Francisco de la Aguada.

Early Defense Efforts

Because of its strategic location in the Caribbean, Puerto Rico became a bone of contention almost from the start, and Spain ordered her settlers to begin building a defense system.[31] Repeated rumors during the 1520s that France planned to attack led the settlers of San Juan to build a wooden bulwark at the "entry to the port." By 1530, the governors' house, Casa Blanca, had been built in stone and fortified, since it was expected to serve as refuge for the settlers in case of attack.

Between 1532 and 1540 the Santa Catalina fortress (present-day La Fortaleza, and the governor's mansion) was built near the bay of San Juan, on the southwest quadrant of the city. Since Santa Catalina faced away from the harbor, in 1540, the settlers began construction of the massive El Morro Castle, a project that took more than a century to complete and devoured thousands of workers. Built on the rocky promontory at the entrance of the bay, El Morro served San Juan and Spain well for cen-

Spanish attack of Boriquén

turies. It was, like Santa Catalina, staffed by Spanish soldiers and equipped with cannons and other war matériel from the Spanish arsenals.

Such military protection, however, was limited to San Juan, the seat of the colonial government and the one authorized port. San Germán and other settlements remained defenseless, and thus subjected to periodic raids from Spain's rivals. As the French attacks on San Germán waned, the British began to threaten the northern capital. Bitter religious differences and England's determination to share Spain's newfound wealth led the two to go to war in the mid-1580s. To fend off the attacks of the English "sea dogs", Spain increased the pace of its fortifications in the Indies. In Puerto Rico, old fortifications were repaired and new ones built. At the eastern entrance of the city, the land bridge (San Antonio), connecting the islet of San Juan to the larger island, was strengthened and the bulwark, El Boquerón, was constructed. In the west, between El Morro and Fortaleza, arose the bulwark of Santa Elena.

For their defense, the Spanish government sent 200 additional soldiers and large quantities of heavy artillery and munitions. But since local funds were insufficient to finance the increasing military operations, the Crown ordered the treasury of New Spain (Mexico) to provide a yearly subsidy ("el situado") to Puerto Rico. Situado funds were sent, albeit irregularly, from the 1580s to the first decades of the nineteenth century.

The Catholic Church

The first Catholic church in Puerto Rico was built in Caparra in 1509, by order of Juan Ponce de León. It was a wooden hut, to be used as a temporary place of worship. Once completed, Ponce de León asked Governor Ovando to send a priest from Hispaniola. In 1511, the King, the regal patron of the church, authorized the Franciscans to build a monastery and a chapel in San Juan, in honor of St. John the Baptist, but for reasons that are not altogether clear, they delayed more than a century in fulfilling that mission.

In 1511, the King also declared San Juan the first episcopal see in the New World and appointed Alonso Manso as the first bishop of the Americas. Upon his arrival in Caparra in 1513, the bishop received an encomienda of 150 Indians as part of the church's endowment.[32]

The community was small and poor and he was not able to obtain the

necessary funds to build a proper church and conduct the expected services. In 1515, Bishop Manso returned to Spain to seek assistance. When
he retuned to Caparra four years later, it was with the grand title of
Inquisitor of the Indies. Thus Manso brought Puerto Rico the dubious
honor of being the first place in the New World to have a Holy Inquisitor.

There are no accounts, however, of inquisitorial trials on the island during his reign. Apparently, he restricted his activities to seeking sustenance
for the church, to offering elementary instruction to the settlers' children
and to demanding that the Indians in the encomiendas be made available
for conversion.

After the Caparra settlement moved to San Juan, in 1521, the modest
wooden church was replaced by a solid stone building. In the 1520s, the
Dominican Order settled in San Juan, and by 1530 had built a convent in
the northwest quadrant of the city. Shortly afterwards, the Order began
construction of a church, which took more than a century to complete. In
other parts of the city, parishioners also built a few chapels in honor of
Santa Ana, Santa Bárbara, San Sebastián, and Santa Catalina.[33]

Despite its meager resources, the Catholic church in Puerto Rico
offered some services and assistance to the community. In the 1520s,
Bishop Manso turned part of the San Juan cathedral into a grammar
school, for the children of his parishioners.

The Dominican House of General Studies, established in the 1520s,
offered limited courses in secondary education. Courses in the liberal arts,
grammar, and theology were provided free of charge to the young boys of
the city. Books, however, were a problem, except for the fortunate few
who had access to the private libraries of the Dominican convent, or the
house of the new bishop, Bernardo Balbuena. With so few schools and
resources, the settlers' educational level was low.

The Colonial Economy

The distant royal hand was present in the economic affairs of the
colony from the beginning.[34] Shortly after the battle of Yagüecas, the
Crown stipulated that, in addition to exploiting the salt and gold mines,
the governor assign one-third of the Indian labor force to the cultivation
of crops for local consumption. The aim, the Crown never tired of repeat-
ing, was to make the island a valuable asset that was also self-sufficient.

To insure itself of receiving its due share of the local wealth and taxes, the Crown appointed, in 1511, an accountant, a commissioner, an overseer, and a treasurer. Their duties included assessing the value of the island's production and trade, and levying taxes and duties. Among these were the *alcabala* (sales tax), *almojarifazgo* (import/export duty, roughly 7.5 percent of the value), *avería* (shipping tax),*diezmo real* (a 10 percent royal tribute), *diezmo eclesiástico* (a 10 church tax), and *regalías* (royalties, demanded of miners and those given land grants by the King).

By the 1530s, the placer mines were nearly exhausted and the island experienced its first economic crisis. As gold production dropped from 20,000 pesos in 1532 to 6,000 the next year, miners, who had purchased slaves on credit, fled with them for fear of ending in debtor's prison.[35] Many of the other settlers also sought to abandon the island after 1534, when some of Pizarro's men arrived with news of the fabulous wealth that could be obtained in Perú.

Fearing the depopulation of the colony, the governor, Francisco Manuel de Lando, threatened to cut off the foot of anyone caught trying to leave. When the cry "May God take me to Perú" proved more powerful than his threats, the governor suggested that the Crown offer financial incentives to those willing to engage in growing sugar cane for export. His idea was to have sugar earnings from sales replace the vanishing gold revenues. Seedlings were easily obtained from neighboring Hispaniola and a few settlers already grew sugar cane successfully. One of them, Tomás de Castellón, had been operating a sugar mill in the jurisdiction of Añasco since 1523.

The royal government accepted Lando's proposal and offered a loan of 6,000 pesos, to build a sugar mill. To mitigate the colony's demands for workers, in 1540, the Crown financed the voyage of fifty Spanish families, and in 1551, authorized forty-five refugees from Portuguese Brazil to settle in Puerto Rico with their slaves. Toward the end of the century, immigration laws were further relaxed to permit 150 free blacks to settle in Puerto Rico.[36]

In addition to supplying settlers, the Crown awarded prospective sugar planters generous land grants, from one to seven caballerías (in Puerto Rico one caballería = 200 acres). The land grants, however, were given in "usufruct", to be used by the grantees for indefinite periods, but never as permanent holdings. Those interested in purchasing individual plots could do so through public auctions. Few could purchase land outright, so the usufruct tenure practice prevailed for centuries.

To develop a viable sugar industry the island needed, in addition to land and willing planters, large investments and lines of credit to finance production. It needed also a skilled and accessible labor pool, a protected, guaranteed market, and dependable means of transporting the sugar from the island to Europe.

Such economic demands were not particularly onerous for Spain, but they surfaced at a time when the metropolis was becoming more concerned about fortifying the island than in developing its economy. Increasing attacks from French and English corsairs led the monarchy to devote much of its resources and energies to defend its ships and the vital Caribbean ports. As its priorities changed, the subsidies to Puerto Rico vanished, and the island's nascent sugar industry stagnated.

Suggestested Readings

Alegría, Ricardo. *Descubrimiento, conquista y colonización de Puerto Rico* (San Juan: Colección de Estudios Puertorriqueños, 1969).

Brau, Salvador. *La Colonización de Puerto Rico* (San Juan: Instituto de Cultura Puertorriqueña, 1969).

Campo Lacasa, Cristina. *Historia de la Iglesia Cátolica en Puerto Rico* (San Juan: Instituto de Cultura Puertorriqueña, 1977).

Caro Costas, Aida R. *Antología de Lecturas de Historia de Puerto Rico (Siglos XV-XVIII)* (San Juan: n. p., 1989).

————. "Esclavos y esclavistas en el primer tercio del Siglo XVI (1530)." In: *Revista del Museo de Antropología, Historia y Arte* (Universidad de Puerto Rico), Vol. 1. No. 1 (1979).

Fernández de Oviedo, Gonzalo. *Historial General y Natural de las Indias*. (Book 16, Chs. 1-18, reproduced in Fernández Méndez, Eugenio, editor. *Crónicas de Puerto Rico*, Vol. 1 (1493-1797) (San Juan: Government Printing Office, 1957).

Fernández Méndez, Eugenio. *Las encomiendas y esclavitud de los indios de Puerto Rico, 1508-1550* (Río Piedras, Puerto Rico: Editorial Universitaria, 1976).

Morales Carrión, Arturo, *Puerto Rico and the Non-Hispanic Caribbean* (San Juan: University of Puerto Rico, 1974).

Moya Pons, Frank. *Manual de Historia Dominicana* (Santiago, República Dominicana: Universidad Católica Madre y Maestra, 1980)

Picó, Fernando. *Historia General de Puerto Rico* (Río Piedras: Ediciones Huracán, 1986).

Silvestrini, Blanca and Luque de Sánchez, María. *Historia de Puerto Rico* (San Juan: Cultural Puertorriqueña, Inc., 1987).

Wagenheim, Kal. *Puerto Rico: A Profile* (New York: Praeger Publishers, Revised Edition, 1975).

Castillo de San Felipe del Morro, completed around 1580, withstood the attacks of Sir Francis Drake in 1595.

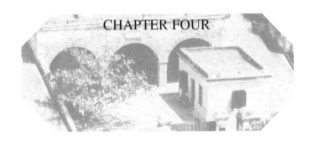

CHAPTER FOUR

Foreign Attacks and Imperial Neglect, 1570s–1699

By the middle of the sixteenth century, Spain had consolidated a mighty empire, a deed that forced her to fight a defensive battle against her rivals from the start. At first her enemies focused on capturing her ships and raiding her major settlements, but by the end of the century they were threatening to despoil her of territory. Because of its strategic location in the Caribbean, Puerto Rico was invaded twice by the British in the 1590s and once by the Dutch in the 1620s.

English and Dutch Attacks

Although England was officially at peace with Spain in the mid-1590s, she did not stop her "sea dogs" from raiding Spanish ships and ports. In early August 1595 Spanish spies reported from London that Queen Elizabeth had authorized Francis Drake and John Hawkins to seize Puerto Rico. The motive for that decision was apparently a cargo of gold and silver, worth about two million ducats, which was being temporarily stored in San Juan.

Convinced that they could take the island easily, Drake and Hawkins set out from Plymouth on August 28, 1595, with a fleet of twenty-seven ships and 4,500 sailors.[1] Poor weather delayed the voyage and they reached the island of Guadeloupe about the middle of November. There, they were spotted by five Spanish frigates which were bound for San Juan. Thus the news of the impending British invasion reached the fort before Drake and Hawkins.

When the invading forces finally entered San Juan Bay on November

22, they found the entrance to the harbor blocked by two sunken ships and the five frigates that had surprised them a few days earlier. They found also a deserted city, except for the 800 seamen from the frigates who had joined the 750 able-bodied men of the city inside the forts.[2]

Having sailed directly into the bay, Drake's ships were subjected to repeated rounds of cannon shots. Efforts to steer the vessels out of the line of fire were unsuccessful. The attack lasted well into the evening, and nearly cost Drake his life, when a cannon shot pierced his cabin. Hawkins had perished earlier in a fever epidemic and many of Drake's men were already showing signs of the disease.

Eager to enter the city before he lost too many of his men, Drake gave the order on November 24 to invade. A group of his men forced their way into the port during the evening and set fire to a few Spanish frigates, not realizing that the light from the burning vessels also made them sitting targets. Their casualties were so numerous that Drake called off the attack and retreated. By late January 1596 Drake, too, had died, victim of the epidemic that killed Hawkins.

San Juan breathed a sigh of relief as both the city and the bullion were spared. England looked to other mariners to continue the attacks against the Spaniards. Three years passed, however, before another Englishman, George Clifford, the Earl of Cumberland, accepted the mission of capturing San Juan.[3]

Fearing such an eventuality, Spain had doubled the number of troops in San Juan, from 200 to 400, increased the level of military funding, and ordered repairs and improvements of the island's fortifications. What Spain could not insure against was the recurring epidemics, one of which decimated San Juan's population the year before (1597) the second British invasion.

This time the island did not receive advance notice of the impending attack, nor did it have the support of Spanish seamen in the forts, as had been the case three years earlier. Consequently, when Cumberland and his 1,400 troops entered San Juan on June 16, 1598, they encountered little resistance.

Having learned from Drake's mistakes, Cumberland avoided sailing directly into the bay, opting instead to land his troops four leagues east of the city. Hoping to gain access to the city over land, he landed part of his men across from the San Antonio bridge, where the islet of San Juan connects with the larger island of Puerto Rico. Artillery fire from the Boquerón fort forced him to retreat momentarily, to replace fifty of his men who were either dead or wounded in the attack.[4]

Two days later, he maneuvered his ships past the Boquerón cannons and landed 200 of his troops about a mile north of the fort, at the Escambrón beach. Encountering no other resistance, the invading troops marched right into the city the morning of June 18. They found the city deserted, except for 400 men quartered in the Morro fort.

Encouraged by the surprising turn of events, Cumberland sent word to Governor Mosquera to surrender at once. Mosquera refused, and Cumberland laid siege to the city. The men in El Morro held out for fifteen days, but on July 1, short of food and ammunition, the beleaguered troops finally surrendered.[5]

With the surrender of El Morro and Fortaleza, Cumberland placed Puerto Rico under British jurisdiction, rounded up the Spanish soldiers in the city and shipped them off to Jamaica. Governor Mosquera and several others disappared before the city fell.

Taking the island, however, proved easier than holding it. In just two weeks after the victory, Cumberland lost 400 men to the same epidemic that had ravaged the city's population the previous year. The settlers outside the city contributed to the invaders' problems, by denying them food and water. Weakened by hunger and disease, Cumberland's forces had trouble defending themselves from the settlers outside the city walls, who grew bolder in their attacks.

Finally, on August 27, barely two months after he captured San Juan, Cumberland made preparations to leave, appointed Sir John Berkeley to succeed him, and looted the place thoroughly. In his retreat, he took the artillery from the forts and an assortment of cargoes waiting at the port. Among the most valuable items he seized were 1,000 boxes of sugar, a few thousand hides, 2,000 quintales of ginger (one quintal = 100 lbs), a ship full of slaves, and another loaded with pearls, from the island of Margarita, which had just docked in San Juan.[6] He even took the church bells and the organ. On September 5, Berkeley, too, abandoned San Juan. His departure ended the British occupation before Spanish reinforcements arrived to the island's rescue.

With the death of Queen Elizabeth in 1603, relations between Spain and England improved temporarily. Her successor, James I, signed a peace treaty with Spain. The Spaniards, however, were still skeptical of England's intentions and continued to order repairs and improvements of Puerto Rico's defenses.

Fear of attacks and disease made staffing the island a problem, since few Spaniards would volunteer for the assignment. Expected to serve their King twenty years or more, before they were free to return to civilian life, Spanish soldiers, when given a choice, preferred to serve their time in places with better prospects for survival. This forced the colonial authorities to depend on the local militia to defend the city whenever the forts were understaffed. Neither paid nor trained for this task, the militia did not inspire much confidence among the city's residents at first, but the fact that it performed well during the British attacks eventually gained it a measure of acceptance.

The next European group to attempt taking San Juan were the Dutch. Subjects of Spain for more than a century, until 1609, when they achieved their independence, the Dutch were particularly angry with the Spaniards, whom they accused of trying to strangle their fishing industry. For years, the Dutch had depended on Portugal for the salt they needed for the fishing industry. But when the Spaniards gained control of the Portuguese Crown (1580–1640), they barred the Dutch from the Portuguese salt mines.[7]

In need of salt, and probably eager to punish Spain, they began mining the salt flats in the Spanish Main, along the northern coast of South America. On the way to and from the salt flats, some Dutchmen discovered that one way to increase their profits was to capture the cargoes of gold and silver sent annually by Mexico and Perú. Another was to engage in contraband trade with the Spanish colonists. Both of these ventures, in turn, required a steadier presence in the Caribbean, and Puerto Rico seemed to be an ideal location to establish a foothold. Thus, on September 24, 1625, Bowdewijn Hendriksz (Balduino Enrico to the Spaniards) led a fleet of eight ships to San Juan.

Worried that Enrico might follow Cumberland's example and land his troops at the Escambrón beach, Governor Juan de Haro deployed some of his soldiers to the area. Enrico, however, surprised the governor by sail-

Dutch view of San Juan (17th century print)

ing directly into the harbor. With part of the men outside the city, the 330 troops assigned to defend El Morro were not enough to repel the attack, nor bar Enrico from landing his men. Once ashore, some of the invaders dug trenches in front of the fort, while the others laid siege to the city, and threatened to burn it if the fort was not surrendered.

The threats were ignored, and the soldiers continued to hold the fort despite shortages of food and ammunition. Meanwhile, Governor de Haro sent small groups of soldiers into the enemy trenches, where on October 5 a group led by Captain Juan de Amézquita reportedly slashed the throats of sixty Dutchmen.[8]

On October 21, Enrico, apparently already weary of the struggle, ordered the governor to surrender the city, or see it put to the torch. Assured that reinforcements would be arriving shortly from the interior of the island, Governor de Haro stayed the course. Enrico carried out his threat and set fire to some buildings.

As reinforcements drifted into the city, the governor increased the attacks on the troops still in the trenches outside the fort, another 200 of Enrico's men were killed before they could be removed to the ships. In retaliation, Enrico continued to set fire to different parts of the city over the next ten days. Failing to force the city to surrender, he finally gave orders to retreat, on November 2, leaving behind guns, artillery, a stranded ship, and hundreds of dead men. The five-week stay in the San Juan harbor had also caused havoc to his ships.[9]

Following the Dutch attack, the cabildo of San Juan presented a plan to the crown for enclosing the city behind massive stone walls that would be interrupted at intervals by bulwarks and entrance gates. The plan was approved by King Philip IV and the eastern and southern walls, covering the most vulnerable areas, were built in just four years, from 1634 to 1638. The northern and western walls took more than a century to complete, in part because these areas were already protected by several fortresses.

Although no other European group threatened San Juan for nearly two centuries, the island's coastal settlements continued to be raided by pirates and privateers, and some of its offshore islands were repeatedly seized by non-Spanish colonists from the neighboring Caribbean.

Beginning in the 1620s, England succeeded in wresting from Spain several islands in the Lesser Antilles. These were rapidly converted into sugar and other plantations, worked by African slaves. In times of peace when slaves escaped it was expected that they be returned to their owners by those who found them. In times of war, however, fugitive slaves were generally confiscated and sold at public auctions by the officials in whose jurisdiction they were apprehended.

That practice was changed in Puerto Rico in 1664, when four slaves (three women and one man) from the British island of Saint Kitts were discovered in Puerto Rico. The governor, Juan Pérez de Guzmán, not only granted them asylum, but encouraged the Council of the Indies (Spain's colonial office) to do the same with future fugitives. He justified his decision to the Council by saying that, "it does not seem proper that the King receive into slavery those who seek his protection."[10]

The Council approved his idea and issued a general asylum policy for the fugitive slaves of her rivals. Reissued at least twice in the next century, the asylum policy became an additional source of tension between Spain and England. Viewed by England as a deliberate aggression, the asylum policy became a convenient pretext for its colonial authorities in the Lesser Antilles to seize the island of Vieques from Puerto Rico. Long neglected by the Spaniards and reputed to be "the best of all the Virgins"

Vieques was seized and occupied by a British group from the island of Anguilla several times between 1683 and the 1690s.[11] Tired of the long droughts in Anguilla, the British nationals sought permission from the governor of the Leeward Islands to colonize Vieques. Once there, they renamed it Crab Island.

Having lost much of the Lesser Antilles to her rivals, Spain was not very well disposed to let the British keep Vieques, and in 1685, instructed the Viceroy of New Spain (Mexico) to send troops to dislodge the intruders. The Viceroy delayed three years in carrying out his mission and by the time the royal forces arrived in December 1688, Vieques was also occupied by Danish settlers, sent from the island of Saint Thomas. Convinced that both the Danes and the British wanted the island as a base from which to trade with Puerto Rico, the royal forces killed all who resisted, destroyed their crops, set fire to their homes, and shipped the survivors back to the islands from which they had come. The effect of such retaliatory measures was temporary. As long as Spain insisted on its asylum policy, the British felt justified in their efforts to occupy Vieques, which they considered an important link in the underground trail used by the fugitives.

The Colonial Government

Prior to the 1560s, both civilians and military men were sent to the island as governors. In some instances the monarchy entrusted the colony to magistrates and judges. But beginning in 1564, as foreign threats to the island increased, Spain turned almost exclusively to the military for governors.[12]

As the island's military role grew after the 1580s, so did the governor's powers. Given the title of Captain-General, he became the maximum authority in both military and civil affairs. His term of office generally lasted two to five years. As the colony's chief military figure, the governor was responsible for the protection and defense of the colony. His jurisdiction extended over every aspect of the armed forces and defense. His discretion over the island's defense budget guaranteed him access to funds for punitive expeditions against Spain's enemies in the Caribbean.

In his role as the Crown's highest representative, the governor appointed the cabildo members (regidores) and other municipal officials; deter-

mined which offices should be auctioned off and which should be awarded for life; presided over cabildo meetings whenever he wished; and
decided on the municipal ordinances to be enforced. Broad judicial powers enabled him to try and judge major civil criminal cases, whether
appellate or of the first instance. Few governors, however, knew much
about the law and thus preferred to delegate these tasks to legal experts.[13]

The governor's responsibilities included overseeing the colony's economic and fiscal affairs, promoting production and exports, and protecting Spain's commercial interests from interlopers. Through edicts and
decrees, collectively known as "Bandos de Policía y Buen Gobierno" he
implemented economic policy, apportioned land, set prices for staple
foods, and fixed the quantities of meat the cattle ranchers were expected
to supply to the settlements in their towns or districts. Many of his edicts
were aimed at curtailing contraband between the island and Spain's competitors, in a futile attempt to capture part of the lost trade revenues.

As admininistrator of the treasury, he monitored the local currency and
enforced the collection of taxes. When his directives in economic matters
were ignored, as they often were, he imposed numerous punishments
ranging from removal of corrupt officials from office, to confiscation of
property, and or confinement to prison for repeat offenders.

Governors sought to control social mores by banning a host of public
activities, especially those that encouraged gambling, such as card games
and cockfights. Penalties prescribed for infractions ranged from fines to
corporal punishment, but the governors were no more successful at curbing gambling than they were at reducing contraband trade. Recreational
activities condoned by the governor were generally those sponsored by
the Church in honor of patron saints or members of the royal family. As
the secular head of the colonial Church, the governor intervened in the
temporal affairs of the institution. He paid the priests' salaries, provided
for religious services and the upkeep of Church buildings and saw to it
that Papal bulls and other religious decrees were respected.

In theory, the governor's rule was absolute, with no legislature or other
group sharing power.[14] In reality, his power was checked by the colonists,
who resisted and disobeyed his laws. All colonial officials, governors in
particular, were monitored by the audiencia, the appellate court of the
region, and were required to submit to a review trial ("juicio de residen-

cia") when their terms expired.

To help him perform his work in the island's remote districts, the governor appointed the *teniente a guerra*, lieutenant governor, as his direct representative. Like the governor, the teniente a guerra had a wide range of powers, including the right to preside over cabildo meetings, to organize and head the urban militia, to enforce the law, and judge minor court cases. The teniente generally served terms of two to four years.[15]

Besides the governor and the tenientes, the island also had its own form of municipal government that, as in other Spanish colonies, centered around the cabildo and the local magistrates. Ideally, the cabildo was the one government agency where the interests of the settlers were represented. As such, its members were to be selected by the community instead of having them appointed by the King or his representatives. However, towards the end of the 16th century cabildo posts and other colonial offices were sold by the Crown to the highest bidders. Cabildo meetings were generally closed to the public, except when review trials ("juicios de residencia") and other extraordinary events required the presence of the entire community. On those occasions cabildo meetings were open to all and referred to as *cabildo abierto*.[16]

Compared to other Spanish colonies, Puerto Rico, because of its meager population, had fewer and smaller cabildos during the first three centuries of Spanish colonization. The first cabildos established in Puerto Rico, San Juan and San Germán, had extensive jurisdiction over these two districts' territory. The jurisdiction of the cabildo of San Juan, for instance, extended over the capital, its own *barrios*, wards, and all the settlements east of the Camuy river. The cabildo of San Germán was responsible for its own municipality, its barrios, and the settlements in the western district. Each of these cabildos had only two regidores (councilmen).

The regidores, generally members of the wealthier families in the region, recomended, or selected the local magistrates. Together, they performed many functions, such as enforcing municipal ordinances, royal orders and edicts, and judicial rulings handed down by the Audiencia (appellate court) of Santo Domingo.[17]

One function of the cabildo was to ensure that local producers complied with the demands of the *abasto público* (public supply), which stipulated the amount of foodstuffs, especially beef, to be supplied regularly to the urban settlements, at government-fixed prices. Cattle growers were instructed to bring a specified number of livestock to the municipal slaughterhouse, where abasto officials inspected, weighed, and established the price the community would pay for the beef. Regidores also had the power to demand that local merchants supply specific quantities of flour and other products. Meeting the demand for foreign imports often became a problem for the cabildo. In the case of flour specifically, shortages occurred regularly because it was subject to a government monopoly. When these shortages occurred, the merchants sought to make up for them with smuggled flour.

In theory, the abasto was a good program, but in reality it was regularly sabotaged by producers intent on obtaining better prices than those fixed by the government. After the 1650s, as competing Europeans turned the Lesser Antilles into commercial plantations, producers in Puerto Rico found ready markets, not only for draft animals, hides, and tallow, but for beef, and other food crops. When Spain's rivals in the Caribbean offered higher prices than those prevailing in Puerto Rico, local producers became inclined to forget their social obligations to the urban settlements. Trading with the Lesser Antilles freed the Puerto Rico growers from the constrictions imposed by the small size of the domestic market and the price structure set by the state bureaucracy. Since commercial transactions with foreigners were prohibited, local officials sought to dissuade the locals with threats of punishment.

Public health was another of the cabildo's responsibilities, but since there were no doctors or hospitals, its work was limited to separating the sick from the healthy during epidemics and whenever slave ships docked at the local port. Its operation of public works was also limited to inspecting the local cemetery and slaughterhouse.

Another of the cabildo functions (reiterated by a 1574 ordinance) was to grant usufruct rights to residents who were able to pay a minimal fee of two ducats for the equivalent of 200 acres, one *caballería*.[18] The revenues earned from these fees were to be used by the councilmen to finance public works in their jurisdiction. The cabildo was also empowered to tax local producers (based on the estimated value of production) and use the income for other projects, such as financing religious festivals and providing economic assistance to widows and other needy persons in their districts. Celebrations of royal deeds, and visits by important officials to the towns, were financed with funds the regidores borrowed from wealthier settlers.

The Colonial Economy

Between the 1580s and the 1640s, the island's small sugar industry declined sharply, in part because it failed to obtain a share of Spain's market, which was monopolized by the Andalusian sugar growers. Without a protected market, the Puerto Rico growers gradually abandoned production, as they were unable to compete with the sugar industry developed by Brazil after the 1580s.[19] Sugar exports (muscovado, or unrefined sugar) from Puerto Rico to Seville plummeted from 20,000 *arrobas* (one arroba = 25 lbs) in 1568 to 333 arrobas in 1650. As production declined, the number of *trapiches*, primitive sugar mills, were reduced from fifteen in 1582 to seven in 1640.

Without gold, or further prospects of reviving the sugar industry, the planters again turned to cultivating food crops and raising livestock for domestic and foreign consumption. The landholders closest to the shore strengthened their commercial ties with neighboring Caribbean markets, where foreign traders waited to penetrate the Spanish New World market.

The foods most commonly planted for local consumption were yucca and other tubers, sweet potatoes, chili peppers, and plantains, a variety of the banana, brought to Puerto Rico in 1516 from the Canary Islands. Ginger, a plant originally from India, became an important source of export revenues for Puerto Rico producers between the 1560s and 1690s, when demand for it increased in Europe.

Ginger was an ideal cash crop for the small farmer because it grew well on any soil, required little investment capital and few workers to tend it. In 1583, thirty-three quintales were exported to Seville. Nine years later, when Seville purchased over 3,161 quintales of the aromatic root, the island's farmers thought they had found an alternative cash crop to sugar. They were not alone in this dream, however. In the 1590s, Hispaniola requested permission from the Crown to become the exclusive producer of ginger. Although such permission was never granted, the sales of Puerto Rico's ginger dropped sharply by the 1650s.[20] Once again the challenge had come from Brazil. In 1646, it had a huge crop of the aromatic root on the European market. As the supply from Brazil and other sources increased, prices for ginger exports declined, and the Puerto Rico growers shifted their attention once more to crops in demand in the neighboring Caribbean markets.

From the 1650s to the end of the century, Puerto Rico producers sought to replace the vanishing ginger revenues with sales of cocoa and tobacco to the Dutch traders, although by the 1690s much of the tobacco was consumed locally.

. As commercial plantations began to dominate the economy of the neighboring islands, their markets for foodstuff and other farm products increased substantially. Puerto Rico, which was primarily devoted to farming, found itself in a good position to offer them not only foodstuffs, but large animals, such as horses and oxen, used to haul the cane from the field and to power primitive mills that ground the sugar cane. They also sold them hides, which they generally used as receptacles for shipping molasses and muscavado sugar.[21]

The rising demand for livestock and its products was easily met by the Puerto Rico ranchers because of the ample grasslands and water sources at their disposal. In the valleys adjacent to San Germán and San Juan, herds multiplied so rapidly that it was feared that they might soon outnumber humans. Herds were so plentiful that cattle were ostensibly killed only for their hides, while the carcasses were left to rot in the fields.

Demand for leather in Europe also gave a temporary, additional boost to Puerto Rico's cattle industry during the last third of the seventeenth century. From the 1670s to 1700, for instance, the island exported (legally) between 6,000 and 8,000 hides yearly to Seville.[22] Trading with Seville, however, was a costly and complicated process for most Puerto Rico producers.

Contraband and the Official Trade Policy

The practice of funneling the kingdom's trade through one port was part of the doctrine of mercantilism that Spain (and later her rivals) adopted during the sixteenth century.[23] Defenders of the doctrine argued that the path to wealth and power of a nation depended on its ability to accumulate the largest amounts of bullion and precious minerals. One way for a nation to achieve such strength was to have exclusive control over certain resources and commercial routes.

Having conquered much of the New World, Spain sought to implement the mercantile doctrine by monopolizing the region's mines and regulating its trade. The mines were operated by Spanish colonists and the trade was regulated by the "Casa de Contratación" (House of Trade), established in Seville at the beginning of the sixteenth century. Defined as captive markets, the colonies were declared off limits to foreign traders.

News of Spain's newfound wealth led her rivals to ambush and raid her inbound ships, as they reached the Atlantic Ocean, laden with riches from her colonies. In 1540, Spain adopted the *flota*, a defensive maritime system, which required that war ships accompany the merchant vessels sailing between Seville and the New World. Since the costs of such voyages were high, the House of Trade limited them to two a year, during the Spring and Fall. The outbound ships sailed together across the Atlantic and, once in the Caribbean, separated into two convoys. One of them went to Veracruz, Mexico and the other to Portobello, Panamá. From these ports, single vessels, known as galleons, were dispatched to other ports in South America and the Caribbean. For the return voyage to Seville, the flota regrouped at Havana, Cuba before venturing into the Atlantic Ocean.[24]

Short of items with which to tempt the Seville merchants, Puerto Rico was haphazardly supplied by the galleons. Fear of losing a ship to the pirates and poachers who lay in wait in the tiny islets and keys apparently outweighed the gains they could realize from the island's trade.

For their part, the island's exporters rejected the limitations imposed on them by the official trade policy, which demanded that all the colony's commerce be funneled through the San Juan port. Shipping from that port entailed transporting their goods on mules over long stretches of land, or in barges along the rivers. Lack of roads, and swollen rivers during the rainy season, added to the difficulties and cost of doing business through the San Juan port. Sea transport was possible and faster, but ran the risk of interception by pirates or other enemies. High shipping costs and excessive trade duties added to the list of disincentives for trading with Seville.[25]

Unable to trade legally with Spain, most Puerto Rico producers turned very early on to contraband with Spain's rivals. Since the island also suffered from a chronic shortage of coins, the traders resorted to the barter system to remedy the problem. It was thus common for local producers to offer agricultural produce and livestock for slaves and manufactured goods from foreign merchants.

Intent on curbing such trade, the imperial government, in turn, prohibited the cultivation of certain crops. In 1602, for instance, it banned the cultivation of ginger, which since the 1580s had been attracting numerous foreign traders to Puerto Rico. That prohibition, like many others, was not only ignored by the islanders, but by many Spanish officials, who found in the illicit trade new ways to increment their meager incomes.[26]

Their willingness to break the law made it possible for coastal settlements such as Aguada, Arecibo, Cabo Rojo and Fajardo to become vibrant economic communities. Visited regularly by a cast of international traders, many of these coastal settlements became so dependent on contraband trade during the second half of the seventeenth century that even Governor Arredondo's death threats did little to deter the offenders. The fact that on occasion members of the church and some governors themselves became involved in the illicit trade added to the government's problem.

By the 1690s contraband trade had become so profitable that few dared to speak against it, for fear of antagonizing the traders. Those who did were swiftly and severely punished. According to the Spanish historian Angel López Cantos, in 1691, a clergyman from San Germán was kidnapped and beaten to a pulp for notifying the San Juan authorities about the illegal commerce in Ponce.[27] When neither local threats nor royal prohibitions did much to curtail the illicit trade, the King adopted a new defensive system.

Setting Up the Guarda Costas

In 1674, the King created a coast guard, staffed it with independent operators from Spain, popularly known as corsairs and privateers, and ordered it to protect the empire's commercial trade routes in the Caribbean. In exchange for this service, the operators were given a share of the trans-Atlantic Spanish trade and a portion of the booty they seized from rival ships.[28]

The idea for the protective system was apparently devised by Flemish and Biscay merchants as a way to break the Seville monopoly that also excluded them from the lucrative New World trade. As smuggling activities increased during the 1690s, Spanish subjects from the Caribbean were also permitted to join the coast guard.

Their job, like that of the Peninsular operators, was to stop any foreign ship they found following a "suspicious course" and to examine its cargo and papers. If the cargo was not satisfactorily explained, and the privateers suspected it had originated in, or was bound for, the Spanish colonies, they were authorized to seize the vessel and escort it to their home port. Once at port, it was up to the trade officials in the colony to determine the legitimacy of the cargo and whether it should be confiscated. Compensation for the service of the colonial privateers was at the discretion of the port officials.

The ample margins of the royal instructions permitted the privateers to interpret the regulations at will. Consequently, not all the ships captured were necessarily enemy ships nor were all brought to the nearest ports, as required by the government. Armed with the official status of defenders of the Crown's interests, many of the privateers resorted to indiscriminately plundering any cargo ship that crossed their path in the Caribbean. The privateers, like the smugglers themselves, could usually count on the protection of some corrupt port officials, who depended on such operations as a way to boost their wages.

One Puerto Rican privateer who distinguished himself in the service of the Spanish Crown was the mulatto Miguel Henríquez. A former shoemaker, Henríquez took to the sea, and by 1713, had garnered from the King the titles "Capitán de Mar y de Guerra y Armador de los Corsos de Puerto Rico" and Caballero de la Real Efigie."[29] His influence at the Spanish court and his reputation as a mariner made him both feared and hated among the inhabitants of the British Caribbean. To them, says Morales-Carrión, Henríquez was the "Grand Arch Villain, the despicable mulatto, who, in the eyes of the King, was more powerful than the governor of the colony."[30]

But, as the Crown belatedly discovered, neither its coast guard nor the threats issued by its colonial officials were sufficient deterrents in what had become a profitable way of life. The illicit trade continued not only because her colonists and rivals were willing to engage in contraband, but because Spain's trade policy was unrealistic and incapable of satisfying the settlers' needs.

The Population Stagnates

Puerto Rico's population remained very small for the first two centuries, in part because the island lacked the allure of mineral-rich New Spain (Mexico) or Perú. Repeated attempts to attract new settlers were only partially successful, and the number of permanent white Spaniards in the colony in the 1670s represented a meager increment over the previous century. In 1672, for example, San Juan had only 800 permanent Spanish residents, while San Germán had 200.[31] Although from time to time the Crown financed the passage of willing settlers, as it did in 1683 and 1691 with two groups (200 families each) of Canary Islanders, its efforts were often frustrated by recurring epidemics. Between 1689 and 1690, for example, outbreaks of smallpox, measles, and spotted fever ("tabardillo") killed 631 of Puerto Rico's residents. As a result of all these obstacles, the island's population in 1699 amounted to barely 6,000 persons.[32]

Church, Education, and Culture

Not yet the responsibility of the state, education in the colony was left to the priests and friars. San Juan, the center of colonial activity, saw two new schools open between 1650 and the end of the century. One of them was founded by the Franciscans, shortly after they settled in the city, in the 1640s, and the other was founded by Bishop Francisco Padilla.[33] Padilla apparently sought to attract the children of the poor to his school by offering courses free of charge. But when lack of clothes failed to bring them in, he appealed to the King for assistance. It is not known if the King answered his petition.

In addition to the schools, the clergy also built convents and churches. The Franciscans built theirs in the southeast section of the city. In 1651, Carmelite nuns built a convent, the first such place for women with religious vocations. By the end of the seventeenth century, San Juan probably had more religious personnel and institutions than were needed by its meager population.

In San Germán, meanwhile, the Dominicans had finished the Porta

Coeli convent and, in 1688, had replaced its primitive church with a fine stone building. A perennial shortage of religious officers made it difficult for Porta Coeli to offer church services regularly. Settlements smaller than San Juan and San Germán had only modest chapels or parish churches and rarely offered religious services.

Despite the island's shortage of schools there were a few noticeable signs of cultural evolution among its settlers. In the literary field, for instance, Juan Troche y Ponce de León (?–1590), grandson of the Spanish conqueror but a native of San Juan, became in 1577 the first Creole to write an account of Puerto Rico. His description of the territory, however, was until recently attributed to the governor and thus known as "Memoria Melgarejo".

This error in turn led literary scholars to attribute the post of first Creole literary figure to the Canon Diego Torres Vargas (1590–1649). Born also in San Juan, Torres Vargas studied theology and canon law at the University of Salamanca. As canon of San Juan's Cathedral, he published, in 1647, a loving account of his homeland, *Descripción de la Isla y Ciudad de Puerto Rico*, in which he calls the island-born "naturales" (later known as Creoles) and defends them from the criticisms of Spanish chroniclers. He describes the island's women as "the most beautiful, hardworking, and sensible of all the Indies" and explains that such virtues were the reason why so many Spaniards came to marry in Puerto Rico.[34]

Two other Creole figures who distinguished themselves in the latter part of the 17th century are the clergyman-poet, Francisco de Ayerra y Santa María (1630–1708) and the adventurer Alonso Ramírez. A native of San Juan, Ayerra spent much of his life in Mexico, where he held numerous posts and won much praise for his poetry. In 1683, his poems were included in an anthology published by the great Mexican intellectual Carlos Sigüenza y Góngora. Two years later, he received a prize for a sonnet he devoted to Sor Juana Inés de la Cruz.[35]

Ramírez, also a native of San Juan, and a carpenter by trade, moved to Havana, Cuba, when he was still quite young. From Cuba, he went to Mexico, where he joined a commercial group bound for the Philippines. Taken captive by English pirates in the Philippines, he spent many years traveling with them before finally settling down in Mexico city.[36] His trials and tribulations were also recounted by Sigüenza y Góngora in the picaresque novel, *The Misfortunes of Alonso Ramírez* (1690).

Suggested Readings

Brau, Salvador. *La Colonización de Puerto Rico* (San Juan: Instituto de Cultura Puertorriqueña, 1969).

Campo Lacasa, Cristina. *Historia de la Iglesia en Puerto Rico* (San Juan: Instituto de Cultura Puertorriqueña, 1977).

Caro, Aida R. "Esclavos y esclavistas en el primer tercio del siglo XVI (1531)" in *Revista del Museo de Antropología, Historia y Arte de la Universidad de Puerto Rico* vol, 1, No. 1 (1979).

———. "The Outpost of Empire." in Arturo Morales-Carrión, *Puerto Rico: A Political and Cultural History* (New York: W.W. Norton, 1983).

———. "The Organization of an Institutional and Social Life." in Arturo Morales-Carrión, Ibid.

Díaz-Soler, Luis.*Historia de la esclavitud negra en Puerto Rico (1493–1890)* (Río Piedras, Puerto Rico: Editorial Universitaria, Universidad de Puerto Rico, 1965).

Elliott, J.H. *Imperial Spain, 1469–1716* (New York: The American Library, 1966).

López-Cantos, Angel. *Historia de Puerto Rico,1650-1700* (Sevilla: Escuela de Estudios Hispanoamericanos de Sevilla, 1975).

Manrique Cabrera, Francisco. *Historia de la Literatura Puertorriqueña* (Río Piedras: Editorial Cultural, Inc., 1982).

Morán-Arce, Lucas. *Historia de Puerto Rico* (San Juan: Librotex Inc., 1985).

Perea, Salvador. *Historia de Puerto Rico, 1537–1700* (San Juan: Instituto de Cultura Puertorriqueña-U. Cátolica, 1972).

Ramírez, Rafael W. *Cartas y relaciones históricas y geográf icas sobre Puerto Rico* (San Juan: Imprenta Venezuela, 1934).

Tío, Aurelio. *Fundación de San Germán y su significado en el desarrollo político, económico, social, y cultural de Puerto Rico* (San Juan: Biblioteca de Autores Puertorriqueños, 1971).

CHAPTER FIVE

The Colony is Reformed, 1700–1799

The death of Charles II (the Bewitched) in 1699, ended the line of the Hapsburg Dynasty which had ruled the Spanish empire since the 1520s, when Charles V ascended the throne. Without an heir, the dying king bequeathed the empire to Philip d'Anjou, member of the Bourbon dynasty, grandson of King Louis XIV, and heir to the French throne.

England, Austria, and other nations in Europe refused to accept Charles II's testament, for fear that France would become the dominant power. Charles, Archduke of Austria, (later crowned Holy Roman Emperor), a contender to the Spanish throne, was particularly adamant about contesting the will. As neither side yielded in their demands, the matter had to be resolved by war, known thereafter as the War of the Spanish Succession (1701–1713).

England, Austria, Holland, Portugal, and Savoy joined forces against France and Spain.[1] Although the major battles in this struggle were fought in Europe, the Caribbean did not escape unscathed. Puerto Rico, for example, became the target of minor invasions by the British in 1702 and the Dutch a year later.

The British attacked Arecibo in August, and Loíza in November. Both groups were repulsed by the local militia. In defense of Arecibo, Captain Antonio de los Reyes Correa and his men reported killing thirty Englishmen while only four in their camp suffered wounds. The Dutch attack on southern Guadianilla was also repulsed by the timely defense of the militia, commanded by Domingo Pacheco. Armed only with spears and machetes (cutlasses) Pacheco's men killed thirty-eight Dutchmen, and forced the rest to retreat. It is not known if Pacheco's unit suffered casualties.[2]

The Treaty of Utrecht (1713) restored peace among the European nations, at a price to Spain and France. Philip d' Anjou ascended the Spanish throne, as Philip V, but had to relinquish the French throne for himself and his descendants, and grant England the coveted Spanish *asiento* (right to supply slaves to her colonies) for thirty-five years.

The asiento limited the British to trading only in slaves, a condition they often ignored. Their insistence on expanding the list of items of trade led to numerous confrontations between the two nations and to seizures of cargo ships by Spanish privateers. In February 1734 a group of Puerto Rican privateers seized a fleet of six British ships which were presumably bound for the North American colonies. The fact that these ships were captured with the consent of the governor, Matías de Abadía, led to angry accusations from the colonial authorities in the British Caribbean.[3]

In 1731, Governor Abadía had been sent to Puerto Rico with instructions to curb the flourishing contraband trade in the region. Tempted by the profits of such trade, he followed a two-pronged course: he became the ringleader of a smuggling operation of local corsairs, which protected French and Dutch traders and punished the British smugglers.[4]

His acts, and the anarchy caused by poachers and privateers, eventually dragged Spain and England into war in 1739. Popularly known as the War of Jenkins' Ear, this armed confrontation played into the hands of Governor Abadía and his corsairs. Called to defend Spain's interests, they felt at liberty to seize and plunder the enemy's ships for their own gain. Ironically, for these dubious services, Governor Abadía was promoted, in 1741, to the rank of brigadier.

Frustrated by what they considered to be Puerto Rico's impunity, British officials in the Lesser Antilles pressured England to seize Puerto Rico. The idea was tentatively considered in 1779, but more in retaliation for Spain's support of the North American colonists in their war of independence from Britain than for the activities of the privateers. The plan to seize Puerto Rico was shelved due to France's objections and the opposition of British West Indian sugar planters, who did not want competition from the much larger Puerto Rico.[5]

The Bourbon Reforms

Shortly after Philip V took control of the Spanish throne, he undertook a series of reforms, to consolidate his power and boost the revenues from the colonies. To achieve these goals, he sought to change the trade system and revamp the inefficient and often corrupt government bureaucracy.[6]

In the Antilles, where contraband remained a major obstacle to Spain's trade with its colonies, the Bourbon court eliminated the privateers and introduced a "free trade" policy. In Spanish terms, free trade meant that the colonies were henceforth free to trade with more than one port in Spain, rather than continue to be restricted to the port of Seville. Since the object of this policy was to channel colonial commerce more effectively to Spain, the Crown also created a number of Spanish-owned trading companies and assigned each of them a portion of the West Indian trade.

Puerto Rico came under the jurisdiction of the Royal Company of Barcelona, which was chartered in 1755 by Ferdinand VI. The Company's charge was to regulate the commerce of Spanish Santo Domingo and the island of Margarita as well. Until 1784, the Company imported many of the foodstuffs sold on the island, such as flour, wine, oil, cheese, olives, and chickpeas directly from Spain and exported to Seville coffee, sugar, and hides.

Despite the Company's efforts to control the Caribbean trade, smuggling remained strong, as it was always more lucrative than the legal trade with Spain. During the decade 1755–65, Spanish merchants complained of having lost an average of six million pesos annually to the illegal trade.[7]

In Puerto Rico, trade revenues collected by the treasury during the 1760s amounted to a meager 10,804 pesos yearly. The problem, as the officials explained, was that Spanish imports were limited to foodstuffs, and the island's shortage of currency forced the importers to barter these for hides, annato ("achiote") and other tropical crops.

Following England's temporary occupation of Cuba during the Seven Years War (1756–1763), Spain sought to strengthen its control over its Caribbean colonies. In 1765, King Charles III sent Marshal Alejandro O'Reilly to investigate the prevailing conditions in Puerto Rico and Cuba, and to offer recommendations that would lead to the improvement of their economies and their military defenses.[8] His distinguished military record in the Spanish wars in Italy had earned O'Reilly numerous titles, as well as the King's trust.

A partisan of ending the ongoing trade monopoly, O'Reilly suggested opening the island's trade and doing away with the one port policy still in effect in Puerto Rico. He explained that the greater part of the colony's trade was conducted out of its illegal ports. Among them, he said, the southern ports accounted for more than 50 percent of the goods smuggled out of the island. The items most often smuggled, according to his report, were livestock, pepper, tobacco and timber. Other ports, on the western and southwestern coasts smuggled coffee and food crops as well. He concluded that the only way to discourage the illicit trade, which had been "so detrimental to the interests of Spain", was to extend the free trade policy to Puerto Rico.

Whether O'Reilly's suggestions in this area were followed is hard to say. Yet in 1765, the King implemented two separate measures with respect to Puerto Rico. He authorized the island to trade with eight ports in the Peninsula and with other ports in the Spanish Caribbean. To cut the costs of the island's trade with Spain, the revised policy reduced the shipping fees and fixed the import-export duties at the rate of 6 percent ad valorem. The island's trade, however, continued to be funnelled through San Juan, and commerce with foreign ports was prohibited as a matter of course.

In 1765, the King chartered a new trade company, Aguirre & Arístegui, and authorized it to supply slaves to Cuba, Puerto Rico and the Island of Margarita.[9] To keep the new company from straying into smuggling activities, he permitted it to supplement its income by importing salt-meat, flour, farm equipment, and clothing for the slaves. The company was also given a tax reduction of ten pesos per each slave it brought to the colonies.

Despite the generous incentives, the Company was caught shortly afterward smuggling flour from Philadelphia. The flour was confiscated, but the Company retained its privileges and even gained a new concession. In 1769, the trade in flour with the United States was legalized, and the Company obtained the concession, with added benefits. It was allowed to import duty free two barrels of American flour for every slave it sold in Puerto Rico.

Such flexibility, however, did not extend to local smugglers. During the 1760s, the monarchy instructed the governor to crack down on illegal traders with every means at his disposal.[10] The governor assigned the task

to the corregidores (district commanders), ordering them to search suspect homes and establishments and to send the confiscated goods to San
Juan. They were authorized also to close unlicensed stores, to prohibit the
cutting of timber, to arrest and to jail any person suspected of smuggling.

In 1776, the Crown also sought the cooperation of the church, exhort-
ing the bishop in Puerto Rico to declare smuggling a sin and to use his
persuasive powers to convince the sinners to abandon their evil ways. Not
sure that the bishop would succeed in his mission, the Crown also
instructed the governor to apply the death sentence to the convicted.[11] The
fact that contraband continued unabated well into the following century
suggests that the results of these measures were limited.

During the last decade of the eighteenth century Spain increasingly lost
more control of her colonial trade, as she was forced to grant a series of
concessions[12] to merchants from friendly nations. In 1789, for example,
before the French Revolution erupted, Spain granted a license to a merchant from Nantes, and permitted slave traders from the French Antilles,
to sell cargoes of slaves in Puerto Rico.

During the early 1790s, when she joined England against France in
support of the Haitian Revolution (1792–1804), Spain found herself
unable to supply her colonies and granted this privilege temporarily to the
United States. She restricted slave traders, however, to bringing their cargoes in ships that did not exceed 300 tons, and demanded that they abandon her ports within twenty-four hours from the time they docked.

With respect to Puerto Rico, the concession granted to the Americans
represented an opportunity to import legally many of the same items
(slaves, flour and foodstuffs) they had been forced to smuggle in for more
than a century. It meant also that local producers, especially the island's
emerging sugar growers, could export their products to the American
market, a much closer and more receptive market than Seville.

Reforming the Land System

In addition to the trade, the Crown sought to reform the island's land
tenure system.[13] Its intentions were to regain control of the plots it had
previously given in usufruct to the colonists and to reassign them to others. Thus, in 1729, the Crown sent a decree to the colony by which it
ordered the cabildo to stop issuing land grants immediately. A subsequent

decree in 1734 clarified that the power to issue land grants belonged only to the Crown, and would be exercised henceforth by its representatives, namely a land commissioner, with the help of the governor.

A 1735 royal decree clarified further that the Crown's vacant lands ("tierras realengas") were to be assigned to those able to cultivate them, and instructed the extant holders to file for legal permits at once. Nothing more was heard from the King until 1746, when he again ordered the islanders to present proper documentation to the authorities within four days. This time, the request came with the warning that land grants issued since April 26, 1618 were null and void, and that such plots would revert to the Crown, unless their holders were able to produce titles and deeds for them.

The King's death in 1747 postponed the process for another seven years. The new king, Ferdinand VI, ordered the Audiencia of Santo Domingo (the appellate court) to appoint a land commissioner to carry out the changes. Ferdinand's decree modified the previous instructions by targeting only the plots that had been awarded since 1700. Although it encouraged landless families to request land from the government, it made clear that obtaining and keeping the plots depended on their ability to cultivate them within a specified time period. It also highlighted the fact that farmers were to be given preference over cattle raisers.

The imminence of the reform galvanized many of the old landholders into action. They complained in cabildo meetings and flooded the governor with complaints and petitions. Faced with a potentially explosive situation, Governor Felipe Ramírez de Estenós tried to stall the project until he had reached a compromise with the landholders of San Juan.

Making use of the traditional prerogative "obedezco pero no cumplo" (I obey but do not execute), he rejected the commissioner sent by the Audiencia of Santo Domingo. In his place he appointed two local commissioners and charged them with the task of distributing part of the vacant lands to landless families.

In 1757, he sent the Council of the Indies a modified reform plan, which had been submitted to him by the councilmen of San Juan. The "San Juan" plan accepted the Crown's order to demolish the large grazing plots ("hatos") near the capital, but requested new plots for the cattlemen in the interior of the island. It requested also that the lands from the dismembered hatos be assigned to individuals capable of cultivating them.

Displaying preference for the farmers, the San Juan plan prescribed that cattle growers keep their animals fenced in to prevent damages to the crops. Violators were threatened with hefty fines and even loss of their plots. Although cattle owners were not specifically required to farm their land, they were advised to offer subsistence plots on their estates to land-less workers.

While the Council of the Indies deliberated over the San Juan plan, Governor Ramírez moved to implement the least controversial portions of the royal plan, namely that which permitted demolition of the hatos near San Juan and granting plots to landless families from the vacant lands in the interior. The King's and the locally owned hatos which had already been converted into sugar farms were exempted from demolition.

When Ramírez' term expired in 1757, many of the hatos outside San Juan were still intact because of mounting opposition from the cattlemen. Rather than confront the unhappy landholders, his successor, Esteban Primo de Rivera, suggested that the Council of the Indies resolve the problem by granting ownership titles to those "occupying" the land. The Council replied rather ambiguously the following year that the land belonged to those who "worked it".[14]

In 1767, the Audiencia of Santo Domingo again sent its own land com-missioner to Puerto Rico, to resume the work assigned by the King 13 years earlier. His arrival provoked such violent protests that the Audiencia not only recalled him, but tabled the project for a few years.

Unable to dislodge the landholders through legal channels (the inter-vention of the Audiencia), Charles III resorted to reducing their holdings. He accomplished this in 1774, when he imposed a land tax (one of Alejandro O'Reilly's suggestions) with the pretext that the island's defense made such revenues necessary. Through the imposition of the tax, and the requirement that plots be planted, he hoped to force the land-holders to relinquish the uncultivated acreage.

This time the landowners did not object. They agreed to pay the tax, on condition that the metropolis grant them ownership titles to their plots. Encouraged by this reaction, the Crown ordered a study of the colony's lands from the cabildo of San Juan. The report, sent in 1775, stated that, excluding the rocky and inaccessible terrain, the island had over 8.2 million caballerías (one caballería = 200 acres) of arable land, of which roughly one-eighth, or 1.3 million caballerías, were being farmed and the rest were used as pasture lands.

The cultivated land, the report went on, was divided into 5,581 farms ("estancias"), of which eighty-seven were sugar plantations, large enough to own their own sugar mills ("ingenios"), 185 were medium-sized estancias of one to two caballerías, and the rest (5,039) were small farms of one caballería or less.[15]

Most of the smaller farms, the report continued, produced staple crops such as rice, manioc, yams, plantains, legumes, and maize, while the large, and medium-sized estancias grew primarily sugar cane, coffee, and other cash crops for export.

Aware of the Crown's intentions to reduce the amount of land devoted to pasture, the report suggested that future demolition of hatos be done on a district by district basis, to protect the island's cattle industry.

Without commenting on the report, the Crown instructed the governor, in 1778, to appoint a land commission and proceed to provide titles to those who "occupied" the land. But, as it often happened in the colonies, the process soon ground to a halt and a decade later the landholders were still waiting for their titles, except in Río Piedras, where a fraction of the land had been surveyed and distributed.

The delay, the governor told the Council of the Indies, was caused by the multiple disputes that resulted from conflicting claims over boundaries and often over the same plots. He explained also that while an expert might help to resolve these conflicts and thus speed the process, there was nothing he could do about the holders who were too poor to pay the taxes and necessary fees to allow them to take possession of their plots.

In 1786, the Council sent an expert land commissioner and a scribe from the Audiencia of Santo Domingo, endowed with the necessary resources to survey and divide the lands of the northeastern municipalities of Loíza, Fajardo and Humacao.

The commissioner, however, left the island within the year, complaining that the topography of most regions made the surveying task difficult, that most inhabitants were "too poor" to secure the titles to the plots they held, and that many of the hatos marked for demolition were either too small, or in areas not conducive to agriculture.[16]

With the commissioner's departure, Puerto Rico's land reform program came to a standtill for nearly three decades. The death of Charles III, and the revolutionary upheavals that rocked France and its colony, Saint Domingue in the 1790s, made Spain's new king, Charles IV, less eager to provoke his colonial subjects.

The respite, in turn, allowed Puerto Rico's landholders to devote themselves to planting coffee, sugar, and other commercial crops abandoned by Haiti since the outbreak of its revolution. The rising demand for cotton, for example, made it possible for Puerto Rico to increase its exports from 2,000 arrobas to 40,000 arrobas annually during the last decade of the century.

The Pace of Settlement Increases

Although the island's population increased by more than seven times in the first two thirds of the century, there are no official reports of these demographic changes until 1765. One can only deduce that an unusual increase was occurring because of the number of settlements that were founded after the 1720s.[17] Añasco, the first of the many municipalities to be officially incorporated during the eighteenth century, was founded around the parish of San Antonio in the western region of the island.

Its history dates back to 1726, when eighty-one vecinos, complaining that they could not attend mass in Aguada during the rainy season, requested permission from the cabildo of San Germán, to found a new town. The San Germán cabildo referred the case to the governor, who approved the petition eighteen months later.

Generally, it took months to verify the requirements stipulated by the Ordinance that guided the establishment of towns. Any town seeking incorporation had to have clearly defined physical boundaries, a specified number of inhabitants, a chapel or church, a prison, a priest, and a teniente a guerra. The lack of any of these, or the objection from any group of neighbors, could stall the project for years.

In the case of Añasco, the objection by a group of forty-seven cattle ranchers from San Germán threatened its incorporation. The challengers, led by their representative, Martín de Burgos, claimed that the site chosen by the founders of the town created problems for the cattlemen since they were not yet ready to fence in their livestock. Burgos explained that a town in Añasco would result in unnecessary legal suits against them, as they could not keep the cattle from causing damages to the farmers who would settle in the area.

The governor, apparently not swayed by their argument, signed the incorporation charter in June 1728. Further efforts by Burgos and the cattlemen to stall the project were equally unsuccessful. Thus, in December 1728, the founders of Añasco made the birth of their town official by signing the deed of incorporation.

The staffing of the municipal government was carried out between February and May of the following year, when the governor appointed one of the leading founders, José de Santiago, to the post of teniente a guerra. Santiago, in turn, appointed the members of the militia, while other founding leaders met with the bishop to work out the details of obtaining a priest for the municipality.

Apparently, all went well with the bishop since shortly after he visited Añasco, a copy of its incorporation charter was forwarded to Spain by the governor.

Añasco's success encouraged others. For example, between 1729 and 1732, a group of settlers in the Manatí river basin sought their independence from the district of Arecibo, by creating the town of Manatí. In 1765, Manatí was among the towns on the island with more than 2,000 inhabitants.

In similar fashion, a group of settlers in the Otoao region petitioned the athorities to create the town of Utuado. The founders of Utuado differed from others, according to Fernando Picó, in that they were predominantly persons of mixed blood, who also owned a large estate in the region. The town was officially incorporated in 1739, but went without a priest for another five years.[18]

The towns of La Tuna (Isabela), Pepino (San Sebastián), Caguas, Bayamón, Guaynabo, Río Piedras, Mayagüez and five others were incorporated in the 1740s. For a time, Bayamón and Guaynabo, lacking the necessary trained personnel to administer the towns were forced to share municipal officers and the teniente a guerra.

Lack of financial resources or trained personnel did not always deter interested settlers or governors from founding new towns. During his tenure Governor Miguel de Muesas approved the incorporation of seven new towns, bringing the total to twenty-nine by 1776. One of the first to receive his approval was Rincón, a settlement in the western region, which gained municipal status in 1771, with only 210 families. Not far from Rincón, Cabo Rojo also obtained a charter of incorporation in December 1771, despite the opposition of the area's cattle ranchers.

Less than ten miles east of San Juan, the settlement of Cangrejos, a site reserved since the previous century for runaway slaves from the West Indies, was incorporated in 1773. The petition to incorporate was presented by the captain of the settlement's Mulatto Regiment, Pedro Cortijo, and fifty-five other settlers. The governor approved the petition, but added a modification: the town of Cangrejos would remain militarily under the jurisdiction of Río Piedras.

Another municipality founded in 1773 was Cayey de Muesas. It received its incorporation charter within six weeks from the time the petition was presented by Juan de Mata Vázquez, perhaps because the founders had been careful to include the last name of Governor Muesas as part of the town's name.

Aguadilla, a fairly popular port on the western coast, was also incorporated during Muesas' Administration. In February 1775, Juan Bernardo de Sosa received approval of his petition to separate the Aguadilla settlement from the jurisdiction of Aguada. Meanwhile, in the north central region of the island, settlers received permission to incorporate the municipality of La Vega. This municipality was subdivided years later into two urban settlements: Vega Alta and Vega Baja.

Under Muesa's rule, three of the oldest settlements: Arecibo, Aguada and Coamo were raised to the status of "villas". Such recognition gave them supervisory powers over neighboring settlements. The new status was presumably conferred because of some service or asset. In the case of Coamo, the distinguishing asset was its thermal springs, whose healing powers the governor had experienced first hand in 1773. Aguada, on the other hand, was recognized for its excellent port, and Arecibo for the bravery displayed by Captain Correa during the British attack in 1702.

During the last decade of the century, another eight towns were incorporated in an effort to keep pace with the growing population. Among them were Peñuelas and Juana Díaz, near the southern shore, Humacao and Maunabo, along the eastern shore, and Luquillo in the northeast.

The Population

Puerto Rico's population in 1700 was estimated at about 6,000 persons. Since no breakdown was provided, it is hard to determine how many of the inhabitants were free or slaves, or how many were women and children. It is suspected that one-sixth of the population consisted of adult males, between the ages of 16 and 60, because of militia records.[19]

It is not until 1765, when the first census of the century was taken, that one gets a glimpse of the changes that had occurred in the society since the early 1700s. The fact that by 1765 the island had 44,883 persons suggests a seven-fold increase over the earlier population, while a simple breakdown of this figure, by status, reveals that 88.8 percent of the total (39,846) were free persons and 11.2 percent (5,037) were slaves.

Further scrutiny of the census demonstrates that the majority of the inhabitants lived scattered in the rural countryside, far from San Juan and the major urban centers. San Germán, still the second most important center on the island, had over 1,000 residents more than San Juan, while other towns in the western district, such as Aguada, Añasco and Arecibo followed close behind, with 3,000 or more inhabitants each (see Table 5.1).

TABLE 5.1
Municipalities with 2,000 or more persons, 1765

San Germán	5,950
San Juan	4,506
Aguada	4,272
Añasco	3,398
Ponce	3,314
Arecibo	3,170
Manatí	2,475
Guayama	2,404
Coamo	2,189

Source: Blanca Silvestrini and María D. Luque de Sánchez, *Historia de Puerto Rico*, San Juan: Cultural Puertorriqueña, 1987, 107.

A review of the composition of the five most populous municipalities indicates that its residents owned nearly one half (47 percent) of the slaves. San Juan, with a smaller population than San Germán, had a larger proportion of slaves to free persons (see Table 5.2).

In terms of age distribution, the census also indicates that 43 percent of the population were children under 16 years of age. The youth of nearly half of the inhabitants augured well for a society plagued by a perennial shortage of settlers and workers.

TABLE 5.2
Population, 1765

Town	Total	Free	Slave	% Not Free
San Germán	5,950	5,373	577	9.6
San Juan	4,506	3,562	944	20.9
Aguada	4,272	3,976	296	7.4
Añasco	3,398	3,199	199	5.8
Ponce	3,314	2,960	354	10.6

Source: Table adapted from figures cited in Silvestrini and Luque,op. cit., pp. 107, 109.

Although the growth of the population between 1700 and 1765 was impressive, the increase that followed in the next three decades was explosive. Between 1765 and 1795, the island's population nearly tripled, from 44,883 to 129,758 persons.

The factors behind this demographic expansion are varied. Natural reproduction was an important factor due to the higher number of females in the colony, but immigration continued to play a major role in the expansion. Spain's deliberate measures after 1778 to attract colonists to the island also yielded better results than did her earlier efforts.[20]

Although Spaniards still had priority over foreign immigrants, the latter were increasingly welcomed, provided they agreed to convert to the Catholic faith, obey the laws of the kingdom, and promised to contribute to the prosperity of the colony.

Among the first Spanish subjects to answer the call to relocate to Puerto Rico were thousands of Canary Islanders. They were apparently lured by the expectation of obtaining land and by the growing commercial traffic between the Canary Islands and the Caribbean.[21] The Canary Islanders' long history of cultivating sugarcane made them especially welcome in Puerto Rico, where landholders seemed intent on reviving its sugar industry.

Despite the government's yearly reports, it is hard to determine how many of the white residents in Puerto Rico (30,640 in 1776) were old or recent immigrants, or how many of these arrived alone or with their families. What is notable from these reports is that by the late 1770s nearly two-thirds of the inhabitants were children under sixteen years of age.

A study of the population of Río Piedras by Fernando Picó makes the case that a growing percentage of the municipality's children (28.9 percent in 1779) were born out of wedlock, many of them the offsprings of plantation owners and slave women.[22]

As the racial composition of the population changed, the census officials replaced the all inclusive "black" category with those of "pardo" and "moreno" in an effort to differentiate the groups' lifestyles. The term pardo, for example, was applied to persons of mixed racial parentage, whose lifestyle resembled that of the whites, while moreno was reserved for free blacks and mulattos who lived by African cultural standards.

With these categories in place, the census officials divided the 1776 population into 30,640 whites, 29,822 morenos, and 4,708 pardos. The same report indicates that the number of slaves on the island had increased by more than 2,000 since 1765 (see Table 5.3).

The population report of 1795 (see Table 5.3) reveals that the proportion of whites (43,330) to morenos (38,954) remained very close, despite the practice of listing the pardos (9,713) separately. The fact that the number of slaves more than doubled, from 7,746, in 1776, to 18,056, in 1795, further suggests that by the end of the 18th century the majority (66,823) of the island's residents were of African ancestry. The 1795 report also found about 2,000 Indians still residing on the island.

TABLE 5.3
Puerto Rico's Population

Year	Whites	Morenos Libres	Pardos	Slaves
1776	30,640	29,822	4,708	7,746
1795	43,330	38,954	9,713	18,056

Source: The numbers for this Table were adapted from Silvestrini and Luque, op. cit., p. 202

While increases in the white and free black populations were in part due to natural reproduction and voluntary migration, the rise in the number of slaves was primarily due to fresh imports. A rising demand for slaves by the island's growers led Spain to grant special licenses to Spanish companies (as in the case of Aguirre & Arístegui) as well as to individuals and groups from France, the French Antilles, and the United States. These licenses were usually accompanied by a reduction of duties for every slave they imported. As a result, Puerto Rico's growers were able to obtain more than 10,000 slaves between 1776 and 1795, and another 5,000 by 1807.

Although slaves were imported at a relatively faster pace during the latter part eighteenth century than had been the case during earlier years, they were by no means the dominant group within the moreno and pardo population. In 1795, for example, the 18,056 slaves on the island represented 20.6 percent of the combined 48,667 moreno and 38,954 pardo populations. The fact that more than 60 percent of the blacks and mulattos in Puerto Rico in 1795 were free was a highly unusual phenomenon in the Caribbean, and one generally attributed to the island's long-established practice of granting asylum and freedom to fugitive slaves from the non-Hispanic Caribbean. The asylum policy, first issued in 1664, and reiterated twice in the eighteenth century, is believed to have created an image of Puerto Rico as a safe haven for blacks and mulattoes (free and slave) fleeing from neighboring Caribbean islands before and after the 1790s.

Spain's latest relaxation of its immigration policy also attracted thousands of white foreign settlers from Europe and the Caribbean. In its effort to expand the island's plantation economy, Spain welcomed any foreign settler who could offer either capital or skills, provided that individual accepted the Spanish king and the Catholic faith. Although planters with slaves and capital were the preferred group, others were also welcomed, as long as they were willing to work and not depend on the state.

One of the earliest foreign groups to take advantage of Spain's latest immigration policy were the Irish.[23] Some of them came by way of the British Caribbean, where they had started out decades earlier as either indentured servants, or as prisoners of war. Others arrived directly from Spain, where they had often distinguished themselves in the service of the Crown.

As with all other foreigners, Irish immigrants in Puerto Rico were closely watched by the authorities for a few years, to insure that they not become a problem to the colony. How much progress the Irish made as a group in Puerto Rico is hard to say. It appears that a select few, namely those with strong ties to the Spanish government, used their positions to move up economically and socially through the acquisition of land grants, tax breaks, and commercial licenses. Thus, by the beginning of the nineteenth century Irish families such as the Fitzpatricks, O'Daly's, Kiernans, Power's and O'Neill's occupied an important place among the largest sugar growers and power-brokers in San Juan.

As the French Revolution spread to its Caribbean colonies during the 1790s, thousands of refugees fled from French-speaking Saint Domingue (present-day Haiti).[24] Eager to capitalize on their skills and capture part of the sugar and coffee markets abandoned by revolutionary Saint Domingue, Puerto Rico's officials welcomed them. For the exiles, Puerto Rico's invitation represented not only safety from political turmoil, but a chance to recreate the plantation system they had left behind. Lured by the fertility of the soil of the island's western region, many of them moved west and soon after established important coffee farms in the rugged lands of Moca, Mayagüez and San Germán, and sugar plantations in the valleys of Aguada, Añasco and Aguadilla.

When the troops of Toussaint L'Overture occupied Spanish Santo Domingo in the mid-1790s, Dominicans, too, fled to Puerto Rico.[25] The Dominicans, however, were much more easily absorbed by the society than the Frenchmen, in part because their migration was smaller, and partly because as Spanish citizens they shared stronger cultural ties with the Puerto Ricans. The Dominican exiles, however, were less likely than the Frenchmen to engage in farming in part because their group consisted of artisans, and professional military men.

Among the groups that settled in Puerto Rico after the 1770s were about 2,000 Spanish sailors, who jumped ship, and a few hundred Spanish prisoners.[26] Ship deserters were prohibited by law from settling on the island, but they were generally given cover by the local hacendados. In most cases they were sheltered because they represented potential workers for the plantations, and occasionally because they were viewed as good suitors for the planters' marriageable daughters.

The prisoners, on the other hand, were brought to Puerto Rico against their will and confined to the island's forts. There they were assigned the highly demanding task of repairing the military structures, a job traditionally done by slaves. Those fortunate enough to survive their prison terms were.permitted, if they wished, to remain in Puerto Rico, provided they agreed to move to the interior. Ex-convicts who had lost limbs or had become handicapped as a result of the work they did in prison were sent with recommendations for jobs to the towns of the interior. In 1774, a total of sixty such cases were referred to the local mayors.

Only a small percentage of the convicts survived the ordeal of prison life. Poorly fed and forced to live in overcrowded, unsanitary quarters, many of them became easy targets for recurring epidemics of smallpox and spotted fever, while others perished as a result of accidents, malnutrition and prolonged exposure to the sun.

But the convicts, like the sailors, were only marginal groups, whose survival or demise played only minor roles in the overall pattern of growth of the island's population. The demographic expansion experienced by Puerto Rico during the eighteenth century not only accelerated the pace of the island's colonization, but helped to lay the foundation for a plantation economy.

Life in the Urban and Rural Areas

The kind of life one led in eighteenth century Puerto Rico depended on a variety of factors, including, among others, place of birth, skin color, social status, and one's relationship to the source of power. Although for most the society was still sufficiently open to permit upward mobility, for a large segment of the inhabitants conditions were far less encouraging.

In his travels through Puerto Rico during 1797, the French botanist Pierre Ledru discovered that the working classes on the island were harshly treated by the hacendados, and that race relations in general were not particularly amicable.[27] His observation, and the fact that in 1795 the island experienced its first slave conspiracy, indicate that racial relations had begun to deteriorate with the increasing importations of slaves and the landholders' determination to revive the plantation economy.

Besides the apparent social and racial divisions, there were also marked differences between the lifestyles of the capital's residents and those of the rural area. Life for the capital's settlers, under the daily scrutiny of the military, the church, and the Crown's officials was generally more regimented than it was for those in the rural areas, where such regulatory instutions did not reach them.

Living conditions between the two groups differed also in other ways.[28] The style, architecture, and levels of comfort of homes and public buildings in the two areas were quite different. Living quarters in the capital ranged from large, spacious homes to multiple units, built close together, while those in the rural areas were typically single dwellings, spaced far apart from one another. The private homes of wealthy San Juan residents were constructed of brick and mortar or stone, and had large windows and covered porches that let in light and fresh air, without exposing its interior to the sun. Most of these living quarters were built around a courtyard, which besides helping to ventilate the house, offered its inhabitants privacy from the outside world.

By contrast, the houses of the poor of San Juan were small one-room dwellings, constructed of scraps of wood and thatched with palm. Often dark and poorly ventilated the homes of the poor had dirt floors and none of the comforts of those of their wealthier neighbors.

The urban centers outside the capital were small places, where local hacendados and the devoted went to do business or to attend mass on Sundays and holidays. Few of the hacendados and cattle ranchers owned houses in the urban centers, as did their counterparts in San Juan. In Fajardo, for example, with a population of 1,200, there were only nine residences and a church at the end of the 1780s. In nearby Humacao there were only three houses and a church in town, even though its population totalled 1,500 persons during the same decade.

The capital, in turn, had several impressive public buildings surrounding a central plaza, many of them constructed of stone, masonry or brick. It had several churches, a few convents, and a cathedral. It had also a hospital, with room for a few hundred patients, and its streets were already paved with cobblestones.

Most rural houses were mere thatch-covered huts, with minimal comforts. Furnishings were generally confined to one or more hammocks, a table, and either benches or chairs, often made by the owner of the dwelling. Beds, when available, were simple wooden platforms, covered with bags of dried leaves.

By comparison, wealthier rural residents lived in the lap of luxury. As more than one traveler observed, the hacendados and cattle ranchers lived more "like Europeans" in their spacious, well-furnished houses. Like their counterparts in the capital, they usually imported furnishings and foods, and enjoyed a life of comfort and abundance, unknown to the poorer classes.

The daily diet of the rural poor consisted of boiled bananas and starchy roots, sweet potatoes, rice, beans, and scraps of meat or cod fish. Coffee, introduced earlier in the century, had already become the national drink, and often represented the first meal of the day for the poorest inhabitants.

Patriarchs, Women, and the Family

The family, in particular the extended family, was the core of the social organization in the colonial society.[29] Kinship and marriage ties united close and distant blood relations into one family. Patriarchal in structure, the family was usually headed by the father or eldest male relative. In times of need, the patriarch was expected to assume responsibility for the entire clan and to provide for its poorest members.

Ideally, all Spanish women, but expecially those of the upper class, were expected to remain confined to their home, tending to husband and family. Reality, however, often forced many of these women to assume control of their households and to support their families in times of crises. It was not uncommon for females to administer family estates or businesses when the males in their families were either sick, absent, or dead.[30]

Although traditionally women's properties were administered by the men in their lives (fathers, husbands, and so on), they remained the legal owners of such properties and could not be deprived of them without due process. Never totally deprived of their juridical personality, women in eighteenth century Puerto Rico were also permitted to represent their interests and those of their family in court. A case in point is the drawn-out court case of María Verdugo Segarra. This woman fought the court of San Germán for many years, to clear her husband, Sebastián González de Mirabal, of the charges against him of having taken part in a conspiracy against the government in 1701.[31]

In addition to its patriarchal structure and its kinship and marriage linkages, the family was also characterized by powerful religious ties, such as the baptismal ceremony which helped to draw friends and neighbors into the family clan.[32] The practice, which required all newborn children to be baptized shortly after birth, gained momentum as the population expanded and social conditions for the poorer sector deteriorated. Before the ceremony was held, the parents of the unbaptized child were required to choose a couple willing to serve as surrogate parents for their child. The couple then confirmed these vows in front of a priest, who besides acting as witness also sanctified the act in the name of God.

To the parents of the baptized child, the godparents became known as "compadres" (co-parents) and were thereafter held as religious kin folk. Known locally as "compadrazgo", the institution represented a form of insurance for the child, as godparents were expected to offer the child's family a helping hand in times of need. These practical overtones probably encouraged many poor persons to seek out their wealthier neighbors as godparents for their children.

For the prospective compadre, however, the request to baptize a child was viewed both as a religious duty and an honor. Often it was also viewed as confirmation of his superior social standing in the community, as well as an opportunity to secure endless favors from the poorer compadre, particularly if he happened to live or work on his estate.

Compadrazgo, however, was more than just an informal sytem of social security and labor relations. Godparents were, after all, considered family, and were thus entitled to love, respect, and other considerations. But godparents, as voluntary religious kin folk, were morally and socially bound by duties and responsibilities not always applicable to blood relatives.

The Church Reluctantly Ordains Creoles

Despite the Catholic church's presence in Puerto Rico since the beginning of the sixteenth century, its ties to the population were still relatively weak nearly three hundred years later. This situation was created in part by the church's persistent poverty and by the nature of the island's settlers, who tended to live scattered throughout the rural countryside, far away from each other and from the municipal institutions.

In theory, every town was expected to support its own church at the time it was incorporated; in reality, very few ever collected enough tithes to hire a priest or to provide the obligatory religious services. Lamenting the poverty of some churches, a visiting Spanish bishop said that they "look more like stables than places where God should be worshipped." Although the terms of the royal patronage required the state to subsidize the church, the island's treasury was often so bare that it could not meet this obligation. Of the twenty-four religious establishments in Puerto Rico in 1770, only two (the cathedrals of San Juan and San Germán) received aid from the colonial government.[33]

Since the perennial lack of funds made it difficult for the bishop to bring trained clergymen from Spain, he permitted a few Creoles to be ordained and sent to the churches of the interior. Never comfortable with this arrangement, the bishop often complained that the creole priests tended to follow the customs of their parishioners and were at times seen at local dances, parties, and cockfights. Fearing that such conduct would likely give the church a bad name, he circulated a series of circulars to rein in the offending priests.[34]

Whether the Creole priests were more prone than their Spanish counterparts to give the church a bad name is debatable. Possibly, as a modern clergyman has argued, they had a different view of their obligations and saw their participation in such activities as a way to gain acceptance. Creole priests, the modern clergyman explains, were invaluable assets to their communities. As messengers of God, they were both expected to explain and to provide help to the community in times of crises. Often the only literate person in town, the priest was also called upon to run the school and to educate the town's children.[35]

Education and Cultural Expressions

The 1765 report issued by Alejandro O'Reilly noted that there were only two grammar schools outside San Juan for the children of the island. While recent studies tend to challenge this figure as inaccurate, the fact remains that there were simply not enough schools to meet the needs of the growing student population.

O'Reilly's report, however, prompted Governor Miguel de Muesas to design a plan in 1770 that would expand education to the interior.[36] To implement it, he ordered the corregidores (military district commanders) to build at least one school in each district, and to staff it with teachers of sound moral standing.

To insure that every family benefited from this educational reform, the governor instructed the parents to send all their children to school, or at the very least half of them. He stipulated also that all children, regardless of race or color, were to be welcomed at these schools.

Although original, and highly ambitious for its time, the Muesas plan never got off the ground because of lack of funds. Far from the time when education became a task of the state, Muesas did what any governor would have done: assign the task of educating the island's children to the parents and the community. Muesas' plan is remembered more for its non-racist ideals than for its achievements.

Unlike the previous century, no books were written by Creoles in the eighteenth century. The most notable accounts of the island and its people were the report issued by the Irishman Alejandro O'Reilly (1765), a general history of Puerto Rico by the Spaniard Iñigo Abbad y Lasierra (1788), and the travel accounts of the French botanist Pierre Ledru (1797).

Where the Creoles seemed to have made a mark during the eighteenth century was in the visual arts. With the influx of new settlers and the rising population, some individuals with artistic inclination devoted themselves to sculpting religious figures and painting sacred and secular scenes of their surroundings.

The best of the pioneer painters was the mulatto José Campeche (1752–1809), whose portraits of colonial life helped to immortalize him.[37] Campeche also created a studio, where he trained his brothers Miguel and Ignacio, his sister Juana, and his nephew Silvestre Andino Campeche.

José Campeche (1752–1809)

The works of his disciples, like his own, were later purchased by collectors from Spain and Latin America.

The rising population and the growing number of churches also increased the demand for sacred images demanded by household shrines and church altars. While in past centuries these had been generally brought from Spain, by the 1790s they were being commissioned to local sculptors, known as "santeros".

The first Puerto Rican to distinguish himself in this art form was Tiburcio Espada, a native of San Germán.[38] A member of a skilled family of artisans, Espada established a workshop in San Germán in 1770. Out of this, he and his apprentices supplied many of the "saints" or religious figures purchased by the settlers of the western region until the 1830s. The saints produced by Espada and his group were said to be typical of the period in that they were carved in wood and given several coats of paint. The only known carving of Espada's work to have survived is an image of the "Virgin del Carmen", which was donated in recent times by his descendants to the Institute of Puerto Rican Culture.

Military Reforms and a British Attack

As noted earlier, part of Alejandro O'Reilly's mission in 1765 had been to inspect the defenses of Cuba and Puerto Rico, to correct those problems that were within his means and to recommend mesures for their improvement.

In the case of Puerto Rico, O'Reilly noted with some disdain that the troops guarding the plaza had adopted the same carefree attitudes of the

civilian inhabitants.[39] Many of them, he lamented, lived totally undisci-
plined lives, and were more prone to spending their days with their mulatto women, in huts outside the forts, than in performing their duties. Their
lack of discipline, he explained, was a reflection of the poverty of the
troops, who lacked even uniforms in which to drill. He said that enlisted
men were paid a meager four pesos a month, a sum which was often
advanced to them, at usurious rates, by the corrupt officers in charge.

To restore morale among the troops, O'Reilly reorganized the military
units and demoted the corrupt officers. He then ordered the troops back
to the forts, to train and carry on with their military obligations. He augmented and reorganized the native militia into five cavalry units and nine-
teen infantry companies. The infantry groups consisted of one hundred
men each, while those in the cavalry had only sixty riders each. Both cavalry and infantry groups were assigned to the five largest settlements,
while the smaller towns were protected only by the infantry.

To supervise the militia troops, O'Reilly appointed Andrés
Vizcarrondo, a Creole, with the title of sergeant-major, and the power to
appoint three assistants of his own. To instill pride among the militia
troops, he suggested that they be brought to San Juan to train, and that
they be given firearms and uniforms. The expenses incurred by these
reforms, he suggested, need not be a burden to the royal treasury, but
should be covered by a modest tax levy on the land.

In preparation for his departure, O'Reilly left a plan in which he outlined the problems he found. He advised future governors that, in addition
to repairing the forts, they needed to keep discipline among the troops. He
declared San Juan a defense station of the "first order" and entrusted its
fortifications to a compatriot, the Irish engineer Thomas O'Daly.

Shortly after O'Reilly's departure, the Crown sent two additional
infantry battalions and one artillery company to San Juan, and increased
the yearly salaries of the military officers from 574 pesos to 1,200 pesos
by end of the 1770s. The average soldier, on the other hand, had to settle
for the much smaller reward of being able to choose between reenlisting,
returning to Spain, or retiring in Puerto Rico. Those who chose the latter
option were given small plots in the island's interior.[40]

Intent on repairing the forts, as suggested by O'Reilly, Governor
Miguel de Muesas (1769–1776) called on 1,000 militia troops from the

western region, on the pretext that they come to San Juan to train.[41] Once in the capital, they were dispatched to the various forts, and assigned to repair them. Unaccustomed to such hard labor, many of the troops fell ill and would have probably perished had it not been for the fact that their mobilization was also a burden to the colonial treasury. Always mindful of unnecessary expenses, the Crown ordered Muesas to return the militiamen to their districts immediately. To continue the repair work, he was instructed to employ the militia units closest to San Juan.

Undeterred by either the shortage of funds or workers, Muesas and other governors continued to improve the island's defenses. The wisdom of that policy became evident less than two decades later, when England again launched an invasion.

English designs on the island were periodically discussed and then abandoned during 1779 and again in 1782. The plan devised in 1779 envisioned invading and occupying the island, but a warning from France forced England to consider the option of obtaining the island through diplomatic means. These efforts also failed, in part because Spain refused to accept anything other than the Rock of Gibraltar (ceded to England in 1713) in exchange for Puerto Rico, and in part because of mounting opposition from her own West Indian sugar planters, who feared competition from the much larger island of Puerto Rico.

After a brief alliance with Spain in the Anglo-French War (1792–1798) ended, England returned to harrassing Spain. In 1796, when the Spaniards reentered the war, this time on the side of France, the English felt justified to retaliate, and sent a punitive expedition against Puerto Rico.

When Lieutenant General Sir Ralph Abercromby and Rear Admiral Henry Harvey, commanders of the expedition, reached the island of Trinidad in February 1797, they found it scantily inhabited and took it without a fight.[42] Unsure of what awaited them in Puerto Rico, they spent more than a month there preparing the invasion.

By the time the expedition got underway in mid-April, England was losing the war in Haiti and was hoping to use Puerto Rico as a safe haven for her Haitian allies before she retreated from the battlefield.

Meanwhile, Abercromby and Harvey reviewed their plans, in what appeared to be a repetition of the antics of the Earl of Cumberland two centuries earlier. Thus, on April 17, 1797, they ordered the sixty frigates and 7,000 troops under their command to anchor three miles east of San Juan. They hoped to force the city to surrender after a brief siege.

To their surprise, Puerto Rico was no easy prey. Three centuries of construction and repairs had turned its capital into a veritable fortress and the more numerous inhabitants were much better equipped to defend it. Rumors of the impending invasion had also led Governor Ramón de Castro to mobilize both the standing troops and the militia. In addition, grateful exiles, French nationals in particular, volunteered their services as privateers.[43]

The combined efforts of all these groups made the invaders' position untenable. Relentless fire from the forts barred them from scaling the city's walls, while the militia prevented them from reaching the eastern landed corridor and penetrating the city on foot. Armed peasants and privateers added to the invaders' problems, as they blocked their access to the food sources.

Short of supplies and under constant attack, the commanders saw their

The main street in Arecibo, on the western end of the island, taken in 1899

troops dwindle by death and desertion. Aware that the city would not be taken by the surviving troops, many of whom were hungry and sick, and worried about their badly battered ships, Abercromby and Harvey chose to abandon their quest and gave the order to retreat on May 2.[44]

The attack of 1797 proved to be England's last attempt to take Puerto Rico. Napoleon's designs on continental Europe and England's shifting interest from the Antilles to the Spanish Main provided Puerto Rico with nearly a century of relative peace. During this period the island's economy was rapidly transformed from one of subsistence farming into one of commercial farming, slaves were imported in larger numbers and the wealthier Creoles became more assertive in their petitions to Spain.

Suggested Readings

Abbad y Lasierra, Iñigo, *Historia Geográfica, Civil y Natural de la Isla de San Juan Baustita de Puerto Rico* (Río Piedras: Editorial Universitaria, 1970).

Campo Lacasa, Cristina, *Historia de la Iglesia en Puerto Rico* (San Juan: Instituto de Cultura Puertorriqueña, 1977).

Caro Costa, Aida R., *Antología de Lecturas de Historia de Puerto Rico (Siglos XV-XVIII)* (San Juan, 1989).

Fernández-Méndez, Eugenio. *Historia Cultural de Puerto Rico* (San Juan: Instituto de Cultura Puertorriqueña, 1970).

Figueroa, Loida, *History of Puerto Rico* (New York: Anaya Book Company, Inc., 1974).

Gil-Bermejo García, Juana, *Panorama Histórico de la Agricultura en Puerto Rico* (Sevilla, 1970).

Lluch Mora, Francisco, *La Rebelión de San Germán* (Mayagüez: Editorial Isla, Inc., 1981).

Morales-Carrión, Arturo, *Puerto Rico and the Non-Hispanic Caribbean* (Río Piedras: University of Puerto Rico, 1971).

Morán-Arce, Lucas, et. al., *Historia de Puerto Rico* (San Juan: Librotex Inc., 1985).

Ortiz, Altagracia, *Eighteenth-Century Reforms in the Caribbean: Miguel de Muesas, Governor of Puerto Rico, 1769-76* (Rutherford, New Jersey: Fairleigh Dickinson University Press, 1983).

Picó, Fernando, *Historia General de Puerto Rico* (Río Piedras: Ediciones Huracán, 1986).

Silvestrini, Blanca G., and María Dolores Luque de Sánchez, *Historia de Puerto Rico: Trayectoria de un pueblo* (San Juan: Cultural Puertorriqueña, Inc., 1987).

Sued-Badillo Jalil and López-Cantos, Angel, *Puerto Rico Negro* (Río Piedras: Editorial Cultural, 1986).

CHAPTER SIX

Creoles Seek Political and Economic Power, 1800–1830s

During the first decades of the nineteenth century a few members of the Creole elite began to demand that Spain loosen its grip on the colony. The turning point in their attitude toward Spain, according to the late historian Arturo Morales-Carrión, came after they had successfully defended the island from the 1797 English attack. That experience, Morales and others contend, helped to forge a national consciousness which had been gestating during the last century.[1] Love of homeland as well as a sense of entitlement that came from their military success were undoubtedly important forces in the Creoles' new political assertiveness. But to understand the degree of success they achieved, one needs to consider other factors as well. For example, Creoles who followed events in Europe sensed that Spain was no longer the power it had once been. Her recent loss of two Caribbean colonies—Santo Domingo to France (1796) and Trinidad to England (1797)—were evident signs of weakness.

It was also fairly evident that by the late 1790s Spain had become a virtual satellite of France, that her diplomatic leverage was shrinking and that she was experiencing economic problems at home. Her most recent efforts to help France against England (1804) had resulted in a humiliating defeat of its fleet at Trafalgar. Her once mighty navy could no longer protect her exclusive trade, and she had been forced to permit her colonies to trade with foreigners, especially the United States during the time she was at war.

Shrinking revenues from the colonies had left the Spanish treasury without needed funds for war, forcing the royal family to take the unpopular steps of raising taxes and confiscating some church property. Neither measure was enough to make up for the vanishing colonial funds, but they did feed the growing dissatisfaction of the Spanish popular classes and some sectors of the clergy. Tired of war, and often critical of the scandals at the court, the King's subjects demanded that Charles IV abdicate in favor of his son Ferdinand VII.[2] By March 1808, Napoleon's troops had occupied Spain, removed Ferdinand from the throne, and sent the entire royal family to France in exile. In the colonies, attentive Creoles watched these events unfold.

From their perspective, an occupied Spain was not only less intimidating, but one which might possibly be disposed to grant concessions in exchange for help. Educated and ambitious, many of the Creoles prepared their plans. In the case of Puerto Rico, where absolutist military regimes had been the norm, and where for centuries the inhabitants had been devoid of rights, the plan called for reforms.

Armed with the language of the Enlightenment and the ideas of the French philosophers, the local spokesmen laced their petitions with a liberal rationale. When their chance came to speak for the colony, they asked for free trade ("comercio libre"), protection of individual rights, equal participation in the economy and representation in the colonial administration.[3]

The fact that a weakened Spain subsequently found it in its interest to make concessions further served to confirm the Creoles' belief that their demands were justified. Yet, the apparent ease with which some of these concessions were secured during the first two decades of the century also helped to nourish the notion that reforms could always be obtained without the need to resort to war.

Meanwhile, in Spain, the Napoleonic invasion (1808) provoked a widespread revolt against the French. Invoking a medieval tradition that held that, whenever the king was absent or could not rule the subjects could rule themselves, the major figures in the various provinces constituted themselves into rebel juntas and proceeded to defend the country in the name of the exiled king. From all of them a Supreme Junta was carved and installed in Seville, with the joint task of coordinating the defense efforts of the provincial juntas and ruling the empire in the name of King Ferdinand.[4] Yet the rights conferred on the peninsular provinces by the medieval tradition were denied to the overseas colonies. Those now in power in Spain insisted on the prerogative of ruling the colonies with or without a King.

By mid-1808, the Spanish government was split into two opposing camps: a rebel government, represented by the Supreme Junta, protected by the British navy; and the occupation government of Joseph I, with headquarters in northern Spain under the protection of France. Each government, in turn, sent envoys to the colonies to seek political support and financial backing. In Puerto Rico, the governor, Toribio Montes, had Bonaparte's envoys thrown into El Morro's dungeons, while those sent by the rebel Junta, were sent back with assurances that Puerto Rico would remain in the Spanish fold.[5]

Such loyalty would soon be rewarded by the ruling Junta, whose dire circumstances as well as a growing liberal spirit had made it more receptive to petitions from the colonies. It proposed to trade the traditional monarchical system, in which the colonies had no representation, for a new governmental structure, which made the colonies integral parts of the kingdom, with direct, representative participation in the parliamentary body (Cortes) that would soon be established. In 1809, the Junta invited to the colonies to send delegates to Seville, to take part in the new representative government of the Cortes.[6]

The larger colonies considered the offer to be too little, too late. They preferred to rule themselves and no efforts from the Junta could deter them from their course. Within fifteen years most of the Spanish colonies in the Americas became independent of Spain. Cuba and Puerto Rico were exceptions.

For the time being, both islands chose to work within the system rather than break with Spain. In the case of Puerto Rico, there were some apparent reasons for this choice. First, the formidable military presence on the island was a deterrent to the Creoles. Second, the number of Creoles harboring separatist sentiments were few. Third, the majority of the Creole leaders appeared to be more interested in developing the economy than in separating from Spain. Not sure that they could win a war against Spain, they chose the pragmatic course of settling for reforms and cooperating with her government.

The Island's First Elections

Following the Junta's invitation to send an island representative to
Cádiz, the governor, Toribio Montes, set out to organize the first Puerto
Rican elections. In May 1809, the five district councils, ("cabildos") on
the island (San Juan, San Germán, Aguada, Arecibo, and Coamo), were
each instructed to submit the names of three eligible candidates. Out of
the fifteen thus chosen, they were to select five finalists (one for each district) and forward their names, with all the pertinent information to the
Provincial Electoral Board in San Juan. The electoral board, composed of
the governor, the bishop, and a member of the San Juan cabildo, would
further narrow the list to three candidates, and choose the winner by lot.[7]

In July 1809, the governor announced Ramón Power y Giralt
(1775–1813), as the winning candidate. Born to a wealthy San Juan family, Power y Giralt had been educated in Spain and France. Like other
members of his class, he had become an officer in the Spanish armed
forces. A lieutenant in the navy, he had served with distinction in the
Spanish campaign which had recently ousted the French from Spanish
Santo Domingo. He was still in Santo Domingo when he was elected to
be the deputy for Puerto Rico at the Cortes.[8]

In preparation for his journey to Cádiz, Power solicited the advice of
the most important Creole figures in San Juan. Among those who coun-
seled him was Alejo de Arizmendi (1757–1814), the first Puerto Rican to
be appointed bishop. After offering a religious service in honor of Power,
Arizmendi is said to have given Power his episcopal ring, as well as some
advice concerning his duty to protect his compatriots' interests. The bishop was among those long suspected by the authorities of harboring ill
feelings toward Spain.

As Power was preparing to go to the Cortes, he learned that the Junta,
which had issued his invitation, had been replaced by a new ruling group
known as the Regency. The Regency, in turn, had annulled the Junta-
sponsored elections and had called its own. Elected once again, Power at
last left for Cádiz in April 1810. With him went a long list of petitions, or
instructions, from the five district cabildos on how Spain could better
serve the island's interests.

The Cabildos Seek Reforms

Of the five sets of instructions presumably taken by Power to Spain, the one for Arecibo was not found and cannot be commented upon here. After the usual proclamation of loyalty to the Spanish monarchy, the rest went on to complain about the "oppressive, arbitrary, and tyrannical" rule[9] of the colonial administration. Such complaints were generally followed by suggestions about the need "to break the chains that keep us down and prevent our development." In typical liberal fashion, some argued that the "laws of humanity demand an end to tyrannical rule." What this meant, at least for the members of the San Germán council, was that Puerto Rico was prepared to rule itself if Spain remained under Napoleonic rule. They warned that if Spain failed to extricate itself from its present occupation, they would consider the Island "free to select the best way to preserve the Christian Faith and insure the peace and tranquility of its inhabitants."

Although there is no evidence that the text of this demand ever reached the eyes of the Spanish deputies, it has been preserved and interpreted by local historians as the first dissident gesture of the Puerto Rican people. Having issued their warning, however, the San Germán councilmen followed in the footsteps of their counterparts, prescribing solutions to the social and economic problems afflicting their district.

Some of the recommendations focused on improving education and requested an increase in the number of primary schools, the establishment of secondary institutions and a university. The latter, they explained, would permit those intent on becoming professionals to remain on the island rather than be forced to go abroad for their education. An educated society, they reasoned, was an asset to both the church and the state. Arguing that ignorance bred delinquency and vagrancy, they called also for the establishment of vocational schools.

Some councilmen saw the need for revamping the island's infrastructure. They pointed out the need for the construction of new roads, the repair and construction of bridges, the improvement of trade routes and channels of communication, new hospitals, and better medical care. The implementation of these reforms, they were convinced, would help to increase demand, raise production, and promote economic prosperity.

But the best way to launch the economy, others argued, was to replace the prevailing subsistence mode of production with one based on commercial farming for export. To accomplish this goal, they offered various suggestions. For example, the San Juan councilmen highlighted the producers' need of workers. Anticipating a shortage of workers if the economy turned to commercial farming, they suggested a way to gain access to the free labor force on the island by ending the "agrego" system, a practice which enabled the landless to squat on public and private lands.

In their view, the squatters ("agregados") on these lands had become "the most predatory worms of the haciendas and estancias" and should be relocated to urban areas, where they could be forced to work for wages. Such a move, they explained, would be beneficial to the planters, as it would free them from the perennial need of having to import slaves from Africa. In addition, wages would turn squatters into consumers and this would help the economy. But the greatest benefit, in their view, would be for the squatters themselves, as they would be given a chance to "improve their economic and moral conditions." Although the San Juan suggestion was not immediately heeded, there is evidence that it gradually found its way into the labor regulations that were adopted later in the century.

Other cabildos suggested offering incentives to planters and merchants as a way to increase production. For the merchants, they recommended ending the government's monopoly on flour and opening the colonial trade to foreign nations for a minimum of fifteen to twenty years. They claimed that for the whole island to prosper the government had to end the exclusive role of the port of San Juan and open the other ports (Aguadilla, Cabo Rojo, Fajardo, Mayagüez and Ponce) which had been scheduled to open since 1804.

In terms of the producers and cattlemen, all the cabildos concurred that it was time to end the "abasto forzoso", the practice which required them to supply meats and other foods to the urban settlements at a fixed price. They called for a lifting of restrictions on wheat farming, and a chance to introduce farm equipment, machinery, seeds, and fertilizers free of duty.

Others concurred that the tax system had to be revised as well, in order to make the tax load more equitable. Thus, they recommended exempting producers from the sales tax ("alcabala"), the excise rum tax, the tithes and other religious obligations. They also expressed the hope that the remaining tax obligations be based on a formula of net income rather than on the traditional system of the assessed value of each industry. Lastly, they demanded that Creole professionals be employed in the colonial administration. In sum, they wanted for Puerto Rico many of the same concessions Cuba had demanded of Spain in 1804.

Ramón Power at the Cortes

The Cortes began its sessions in Cádiz on September 24, 1810 and the very next day elected Ramón Power y Giralt as its Vice-president. News of this rare event was widely celebrated in Puerto Rico, especially by the liberals who saw in Power their best hope for change.

The island's small elite was ideologically divided into two camps.[10] The peninsulares, or Spanish-born residents, along with a small group of Creoles, followed the conservative doctrine, and viewed Power's work as a potential threat to their privileged positions. They mounted a quick defense by rallying around such issues as centralized government, exclusive trade, and the continuation of autocratic rule.

The liberal camp, on the other hand, was mainly made up Creoles in favor of such ideas as elective government, the right to representation in colonial and metropolitan affairs, guaranteed individual rights, free trade, and broader access to the colonial economy. Among them was also a much smaller group that favored self-rule. Although the latter were labeled separatists by the authorities, they were in reality radical reformers. What they wanted was greater power for themselves, not necessarily to break with Spain.

Meanwhile, in Cádiz, Ramón Power worked with other deputies to revoke a decree issued by the Regency the previous September, which gave the colonial governors extraordinary powers ("facultades omnímodas").[11] It had come as a reaction to the outbreak of violence against the Spanish government in South America. The implementation of such a decree would give the governor in Puerto Rico the power to suppress any and all reforms on the pretext of national security. Viewing it as an unnecessary stumbling block, Power resolved to have it revoked.

Aware that not all members of the Cortes supported the decree, Power set out to show his colleagues that the new order ran counter not only to the interests of the Regency, but to the very principles for which the Cortes stood. Enough delegates obviously concurred, for the decree was abolished in February 1811, leaving the path clear for Power to make his demands on behalf of Puerto Rico.

Between 1811–1812, he obtained approval from the Cortes for a bill which contained most of the reforms outlined by the cabildos. The "Ley Power", as the new act was known, was promulgated in Puerto Rico in 1812 amid joyous celebrations.[12] With the new law, Puerto Rico obtained the right, for the first time in its history, to establish the office of intendancy, or treasury, separate from the office of the Governor and Power received authorization to appoint an intendant. The Ley Power also authorized the cabildos to open the ports they had requested, permitted the export of cattle from Puerto Rico, and abolished the "abasto forsozo" and the government's flour monopoly.

Still in Cádiz, the island's deputy, like other members of the Cortes, helped frame the first Spanish Constitution, a liberal document that curtailed the powers of the King, insured the right to representative government, and guaranteed the rights of individuals throughout the empire. It was the first document of its kind in the history of the monarchy and it was extended to the overseas territories of the kingdom. It was expected that in the future no King would be able to rule without the help of the Cortes. As the law was extended to the provinces, it was similarly expected that no local ruler be allowed to rule in absolute fashion.

The extension of the 1812 Constitution to the overseas territories was welcomed in Puerto Rico, for it meant that the island was officially recognized as a province of the Spanish kingdom, and in theory entitled to the same privileges as the provinces in the peninsula.[13] It meant also, at least theoretically, that all the free inhabitants of Puerto Rico had been transformed from colonial subjects into Spanish citizens. As citizens, they were presumably entitled to the same rights and duties as all other Spanish citizens. But as we shall see shortly, only a chosen few would be considered worthy of this citizenship.

Nevertheless, most inhabitants on the island, except the slaves, found comfort in the fact that they were able to enjoy freedoms never known before. During the constitutional period (1812–1814), they thrived under the guarantees that permitted them to speak freely, write and publish their ideas, and meet with others of similar ideas without fear of reprisal or persecution from the authorities. They found comfort also in the fact that violations against their persons, homes, and properties were punishable by law.

In addition to these individual rights, the Constitution stipulated the right of the provinces to be represented at the Cortes. Puerto Rico, as one of these provinces, was no exception. The irony, as the Creoles soon discovered, was that the representation they were guaranteed at the Cortes was significantly less than that exercised by the peninsular provinces. The problem was that their representative rights were not proportional to the island's population. The formula of proportional representation had been discussed and discarded by the Cortes, presumably for fear of being overwhelmed by hordes of deputies from the overseas territories. Claiming that the issue in question was the numerical superiority of the overseas provinces, the Cortes did its best to hide its ethnic and racial biases. Careful not to antagonize the mixed-bloods, as France had done with the mulattoes of Saint Domingue a few years earlier, the Cádiz legislators devised new guidelines regarding citizenship in the overseas provinces.

According to the new rules, Spanish citizens were those born either in the Spanish peninsula or in any part of the empire whose parents, on both sides, could trace their ancestry to Spain. All others born within the empire would be considered Spanish subjects, but not citizens. For these individuals Spanish citizenship was conditional. They could earn it, via government dispensation, provided they also met a series of stiff requirements. Such citizenship could be obtained by the few who, having performed great feats for the Spanish government, were also free persons, legitimately born to couples married by the Catholic church, and who earned their living by means of a profession or trade.[14] In truth, the Cádiz lawmakers were able to perpetrate this hoax because they understood that the Creoles' concerns did not extend beyond their own narrow circle.

It was within these restrictive guidelines that voting rights were extended to the island's male citizens, over twenty-five years of age, who qualified to register to vote in any of the five districts. As can be surmised, neither non-white males nor women were considered worthy of representation. In Puerto Rico, as in the rest of the Americas, the right to vote for women, the illiterate, and the poor would not become a reality until the present century.

When it came to the question of representation in the affairs of the local government, the Constitution was even less generous. It did not provide for the establishment of a local legislature, and thus continued to deprive the creoles of the means to share power with the colonial administrators.

Instead of an elective legislature, the Constitution provided for the creation of a "Diputación Provincial", or provincial deputation in which certain members of the society could take part. The Diputación was a partly elected, partly appointed body of nine members whose role and function was determined by the governor. Of the nine seats assigned to the Diputación, seven were filled by elected members and the other two went to the governor and the intendant as ex-officio members.[15]

The work of these members generally revolved around such tasks as assessing the value of the districts' wealth for purposes of taxation, apportioning the tax load among districts and municipalities, reviewing the accounts of the municipalities, suggesting ways to cut expenditures, and supervising public works and government buildings.

The Diputación's supervisory role in the affairs of the cabildos (the only representative body for the Creoles) was in reality the usurpation of their power by the Governor. The fact that the Cortes, too, could implant its laws or abolish any cabildo ordinance further suggests that the political changes introduced under the constitutional period were rather limited. Nonetheless, the first constitutional period (1812–1814) provided a welcome respite from the traditional colonial system.

Implementing Power's Reforms

The intendant Power y Giralt appointed to Puerto Rico was the experienced Alejandro Ramírez,[16] who at the time was serving the Spanish government in Guatemala City. Appointed in January 1812, Ramírez did not reach his new post until the following February. Nonetheless, his arrival was a historic moment for Puerto Rico, as it signaled the beginning of a reform period for the colony.

When Ramírez arrived in San Juan in February 1813, he found the colony in the midst of a fiscal crisis. The problem, as he immediately discovered, stemmed from the fact that the island lacked the funds to pay for its own administration. In the past, local officials had depended on the situado (the yearly sum sent by the treasury of Mexico), but when that colony declared war against Spain, in 1810, its subsidy to Puerto Rico stopped. To cover the gap left by the situado Governor Salvador Meléndez issued a paper currency in August 1812. Poor management, however, soon led to inflation and devaluation.[17] Thus, by the time Ramírez assumed his post there was much grumbling among the inhabitants, who had lost faith in the paper currency.

Ramírez' first task was to contain the inflationary trend by recalling part of the paper currency. Faced also with a shortage of coins, Ramírez authorized the circulation of the "macuqina", a silver coin from Venezuela, in place of the withdrawn bills. To restore faith in the remaining paper currency in circulation, he mounted a press campaign to explain it was backed by pledged revenues.

The lack of an accepted, widely circulated currency was a problem Puerto Rico endured for most of the century. The macuquina, adopted in 1813 as a temporary measure, remained in circulation until 1857. Other foreign coins also circulated freely in Puerto Rico until 1848, when they were replaced by the Mexican silver peso.

Since one of the government's problems was its inability to generate sufficient revenues to cover its own expenses, Ramírez' next step was to reform the tax system. He managed this by implementing many of the recommendations proposed by an 1813 decree issued by the Cortes. For example, he abolished all customs barriers within the island and eliminated the hard to collect indirect taxes. He replaced these with new taxes that were easier to collect, such as those levied upon personal income. The tax load was henceforth based on the assessed value of the wealth of individuals and communities.

To make tax collection more efficient, he replaced the private collectors of the old tax-farming system, which brought in only a fraction of the revenues collected, with paid government officials. Although the tax revenues nearly doubled the following year, they were still insufficient to sustain government operations. To make up the deficit, Ramírez levied a tax on rental property, and established a lottery.

In 1814, Ramírez fulfilled another of Power's requests when he established the *Sociedad Económica Amigos del País*, an economic society which had been operating in Spain and Spanish America since the previous century. The Sociedad was considered a good educational vehicle to promote and exchange ideas about the latest discoveries in science and agriculture. Its statutes were approved by King Ferdinand soon after he returned to the throne. Once established, the Sociedad not only focused on agricultural improvements, but offered courses in such fields as geography, the natural sciences and commerce.

To convey his plans for the economy and allow the inhabitants to exchange ideas, Ramírez founded the newspaper the *Diario Económico de Puerto Rico*. The Diario was the second government publication to be founded on the island since the printing press was introduced in 1806. The first was *La Gaceta*. The purpose of the Diario, according to its first issue, was to "convince the wealthy of their duty to contribute to the development and enlightenment of their compatriots."

Still grappling with the reality of their limited political powers, the Creoles, meanwhile, were confronted by a tragedy. Their benefactor and compatriot Ramón Power had died, victim of a yellow fever epidemic that engulfed much of Cádiz in 1813.

To replace him, they elected José María Quiñones, a liberal lawyer from San Germán, who had gained stature among the Spaniards when he served as one of the judges in the Audiencia of Caracas, Venezuela.[18] But Quiñones arrived in Cádiz shortly before the first constitutional period ended and the King restored the absolute monarchy. Unable to obtain any new concessions from the vanishing Cortes, he resorted to petitioning the King to let the island keep Intendant Ramírez.

The Return of Absolutism (1814)

Although most liberals in Spain fought for the safe return of their King, they did not wish to return to the old system of government. As soon as Ferdinand regained the throne, he abolished the Constitution, dissolved the Cortes, and unleashed a persecutory campaign against the liberals.[19] With the support of the loyalists, he also sought to impose his will on the Spanish rebel colonies. He was only partially successful on either front.

In Spain, where political divisions ran deep, his recalcitrance merely added fuel to the feud which had been brewing for some time between liberals and conservatives. The rivalry between these two groups erupted intermittently into open warfare and kept Spain politically unstable until the mid-1870s. In the colonies, the King's policies further confirmed the rebels' beliefs that they were better off without Spain.

In Puerto Rico, where the idea of insurrection had few supporters, the return to absolute rule was accepted with resignation. With the return of absolutism the island was restored to its earlier colonial status, elections were discontinued, and the governor was given back most of his old powers. The island's military role was augmented, its troops were reorganized and periodically dispatched to protect Spain's interests in rebel South America.[20] Deprived of personal guarantees, the island reformers strove to obtain economic concessions from Spain.

With war threatening the empire, the King found it in his interest to keep Puerto Rico loyal by granting it some of these concessions. Thus, in October 1814, he asked the San Juan cabildo to send him a list of suggestions on how to develop the economy and increase the island's population. Less than a year later (August 1815), he apparently accepted the Creoles' suggestions and issued the "Cédula de Gracias", a decree which provided for a variety of social and economic reforms. These were guaranteed for a period of fifteen years, unless they were otherwise extended by subsequent decrees.[21]

Implementing the Cédula de Gracias (1815)

The task of implementing the terms of the Cédula de Gracias fell initially (1815–1817) upon the Intendant Alejandro Ramírez. Since one of the aims of the King was to promote the island's population, the decree, like so many earlier measures, liberalized the entrance requirements of prospective immigrants. Thus, citizens from friendly foreign nations were permitted to settle on the island, provided they were, or became, Catholics and swore allegiance to the Spanish monarchy. Although whites were the immigrants of preference, the policy was flexible enough to accept mulattoes and free blacks who might wish to settle in Puerto Rico. They, like the white immigrants, would be entitled to free plots of land and tax exemptions, although not necessarily in the same proportion.

Once on the island, white heads of household were given six acres of land for each member of their families, and another three acres for each slave they owned. Free black and mulatto heads of family, by contrast, received one half of this amount, three acres for each member of the family and one and half acre for each slave they owned.

With regard to tax holidays, white families received ten-year exemptions from various taxes, such as the tithe, the "alcabala" (sales tax), and the slave tax, while the non-white families were exempted for only five years. After the grace period ended, all immigrant families were expected to pay a slave tax of one peso a year for each slave they owned.

Anticipating that not all who came to the island would stay permanently, the Cédula stipulated that any newcomer who wished to leave Puerto Rico was free to do so, provided he paid a 10 percent tax on all the profits he had earned since his arrival. For those who left during the first five years, before they could become naturalized citizens, there was the added burden of having to relinquish their rights to the land they had been given.

Obtaining Spanish citizenship was also a necessary step for those immigrants who wished to engage in local commerce and overseas trade, since the laws also barred foreigners from such activities. With citizenship also came the rights to purchase additional land plots, to bear arms, and to travel abroad. But more importantly, citizenship made it possible for newcomers to dispose of their estates as they wished. In case of death, for example, they could bequeath their properties to their relatives, even if these did not live in Puerto Rico.

Although there is no statistical breakdown of how many immigrants the Cédula attracted to Puerto Rico, there is evidence that between 1815-1834 the island's population grew by 38 percent, or 138,000 persons. Even after making allowances for natural reproduction, it is safe to say that the majority of the new inhabitants were probably the result of immigration. The impact of this demographic expansion on the environment, the society and the economy will be discussed in other sections of this work.

The economic growth envisioned by the metropolis required not only the development of a plantation economy, but the ability of the island to sell its products in the overseas markets. To make the latter possible, the government was forced to open the island's trade as part of the incentives package. Thus, in addition to the land grants, the tax holidays, and the importation of slaves, the government authorized Puerto Rico to trade with various foreign and Spanish ports for a period of fifteen years.

Although such trade concessions were made under the banner of free trade, the terms were not equally applicable to all nations. For example, all trade originating in Spain and transported in Spanish ships could enter Puerto Rico duty free. Hence, farm implements and industrial machinery, which were generally purchased in Spain, entered the island in this manner. Black slaves imported directly from Africa by local traders, in Puerto Rican or Spanish ships, were also able to escape the tariff. But slaves brought in any other way were charged a 3 percent head tax. All purchases made in the Spanish colonies were subject to a 2 percent tax.

The terms by which the island could trade with friendly foreign nations were slightly more complicated, depending on what items of commerce were involved, whether these competed with those sold by Spain, and what ships were used to transport them. For example, if the items in question were manufactured goods that originated in the foreign nation, and were similarly transported in foreign ships, the duty paid was 15 percent. But if the same items were shipped in Spanish vessels, the tariff rate was only 3 percent. If, on the other hand, the goods originated in Spain, but were carried in foreign ships, the rate of duty fell to 2 percent.

Puerto Rico exports to foreign nations, if carried in Spanish vessels, paid 2 percent duty, but if shipped in foreign vessels, paid 5 percent. Tonnage charges also varied according to the origin and destination of the ships. Generally, foreign vessels paid anywhere from four to eight "reales" a ton.

The Cédula did not authorize Puerto Rico to trade with other territories in the Caribbean, except in case of emergency. Since much of the island's commerce depended on the various European outlets in Caribbean, the Governor took advantage of the loophole in the law and declared a state of emergency while Intendant Ramírez took care to adjust the tariff rates so that they would benefit the Spanish vessels and merchants.[22] Consequently, exports from Puerto Rico to any non-Hispanic Antillean territory, if carried in Spanish ships, paid a 5 percent duty. Imports, on the other hand, if carried in foreign vessels, paid the full 15 percent rate. Those transported in Spanish vessels paid 12 percent of the rate for manufactured goods and 8 percent for food imports.

In addition to the trade regulations, the Cédula appeared intent on reducing the island's dependency on foreign shipping as well. Thus, it encouraged the establishment of a local shipping industry. But to achieve this in a relatively short time, the Cédula stipulated that foreign vessels purchased by the island within the following three years would be considered part of the Spanish fleet and thus qualified for the same tax exemptions.

The Second Constitutional Period, 1820–1823

The struggle between the King and liberal forces in Spain resulted in a temporary victory for the latter in January 1820, when some sectors of the imperial armed forces came to their support. The feud between liberals and conservative loyalists had led both camps to seek allies abroad as well as at home. The King's faction, for instance, sought to keep itself in absolute control by appealing for help to several European powers, particularly the French monarchy. The liberals, in turn, appealed to some sectors of the Spanish armed forces, which favored restoring the constitution of 1812.[23]

In January 1820, a revolt broke out among the troops that were in Cádiz waiting to be sent to South America. The commander of the troops, Rafael de Riego, issued a call to arms to other military groups. When these were seconded, the King felt compelled to meet the rebels' demands. Thus, he restored the constitution, reconvened the Cortes, permitted elections, and tolerated the exercise of civil rights. As in the first constitutional period, loyal colonies, such as Puerto Rico, were again made provinces of Spain with the same privileges and limitations as before.

This time, elections in Puerto Rico were marred from the start by divisions between conservative and liberal camps.[24] The two struggled, often violently, for the only seat at the Cortes. The victory, however, went to the liberal creoles. To represent their interests at the Cortes they chose Demetrio O'Daly, a military officer, native of San Juan, who happened to be stationed in Spain at the time. A staunch defender of the 1812 Constitution, O'Daly had been among the military officers who seconded Riego's call to arms. Thus, from his compatriots' viewpoint, he was the best candidate to represent the island's interests in Spain.

The instructions forwarded to O'Daly by the Puerto Rican cabildos were essentially similar to those given to Ramón Power ten years earlier. They differed mainly in one respect. They sought not so much to obtain new economic concessions, as to preserve those conferred five years earlier by the King under the Cédula de Gracias. The advice the cabildos gave O'Daly, and the deputy who followed him, was to first negotiate the continuation of the reforms they already had and then ask for new ones.

Reassured that the King's concessions would remain intact, O'Daly moved to bring the island greater political reforms. He introduced a bill in the Cortes that proposed to limit the Governor's powers by dividing the provincial office into two branches of government: a civil and a military. The bill was approved as the "Ley O'Daly" (O'Daly Law) and a civil governor was appointed. In May 1822, the Spaniard Francisco González de Linares arrived in San Juan to occupy the new post.[25]

Nevertheless the Creoles' hopes were soon dashed, for González de Linares was no champion of liberal causes. He had been a businessman in Venezuela and was apparently being rewarded for the financial support he had given the loyal forces against the revolutionaries. His appointment placed in doubt O'Daly's plans to reform the island's government.

When O'Daly's term as deputy expired in 1822, his seat was taken by the liberal José María Quiñones (1822–23), a native of San Germán. Like O'Daly, Quiñones' instructions were to defend the existing reforms first and then present his new demands. Since Quiñones also favored political change, he joined the Cuban deputies Felix Varela and Leonardo Santos Suárez in drafting and submitting a bill that called for gradual self-rule.[26]

Arguing that their homelands were socially and economically different from the other provinces of Spain, they proposed that these be ruled by "special laws", or measures that better reflected their special needs. The aim of these "special laws", although not stated explicitly, was to remove the two islands from the assimilationist path they were on, and place them on the road to eventual self-rule. Although this bill, too, was approved by the Cortes, it was never implemented. In 1823 French troops marched into Madrid once more, only this time, they came to help Ferdinand restore his absolute monarchy.

Absolute Rule Once More

With the restoration of absolutism in Spain in 1823, Puerto Rico lost its provincial status and became a colony once more. As the constitution vanished, so did the electoral rights and personal guarantees. Deprived of constitutional rights, the Creoles, particularly the outspoken liberals, had to adopt a low profile, to avoid antagonizing the repressive regimes that followed.

The first despot to arrive in San Juan was Marshal Miguel de la Torre,[27] a seasoned Spanish veteran from the Venezuelan front. He had been recruited in 1822 for the post of military governor of the island by his friend, the civil governor, Francisco González de Linares. When the King ended the second constitutional period, the civil governorship in Puerto Rico was suppressed, and La Torre was promoted to Captain-General.

Having suffered defeat at the hand of the Venezuelans, La Torre harbored enormous resentment against the Latin American revolutionaries, and Simón Bolívar in particular. Thus, he viewed his new post in Puerto Rico as a welcome opportunity to retaliate against his enemies in the name of Spain. Constant rumors that Bolívar was planning the liberation of Cuba and Puerto Rico gave La Torre the excuse he needed to place the island under a state of siege for the next fifteen years.

Intent on redeeming himself after his defeat in Venezuela, La Torre wanted very badly to insure stability in Puerto Rico. He increased the military forces, recruited loyal Spaniards into the militias, and established an extensive espionage network.

To keep abreast of any threats in the farthest corners of the island, he organized a series of special juntas ("juntas de visita") from among the most conservative elements of the district. To these, he assigned the tasks of keeping him informed on a variety of activities, and organizing receptions for him whenever he chose to visit their districts.

La Torre also unleashed a campaign of hatred against revolutionary and democratic ideals. He personalized these with examples from the Latin American revolutionary fronts, accusing them of every despicable crime. Through the government newspaper, *La Gaceta*, he conveyed the image of the revolutionaries as rapists and terrorists, bent on destroying the civilization they had inherited from Spain. He warned repeatedly against the dangers of democracy, which he described as anarchy. To those who dared to challenge his wisdom, he promised a bleak future.

In the implementation of his policies, La Torre was careful not to antagonize the wealthier classes. He continued to implement the economic reforms prescribed by the Cédula de Gracias. Land plots were distributed, foreign trade was expanded, and the importation of black slaves was encouraged, often in violation of the Anglo-Spanish treaty of 1817. After England abolished the slave trade in her empire in 1807, she began to push other powers,[28] particularly those with colonies in the Caribbean (Sweden, 1813, Holland, 1814, France, 1815, Spain, 1817) to do likewise. For Spain, with its new plans to revive the sugar economy in Cuba and Puerto Rico, the treaty came at a particularly bad time. But rather than provoke England, Spain agreed to end the slave trade within three years. Unofficially, however, she let the colonial rulers violate the agreement for several decades.

To meet Puerto Rico's demand for slaves, La Torre resorted to the old Spanish practice of issuing licenses to individuals and small trading groups with access to slave sources in Africa or the Caribbean and the ability to withstand English pressure. The net result of these practices was a rapid increase in the island's slave population. Between 1820 and 1834, for example, the official count of slaves in Puerto Rico nearly doubled from 21,730 to 41,818. For the next two decades slaves would constitute 11 per cent of the island's total population.

Ironically, La Torre's willingness to help local producers obtain slave labor brought additional problems to his administration. Already in the 1820s slave conspiracies began to threaten the colonial tranquility he was determined to protect. Rather than take any chances, he drafted a stringent slave code which prescribed specific punitive measures against any slave who challenged the system.

The Slave Code and Military Justice

A growing fear of slave revolts had come to permeate the Puerto Rican society. This fear was due in part to the rising number of slaves on the island, and partly to what was known about slave uprisings in the Caribbean since the Haitian Revolution.[29] The fact that black, independent Haiti had become a source of inspiration and a haven for runaway slaves also convinced the authorities in Puerto Rico that they could not relax their guard. Moreover, the 1822 Haitian invasion of neighboring Santo Domingo, in the name of liberating the slaves, only compounded their fear. Thus, when slave conspiracies were uncovered in Bayamón (1821) and Naguabo (1823)[30] it was natural for the authorities to blame them on Haiti rather than on the inhumane system that produced them.

Stories of conspirators' plans to destroy the haciendas, kill the whites in the towns, and take over the island spread fear among many sectors of the society. In their haste to find protection from the slaves, the white Creoles permitted the military to encroach on the area of civil justice. Without hindrance or resistance, the Governor created a military tribunal and charged it with the tasks (which had previously been the realm of the civil courts) of investigating, trying, and sentencing those who committed crimes again the state.

Shortly after its creation, the military court was given jurisdiction over the Bayamón slave conspiracy. Dozens of suspects were rounded up and seventy-nine were charged and arrested in connection with the conspiracy. Of those only seventeen were actually found guilty and sentenced. Two, believed to be the leaders, were executed as a deterrent to other conspirators, two were sentenced to terms of six years in prison, and the remaining fourteen were returned to their owners, with instructions for punishments.[31]

In an effort to prevent other conspiracies, the Governor promulgated a slave code in 1826. The document, known as the "Reglamento de los Esclavos" (Slave Regulation), was essentially a rewritten version of the Spanish Slave Code of 1789. It differed from the earlier code, according to Guillermo Baralt, in its methods and intent. The aim of the imperial code, Baralt explains, was to prevent slave uprisings, by reducing the harshness of the slave system, while the intent of La Torre's code was to intimidate the slaves into submission by subjecting them to much harsher conditions.[32]

Nonetheless, the new code also contained a series of provisions that ostensibly sought to create a more humane climate for the slaves. According to these provisions, slave owners were expected to work their slaves no more than thirteen hours a day during the sugar harvest (days of eighteen hours were the norm), and nine hours at other times. They were similarly expected to reduce the harsh punishments for slave offenses, to feed all slaves three meals a day, to give them medical attention when they were ill, and to supply each of them with at least two changes of clothes every year.[33] The problem with these provisions was they were not easily implemented since no institutions were created to enforce them. Nor was there any prescribed punishment for those who violated them.

The portion of the code that was more often enforced was the one designed to prevent future conspiracies, for it gave those lording over the slaves more power over them. With the promulgation of the code, owners and overseers were expected to contain the slaves within the places they worked. The idea was to curtail communication between neighboring groups of slaves in the hope that this would prevent them from conspiring against the system. To accommodate those owners who either hired out their slaves, or sent some of them on errands to neighboring haciendas and towns, the code added a provision requiring them to give the slaves written permission every time they left the premises. Those who knowingly violated this regulation ran the risk of being fined or possibly losing the slave in question, unless it was determined that the slave was a runaway.

To ensure the safety of haciendas, where the slaves were primarily concentrated, the code required that they be locked up at night. All work tools, particularly those used by the field slaves, were to be removed and locked up as well at the end of each day. Slave holidays and festivities were also reduced by the code, in the belief that during these activities conspiratorial plans were hatched.

Unwilling to leave any aspect of such an important task to chance, the authorities also tried to enlist some of the slaves into cooperating with the government with offers of rewards. Any slave who denounced a conspiracy was promised a certificate of freedom and a cash award of 500 pesos. Yet, despite these generous incentives only four of the fourteen conspiracies[34] that were discovered between 1826–1848 were denounced by fellow slaves. As the figure above indicates, slaves continued to conspire despite the harsh regulations. They also resisted the inhuman system in other ways. Some ran away to the hills, others roamed around the towns and mixed with the free blacks, and those who stayed retaliated by destroying the master's property and sabotaging their work.

In addition to their preventive measures against slave revolts, the colonial authorities were called upon to protect the coastal settlements from periodic attacks from privateers and pirates, and to prevent the South American revolutions from spreading to Puerto Rico.

Impact of Latin America's Wars on Puerto Rico

Concern over the impact of Latin America's revolutionary wars on Puerto Rico began early in 1810, when the Junta of Caracas (Venezuela) rose against Spain and invited the San Juan city council to do the same. Although, as noted earlier, the island's elite decided to remain loyal, there had been echoes of nationalism to remind the authorities that all was not well. The members of the San Germán cabildo, as indicated, made the point that they were ready to rule the island if Spain continued under Napoleonic rule. In San Juan, Bishop Arizmendi was reported to have said that Puerto Rico should follow the Caracas example. An anonymous flyer, which was nailed to the bedroom door of the officer who was recruiting in San Juan, warned that "not a single American will be taken from this island to fight against our Caracas brothers."[35]

Although no plots to liberate the island were hatched for the next twelve years, the authorities continued to take precautionary steps. Puerto Rico, which had always been a military garrison, became during this insurrectionary period one of Spain's two best military bases in the hemisphere. Spanish royal forces turned to Puerto Rico and Cuba for reinforcements, provisions, supplies, weapons and war subsidies. Puerto Rico was also a haven to which the wounded and the sick were sent to rest and recuperate from the ravages of the wars. And when the wars finally ended, Puerto Rico became one of the destinations for thousands of exiles, and hundreds of displaced soldiers from the Latin American front.[36] In gratitude to Spain for this opportunity to start anew, some exiles sought to cooperate with the authorities to keep the island safely under Spanish control.

Despite the government's efforts to keep the revolutionary spirit from infecting the island, some separatists in Puerto Rico made plans to break the colonial ties with Spain.[37] To help them prepare an invasion, they enlisted the help of Guillermo Lafayette Ducoudray Holstein, an ex-general of Bolívar's rebel camp. Although it is not clear who were the main figures behind the plot, there is evidence that Ducoudray received 25,000 pesos from the conspirators to purchase weapons, a few vessels, and other war matériel for an invading expedition. The attack, scheduled for the end of September (1822), was expected to begin in the western city of Mayagüez with the 500–600 men Ducoudray would be transporting to the western harbor. There, they would presumably be joined by local fighters. Once liberated, Mayagüez would become the capital of the Republic of Boricua, and the base for other attacks. The organizers expected to get slave support for their project, even though they had made no plans to emancipate them.

But as it had happened with the slave conspiracies, the rebel plot was denounced a few days before they were ready to strike. Three informers (presumed to be Venezuelan exiles) from the eastern town of Fajardo reported the plan to the governor. A few days later, La Torre also received confirmation from the governor of the island of Saint Bartholomew. In his report, the neighboring governor stated that Ducoudray already had three of the nine ships bound for Puerto Rico docked at the port of Curaçao.

Acting on this official dispatch, La Torre persuaded the Dutch authorities to confiscate the rebel ships and issue an order for the arrest of Ducuodray. In Puerto Rico, meanwhile, he began an investigation, ordering the arrest of Pedro Dubois and one named Romano, for their alleged roles as intermediaries between the separatists and Ducoudray. Convicted of plotting against the state, the two were summarily executed a few days after they were arrested.

Shortly after this conspiracy was aborted, the Governor received other reports from his agents that another expedition to liberate Puerto Rico was being planned in Mexico with support from Gran Colombia (Venezuela, Colombia, Ecuador).[38] The leader of this expedition was reported to be the Puerto Rican soldier José Antonio Valero. A native of Fajardo, Valero was a trained military officer who had joined the rebel forces of Mexico and Gran Colombia after deserting the Spanish army.

Although neither this nor other rumored invasions materialized, they provided the authorities with added justification to search, arrest, jail and/or deport dozens of Creoles in the following decades. In October 1824, for example, a group of Creoles from Mayagüez were accused of seditious acts and imprisoned at the El Morro Castle.[39] Also charged for similar acts were the public scribe of Añasco José Barbudo, his sister María Mercedes Barbudo, then residing in San Juan, and a well-known agitator from the capital, José Ignacio Grau.[40] José Barbudo was held in the municipal jail of San Juan until November 19, 1825, when he was shipped to Spain. José Ignacio Grau was kept at Fort San Cristóbal and

María Mercedes Barbudo was exiled to Havana, Cuba. Accused of using her home to distribute rebel propaganda she received from Bolívar's forces, María Mercedes Barbudo was prohibited from returning to Puerto Rico until she was able to provide evidence that she had abandoned her separatist ideals. There is no evidence of her return to Puerto Rico.

Besides the fear of domestic threats from conspiring slaves and separatists, colonial authorities were also periodically challenged by the activities of pirates and privateers. For example, beginning in January 1817, privateer vessels in the service of the Buenos Aires (Argentina) government, but staffed by American mercenaries, raided the eastern port of Fajardo in search of arms, gunpowder, and foodstuffs. The port was defended by the local militia, but at a cost of lives to both sides. The attack became a personal humiliation for governor Salvador Meléndez as well, who found himself obliged to negotiate the exchange of prisoners with the commander of the raid, the American-born Thomas Taylor.[41]

Eight years later, when La Torre was in command, a number of Venezuelan ships landed at the western port of Aguadilla and seized the Punta Borínquen fort. The fort was recaptured after a violent attack by Spanish troops. The authorities later claimed that the Venezuelan attack had been in fulfillment of a pledge Bolivar had made to the Puerto Rican Valero at the Battle of Ayacucho (Perú) a year earlier.[42]

Although neither these nor other the Latin American expeditions succeeded in arousing the Puerto Rican population against Spain, they remained a constant source of worry to the authorities, the merchants and settlers in the coastal areas. Until 1825, when most Latin American colonies became independent of Spain, Puerto Rico continued to be a target of the privateers serving Buenos Aires and Gran Colombia. Generally, many of the privateers bound for Puerto Rico used the Caja de Muertos Key, off the southern coast of the island as a place of operations. From this point, they proceeded to attack the nearby ports, raid the coastal settlements and kidnap the wealthier settlers for ransom. Hardest hit among these settlements were Humacao, Aguadilla, Ponce, and Guayama, which had their warehouses sacked and some of its residents kidnaped on several occasions. The raiders' practice of intercepting and seizing the cargoes of inbound and outbound ships further disrupted the maritime trade of the entire Caribbean region.[43]

Unwilling to give ground to the privateers, the Spanish government authorized Cuba and Puerto Rico to arm their own privateers. As in the past century when Spain had resorted to a similar practice, the result was greater anarchy in the Caribbean sea lanes, and an increase in illegal trade. Hard hit by the rising cost of insurance, Spanish merchants often resorted to shipping their cargoes in neutral, mainly American-owned, vessels as a form of protection.

Since the activities of the privateers also affected American and English trade in the region, these nations applied pressure on the governments of Spain and the rebel colonies to suppress them. Although Buenos Aires and Gran Colombia made some efforts to restrain their privateers in the early 1820s, they continued to create havoc in the Caribbean until the wars of independence ended. After that, many of them simply became pirates.

Intent on removing these unwelcomed guests, the United States organized a permanent West Indian Naval Squadron in 1822 to patrol the area. Since some of the groups disrupting the trade were from Cuba and Puerto Rico, the United States demanded Spain's cooperation in ridding the area of the interlopers. When Spain failed to cooperate, the Squadron retaliated by harassing her ports. One such incident occurred in the eastern town of Fajardo when the Squadron's commanding officer, Commodore David Porter, landed some of his men at the port[44] under the pretext that he was pursuing some pirates he believed to be hiding there.

Local authorities denied the charge and, when Porter threatened to destroy the town unless the pirates were produced, the locals took up arms against the Americans. Surprised by the hostile reception, Porter evacuated his men, but insisted on an apology from the colonial officials. No apology was issued, but the incident was finally resolved when Spain agreed to help the United States rid the Caribbean of the international pirates and the United States proceeded to court martial and suspend Porter from service.

In 1826, when the newly independent Latin American republics (except Haiti, which was not invited) met in Panamá, to discuss the idea of forming a federation of Latin American nations, the authorities in Puerto Rico began to fear that Bolívar might finally succeed in securing support for the liberation of Cuba and Puerto Rico. In anticipation of such an event, La Torre revamped the island's military operations and placed nearly 10,000 troops on the alert.

As it turned out, the Panamanian convention did not approve either plan, in part because of internal rivalries between the new nations and in part because of pressure the United States exerted on them to leave Cuba and Puerto Rico in Spanish hands. According to Henry Clay, the United States Secretary of State, his government opposed the liberation of Cuba and Puerto Rico because it believed that "neither island [was] competent demographically or politically to rule its own destiny."[45]

Whether the islands' perceived lack of political competence was the real concern of the United States is called into question by Henry Clay's message to Spain a year earlier. Rumors that Spain was planning to recapture its lost territory in Latin America elicited a warning from Secretary Clay that the United States "[would] not remain indifferent" if any part of the hemisphere was attacked. The rationale for this veiled threat was similar to the one offered by the Monroe Doctrine (1823), namely that any interference in the region by any European power disturbed the economic and political interests of the United States.

The message, which the United States government sent Spain demanding her recognition of Latin America's independence, ended with a curious note of reassurance with respect to her remaining colonies. It said in essence that the United States had "no desire" to take Cuba and Puerto Rico, but added that, "even if it did", it was "not able to take them" because its "diplomatic policy prohibit[ed] it."[46]

Thus, when the new republics met in Panamá, Secretary Clay was able to point to the text of his earlier message to Spain as an indication of his country's efforts to help them safeguard their independence. Eager for international recognition, the leaders of the new nations could not ignore the United States' friendly offer. But, whether their decision to abandon Cuba and Puerto Rico to their colonial fates was made in response to the United States' offer, or whether other events, such as the death of Bolívar, played a much larger role is a question that continues to be debated by local scholars. In all fairness, it should be remembered that shortly after the Spanish American republics won their independence, they were besieged by so many problems that the last thing they needed was to provoke another war with Spain or risk antagonizing the United States.

Given the events in and around Puerto Rico in the 1820s, Governor La Torre's preoccupation with the island's safety is understandable. As stated earlier, he also took steps to help the economy and occasionally sought to ingratiate himself with the inhabitants. In 1826, for example, he appointed two doctors to care for the poorer classes of the capital who were then afflicted by a rash of food poisoning. Aware also that education was of great interest to his subjects, he occasionally utilized city funds to open and finance primary schools. Always eager to please the wealthier classes, he also authorized the establishment of San Idelfonso, a private secondary school in the capital. He constructed or repaired the roads and bridges leading to and from San Juan, and supported the opening (1829) of the San Juan Theater.[47]

But no matter how he much he tried, La Torre never won the affection of the Creoles nor shed the harsh image they had of him. A believer in the notion that "a happy people don't conspire", he apparently authorized more private parties, gambling houses and public festivities than any governor. For these practices, his enemies soon named him the "governor of the three b's", a reference to the dances ("bailes"), the drinking ("botella") and the gambling ("barajas") that he permitted.

Among the educated and dissident circles, he was generally accused of using these distractions to keep the inhabitants from focusing on the abuses of the military, the nightly curfews, the press censorship, the arbitrary searches and arrests, the imprisonment, the exile and deportation of those suspected of opposing his system.[48] By the end of his term, he had built a military machinery capable of squashing any revolt from within. As a result, the following decades proved to be a political dead end for local reformers.

Impact of the Economic Reforms

As a result of the Cédula's incentives, and the provisions of an 1824 decree, which opened the Spanish West Indian ports indefinitely to foreign traders, the island's economy was gradually transformed from its predominantly subsistence nature to one based on commercial farming for export. As the manufacture of sugar, rum, cigars, and other minor industries made some advances, the value of the island's foreign trade increased from 269,000 pesos in 1813, to 7.8 million pesos in 1835.[49]

According to economist James Dietz, the average yearly value of Puerto Rico's trade between 1828–1832 was 5.5 million pesos.

It is ironic that the very measures Spain designed to recover control of the island's commerce ended up benefiting her competitors as well. The fact that the island's productive energies were devoted to sugar cane, a commodity of little use to Spain, had much to do with the fact that by 1830 the United States had become Puerto Rico's second largest trade partner after Spain. The importance of the United States for the island was recognized by George Flinter, an Irish officer serving Spain in Puerto Rico, when he noted that "the U.S. not only provides an inexhaustible and cheap supply of life necessities, such as salt, fish, flour, butter, lard, grain, lumber, staves [and] articles of furniture, but is the surest market for the planters' productions."[50]

With the increasing privatization of the plots after 1815, many islanders devoted the best soil to planting commercial crops, such as coffee, sugar cane, cotton and tobbaco. Of these, sugar and coffee dominated the island's economy during different periods during the century. Introduced in 1736, coffee was until the early 1800s the preferred cash crop of the peasants and small producers of the interior highlands. Part of its attraction, explains historian Laird Bergad, was that coffee could be grown in conjunction with food crops.[51] Plantains and bananas, he states, were of great use to coffee groves since they provided the shade needed by the coffee trees. Since both of these grow high above ground, they made it possible for the farmers to intersperse them with crops of starchy tubers, beans, squash, and other staples of their daily diet.

Harvesting and processing the coffee beans, continues Bergad, were also relatively simple operations that could be performed by members of the farmer's family without the need of machinery. By 1812, there were 9,493 cuerdas (one cuerda = .97 acre) planted in coffee, which yielded approximately 3,905 tons of coffee beans, and generated 512,261 pesos in export revenues.[52] That year, sugar occupied 5,765 cuerdas, produced 838 tons, and brought in 508,375 pesos in export revenues. According to Bergad, before the sugar culture began to dominate the export sector in the late 1820s, the value of coffee exports was roughly equal to that of sugar. A decade later, however, sugar surpassed coffee in economic importance and remained the island's leading export until the 1870s.[53]

A host of fortuitous events, such as the rise in world market prices for sugar, the favorable colonial climate ushered in by the Cédula de Gracias, the availability of virgin soil, and the growing presence of slaves and free laborers, paved the way for the expansion of the island's sugar industry for the next three or four decades.

According to the official data, exports of muscovado sugar produced by Puerto Rico averaged 14,595 tons in 1828–1832.[54] Trade statistics indicate that during the decade of the 1830s 75 per cent of Puerto Rico's sugar exports went to the United States. In exchange, the islanders bought from the Americans much of the technology, manufactures, and food-stuffs they needed.

In 1827–28, the governor's secretary, Pedro Tomás de Córdova report-ed that Ponce and Guayama, in the south, and Mayagüez, in the west, were the dominant producers of sugar, about 1,000 tons each. The com-bined output of the three municipalities, he said, accounted for more than one half of the island's exports, even though they only owned eighty-eight of the 276 sugar haciendas.[55]

Encouraged by the rising world market prices, reports historian Francisco Scarano, some sugar planters modernized their estates, adopt-ing more efficient techniques in the field and replacing old machinery and the ox-driven grinders ("trapiches") with steam-driven mills in the facto-ry. In his study of the Ponce sugar industry, Scarano found that in 1828 five of the region's forty-nine haciendas had adopted many of these mod-ernizing practices and were thus as productive as their counterparts had been in the past century in the Non-Hispanic Caribbean.[56]

The existence of large, fertile lands near major coastal ports in the west and south lured established residents from San Juan and San Germán to expand or form new settlements along the coastal upland areas of the western and southern regions. Promises of land and tax exemptions, as were offered by the Cédula de Gracias, also attracted thousands of foreign settlers, traders and financiers. In the struggle for land and power that ensued between the old and new settlers it was generally the wealthy for-eigners who displaced many of the Spaniards and Creole brokers.

As Scarano's study indicates, in 1828 foreign immigrants owned 80 percent of the haciendas of Ponce, and foreign merchants, namely through their commercial houses in the Danish island of Saint Thomas, supplied the bulk of the investment and finance capital utilized by the haciendas. Most immigrant planters in the sugar-producing regions were French citizens from Corsica, Haiti, and Louisiana, although a few others were citizens of the United States, Holland, England, Germany, and Venezuela.[57]

The economic prosperity generated by the sugar industry gradually transformed the once sleepy villages of Mayagüez and Ponce into the second and third most important cities in Puerto Rico. With the wealth obtained from the sugar exports the hacendados, as part of the new rural elite, built sumptuous homes, purchased increasing number of slaves, contributed to the beautification of the cities, sent their sons to study abroad, consumed greater quantities of imports, and paid for recreational services previously unknown in the region.[58] In time, they also bought the best arable land and displaced the food producers. With the newly acquired wealth, many of them also secured political clout with which to defend their acquisitions and status. So long as the world prices held and the government protected them, the island's sugar producers did well.

For the others, especially the free workers, the slaves, and the displaced, the expansion of the sugar industry was not to their benefit. The effects of the commercial plantations on these groups will be discussed in the following chapter.

Suggested Readings

Baralt, Guillermo. *Esclavos Rebeldes: conspiraciones y sublevaciones de esclavos en puerto rico (1795-1873)* (Río Piedras: Ediciones Huracán, 1981).

Bergad, Laird W. *Coffee and the Growth of Agrarian Capitalism in Nineteenth-Century Puerto Rico* (Princeton: Princeton University Press, 1983).

Camuñas, Ricardo. *Hacendados y Comerciantes en Puerto Rico en Torno a la Década Revolucionaria de 1860* (Mayagüez, Puerto Rico: n.p. 2nd edition, 1994).

Caro de Delgado, Aida. *Ramón Power y Giralt (Compilación de Documentos)* (Barcelona, Spain: Imprenta Manuel Pareja, 1969).

Coll y Toste, Cayetano. *Boletín Histórico de Puerto Rico*. 14 vols. (San

Juan: Tipografía Cantero Fernández, 1914–1927).

Córdova, Pedro Tomás de. *Memorias geográficas, históricas, económicas, y estadísticas de la isla de Puerto Rico*. 6 vols. (San Juan: Imprenta del Gobierno, 1831–1833).

Cruz Monclova, Lidio. *Historia de Puerto Rico (Siglo XIX)*, Vol. I (1808–1868) (Río Piedras, Puerto Rico: Editorial Universidad de Puerto Rico, 1970).

Dietz, James L. *Economic History of Puerto Rico: Institutional Change and Capitalist Development* (Princeton: Princeton University Press, 1986).

Figueroa, Loida. *History of Puerto Rico* (New York: Anaya Book Company, Inc., 1974).

Flinter, George. *An Account of the Present State of Puerto Rico* (London: Longman, 1834).

González Vales, Luis E., *Alejandro Ramírez y su Tiempo* (Río Piedras: Editorial Universitaria, 1978).

Nistal-Moret, Benjamín, *Esclavos Prófugos y Cimarrones: Puerto Rico 1770–1870* (Río Piedras: Editorial Universitaria, 1984)

Scarano, Francisco. *Sugar and Slavery in Puerto Rico: The Plantation Economy of Ponce, 1800–1850* (Madison, Wisconsin: The University of Wisconsin Press, 1984).

Whitaker, Arthur P. *The United States and the Independence of Latin America, 1800–1830* (Baltimore: Johns Hopkins University Press, 1941).

*Nineteenth century neo-classical Palacio de Santa Catalina
in San Juan*

CHAPTER SEVEN

Sugar, Slavery and Absolute Rule, 1830–1867

During the middle third of the nineteenth century Puerto Rico's economy came to depend more and more on the export sector and the fluctuations in prices and demand created by the international market. Between 1814 and 1854 the island's volume of foreign trade increased over 2,000 percent, and its economy enjoyed a favorable trade balance for more than three decades, as exports revenues exceeded the cost of imports.[1] That trade advantage, however, started to disappear by the 1860s, as the islanders began to spend more on imported manufactures and foodstuffs than was generated by their exports.

Sugar Takes the Lead

Increased foreign demand for sugar and other commercial crops led to increased production in Puerto Rico between the 1830s and 1850s. Although coffee, tobacco, and food crop production also expanded during this period, sugar became the island's dominant export. Increased production, in turn, led to a change in land usage, as more plots were devoted to commercial crops than to subsistence farming.[2] Sugar acreage, for example, rose from 11,103 cuerdas in 1830 to over 55,000 cuerdas in 1862, and that of coffee increased from 9,000 cuerdas to 34,000 cuerdas in the same period.[3] Since sugar grew best in the valleys and coastal plains, its expansion led to an increasing concentration of land in the coastal areas and a gradual displacement of squatters and subsistence farmers. Those displaced by sugar's expansion moved to the highlands of the interior, where available plots and soil conditions made it possible to plant coffee and food crops.

The expansion of Puerto Rico's sugar industry was most evident between the 1820s and 1840s. By mid-century Puerto Rico was, after Cuba, the second major exporter of sugar in the Caribbean, and the second foreign supplier of the United States market.[4] Its output during these decades represented 5 percent of the world's sugarcane production. Compared to Cuba (eight times larger in area) Puerto Rico produced 23 percent as much sugar in 1838–42, and 16 percent as much in 1848–52.

Its exports of muscovado (raw sugar) increased from 39,664 tons in 1838–42, to 52,622 tons in 1848–52. By mid-century, cane sugar, and its by-product molasses, represented over 75 percent of Puerto Rico's total exports. In comparison, its coffee exports suffered a relative decline during the 1830s, but stabilized thereafter at about 5,000 tons annually until 1852.

The combined value of sugar and molasses exports during the 1840s equalled approximately six times the value of the island's coffee exports. During the 1840s, coffee accounted for approximately 12 percent of the island's exports.[5]

Much of the sugar's success was in part due to the fact that until the 1840s Puerto Rico's sugar exports cornered a relatively larger share of the United States market in comparison to Cuba. Until then, Cuba's exports to the United States consisted primarily of refined and semi-refined sugars, while those of Puerto Rico were the cheaper muscovado and molasses products.

Of the sugar produced in Puerto Rico, Spain purchased a minimal fraction of its exports compared to what was purchased by the United States and other foreign nations. In 1845, for instance, Spain purchased 4.8 percent of Puerto Rico's total exports; the United States 42 percent; Great Britain 18 percent; France 12.5 percent; while another 22.8 percent went to other destinations.[6]

Pressured by its domestic sugar industry to protect the Spanish market from competing sugar imports from the colonies, Spain not only bought very little of Cuba's and Puerto Rico's sugars, but what it bought was saddled with high duties. In 1845, for instance, the duty paid by Puerto Rico's sugar exports to Spain was 57 percent ad valorem. This practice led some observers to complain that the excessive levies charged by Spain were the major cause for the trade imbalance that existed between the colony and the metropolis.

Unable to control the island's growing foreign trade, the Spanish merchants lobbied to end it, or at the very least to curtail it. But since the revenues generated by the trade's duties and shipping fees were sorely needed by local officials to sustain the colonial administration, Spain allowed the island's foreign trade to continue and develop.

Yet despite Spain's acquiescence to the island's sugar industry, its growth stagnated during the late 1840s due to a combination of external and domestic forces. Among the external forces that most affected the industry's future were the shifting and contraction of markets, price fluctuations, and increasing competition from other sugar-producing nations. By 1850, for example, a substantial portion of the sugar consumed in Austria, France, and Germany came from beets rather than from cane, and was produced locally by beet growers. The fact that the beet sugar growers also competed for the remaining European market further compounded the problems of the cane sugar planters.[7]

Cuba, for its part, sought to make up for its losses in Europe by shifting part of its production to raw sugar and molasses, and by expanding its share of the American market. Cuba's ability to supply a whole line of cane products in great quantities and at fair prices led the United States to reduce the amounts of sugar products it previously purchased from Puerto Rico.

The damage to the economy that loss of the European market brought about for Puerto Rico was temporarily compensated by purchases from Great Britain, which in 1845 opened its market to foreign sugars. As a result of the new British policy, Puerto Rico's sugar exports to the U.K., which had averaged from 3,600 tons annually during 1841–45, nearly tripled to more than 9,000 tons yearly for 1846–50.[8]

But as other cane-growing areas such as Java, the Philippines, and Brazil also increased production during the 1840s, the island's access to the British market was soon marred by the reality of declining prices for cane sugar. Thus, by the late 1840s, several observers of the island's industry were lamenting that the price obtained for a ton of sugar was well below what it cost to produce it.

Besides the problems of contracting markets and price declines, Puerto

Rico's sugar planters also endured a host of domestic challenges, ranging from recurrent, long periods of drought during the 1840s, the dwindling of the slave labor pool, and the effects of the perennial shortage of finance capital that resulted from the lack of banking and credit institutions on the island.

By the 1850s, the bonanza of the last two decades was over and many of the sugar planters either went into debt or lost their haciendas to foreclosure. The survivors were kept afloat by occasional large sales to one nation or another. In the 1860s, for instance, larger purchases were made by the United States, whose own sugar production had declined as a result of its Civil War. When the American demand again declined after the war ended, many of the planters who were still in debt went under. By the 1860s, loss of the small and medium sugar haciendas to foreclosure had become common.

Slaves and Free Labor in the Haciendas

Until recently, traditional historiography conveyed the impression that life on Puerto Rico's sugar haciendas was better than in other sugar-growing areas. These studies generally maintain that free laborers and slaves worked in harmony under the paternal guidance of the hacendado. They contend that free workers performed most of the work in the haciendas, since the number of slaves there was small and their production ostensibly insignificant.[9]

Such conclusions were reached because of lack of detailed studies of the sugar haciendas; the practice of scholars to rely on official documents, such as slave codes, which prescribed humane treatment for the slaves; the tendency to conclude that since slaves rarely exceeded 12 percent of the population, they were only marginal to the economy; the readiness of many to accept the flattering "evidence" provided by at least one of the island's visitors.

Among the most often cited sources that affirm the kindly treatment slaves enjoyed in Puerto Rico are the reports of George D. Flinter (already cited) on Puerto Rico's economy and slave system, published in London between 1832 and 1834. In his first book,[10] published simultaneously in English and Spanish in 1832, Flinter contends that the island's planters were so benevolent that their slaves were much better off than the free laborers of Europe. A comparison of the Spanish with other slave systems in the Caribbean led Flinter to conclude that Puerto Rico's slaves were treated in strict observance of the laws; that they were permitted to own property; and that those who did not own land were allowed to cultivate their own subsistence plots on the plantations. As a further indication of the humane treatment they received, Flinter reported that Puerto Rico's slaves were encouraged to marry, or form stable unions and live in family units. He implied that the increase in the slave population was due to natural reproduction rather than to recent importations.

To convey the "convenience and happiness that black slaves enjoy[ed]" in Puerto Rico, he stated that the living quarters of married slaves were the same as those of the free laborers. Married slave quarters, like those of the free workers, were generally built above ground, with walls and roof thatched with palm, and floors covered with palm boards.

The furnishings of the married slaves quarters, like those of the laborers' homes, he explained, were rustic items made by the slaves themselves. In both living quarters, the hammock played an important role as a place to sit during the day and as a "bed" in the evening. Kitchen utensils in these quarters were generally fashioned from gourds and coconut shells. In both quarters the walls were devoid of decoration except for a crucifix and a few pieces of clothing. The beams in both quarters were used to hang bananas and ears of corn.

These observations led Flinter to claim that in the daily struggle for survival the slaves were better off than the free workers, since the slaves had all their basic needs covered by the master, whereas the free laborers could only depend on themselves.

Although less flattering information was reported by the well-known abolitionist Victor Schoelcher, during his visit to Puerto Rico in 1841, Flinter's arguments, so beneficial to the government and the planter class, prevailed.

According to Schoelcher, Puerto Rico's sugar economy could not be sustained without the work of the slaves, whose world was far from the idealized portrait presented by Flinter.[11] He questioned the beneficial aspects attributed to the slave codes by saying that they were routinely violated with impunity by most masters and overseers.

In support of his thesis, Schoelcher quoted from a testimony he obtained from a local hacendado. In the words of his witness, slaves were most "unhappy creatures bowed under the great evil of slavery." During the harvest season "a slave's work day", the witness continued, "began at three o'clock in the morning and continu[ed] until eight o'clock in the evening". The compensation for such work, the witness added, was "the pleasure of eating cane." Slave work, he said, was "limited only by the pleasure of the master." Sundays and holidays, the days slaves were supposed to rest, were rarely observed, as they were made to work "two hours in the mornings and [another] two in the evening."[12]

Recent studies of the sugar haciendas and the lives of the slaves have begun to question the assertions made by Flinter and to corroborate those of Schoelcher. Benjamín Nistal's study, for example, makes available a wealth of data about the hundreds of runaway slaves who willingly exchanged their lives on the haciendas for the unknown risks of the bush. The fact that many of them fled the haciendas more than once, knowing full well the repercussions of being caught, can only be viewed as an indication that slaves did not enjoy the pleasant life Flinter described.[13]

Others, as Guillermo Baralt discovered, stayed on the haciendas only to organize their fellow slaves to revolt, kill their masters and overseers and set fire to the sugar fields.[14] The object in each of these cases was freedom from slavery. In this quest, they risked not only being apprehended and returned to the haciendas under worse terms than before they left, but going to jail, or being killed for their efforts. When runaway slaves were captured, they were either flogged or tortured in front of other slaves, in the hope of terrorizing those with similar plans. Leaders of conspiracies were executed at once.

The point, however, is not whether slaves in Puerto Rico were treated kindly or harshly, but that they were kept in bondage and deprived of the most basic human rights by a system that stood to gain from their labor. The exploitation of one racial group by another in turn helped to perpetuate social inequities and racism.

The works of Francisco Scarano and Andrés Ramos Mattei question another of Flinter's assertions, namely that Puerto Rico's sugar industry relied more on free than on slave labor.[15] After careful studies of Ponce's sugar haciendas, they conclude that slaves were in fact the primary source of labor in the larger estates, and that free laborers provided supplementary labor. They explain that free laborers tended to be hired by the smaller sugar estates, which lacked the needed number of slaves to plant, cut, and process the cane. They argue further that the presence of free laborers in the area did not automatically translate into a labor force for the estates because most of them tended to avoid working for the sugar plantations as long as they had access to subsistence plots. For their part, the planters, too, preferred to work with the slaves in part because they had total control over them and because many of the slaves came from sugar-producing areas and were thus skilled and familiar with that industry.

As long as free workers continued to have access to uncultivated plots, and the slave trade remained undisturbed, the sugar hacendados saw no need to change their attitudes in favor of the free laborers. Between 1828 and 1834, for instance, the number of free workers in Puerto Rico increased by 49,000 persons compared to the number of slaves, which rose by 10,000.[16] Yet, the planters remained reluctant to employ the free workers, under the pretext that they lacked the discipline and stamina required by the sugar industry. Many also were still convinced that only the slaves were able to withstand the harsh conditions bred by the sugar estates.

They claimed to know from experience that free laborers who sought work in the sugar haciendas were selective about the jobs they accepted. Generally, they agreed to do the planting, cutting, and hauling of cane, but refused any job involved with the processing of the cane at the mill. The long hours, grueling schedules, and constant exposure to the excessive heat and noise generated by the grinding mill and the boiling houses they willingly left to the slaves.

In addition, the planters regularly complained that even when the free workers were willing to work in the estates they could not be expected to put in a full week, as they were prone to take off at the slightest provocation as soon as they had earned enough to supplement the output from their subsistence plots. The planters also complained that the work of this group was more costly than the work of slaves.[17]

By the late 1840s, when Spain, under pressure from England, agreed to eliminate the slave trade, the planters were forced to revise their views and find new ways to harness the reluctant free laborers. The fact that the agreement to end the Spanish slave trade gave the English the right to patrol the trade routes and to emancipate the slaves found aboard slave ships increased the costs of clandestine slaves beyond the reach of most planters in Puerto Rico.[18]

As the major European powers abolished slavery in their Caribbean colonies, between 1834 and 1838, the planters in Puerto Rico became aware that it would only be a question of time before Spain was forced to do the same. When violence erupted following the emancipation process in some of the Caribbean islands, many in Puerto Rico began to worry about the wisdom of continuing to import slaves. Faced with the reality of a declining slave labor force, the Puerto Rico sugar planters pressured the colonial rulers to compel the free laborers to work for the haciendas. Convinced also that free labor would increase their production costs, they instituted a system of piecework. To ensure that they had enough hands during harvest time, they often withheld the workers' wages from one week to the next.

The "Libreta" System

The desire to control the island's free labor had first surfaced in the instructions given to Ramón Power in 1809. The argument then, as later, was essentially the same: the island needed stricter laws to end what the planters perceived to be a problem of vagrancy.

But as long as slaves had been available, the government had done little to regulate the free laborers until 1838, when it finally devised a series of anti-vagrancy laws, known officially as the "Reglamento de Jornaleros" (Workers Regulations).[19] Through these measures, Governor Miguel López de Baños sought to create a labor pool for the benefit of the hacendados, by redefining the status of those without property. According to the Reglamento, any person sixteen years old or older without any visible means of support was considered a "jornalero" (wage earner) and required to find gainful employment at once. Violators were subjected to stiff fines, prison terms, and forced to work on public projects at half pay.[20]

Complaints by the local Audiencia (Court of Appeals), established in Puerto Rico six years earlier, that the Reglamento violated the rights of the free workers, led the Madrid government to abolish it in 1839. But renewed pressure from the hacendados, following the abolition of the slave trade in 1845, led another governor, Juan de la Pezuela, to issue an even more stringent Reglamento in 1849, which remained in effect until the 1870s.

Known locally as the "law of the libreta", the Reglamento issued by Pezuela not only sought to convert the landless into wage workers, under terms similar to those established earlier by López de Baños, but created the mechanisms to implement it. He created municipal vagrancy boards, or juntas, and requested that they register the landless adults in their areas and issue each jornalero/a a passbook, or "libreta". Once registered, the worker was required to carry the libreta at all times and to present it to prospective employers whenever he or she sought work. The employer, in turn, was required to record the number of days the jornalero worked, wages received, conduct, attitudes, and any debts he/she had incurred. To ensure that workers complied with the law, the vagrancy boards conducted monthly inspection of the libretas. Those who through no fault of their own were unable to find work had to notify the board to avoid the punishments prescribed by the law for voluntary vagrants.[21]

Efforts to escape the effects of the new labor law created a desperate rush for land, as many jornaleros sought to lease, rent, and otherwise stake their claim to public and private plots. Those unable to obtain land by these means attempted to escape the effects of the new law by offering their services to landed relatives and friends in exchange for subsistence plots. In other cases, they also entered into sharecropping arrangements with neighboring hacendados.

Aware of the jornaleros' ploys to escape working for the haciendas, the planters pressured the governor to tighten the loopholes in the Reglamento. In 1850, Governor Pezuela complied, ruling that anyone wishing to avoid the classification of jornalero had to have access (via lease, rent, or purchase) to at least four cuerdas of land. Those who failed to obtain this much land were instructed to move their residences to the nearest town at once, where they were to be assigned home plots.[22]

As the island's population expanded during the 1850s and 1860s, competition for the arable acreage increased among the commercial planters, and the price per acre rose well beyond the reach of most jornaleros. As a result, by 1865, 10 percent of the island's inhabitants (60,000 persons) were classified as jornaleros. For these, survival demanded that they sell part, and sometimes all, of their working days to the estates.

By routing the landless away from the subsistence plots the colonial government sought to end the so-called problem of vagrancy and to compensate the planters for the slaves they had lost. With the enactment of the Reglamento (1849–1873) the planters obtained a legal tool with which to compel and keep the landless on their estates.

Unable to obtain land, and pressured by the restrictive terms of the Reglamento, many jornaleros were often powerless to resist the abusive practices of unscrupulous hacendados. In many cases they were underpaid for their work, while in others their wages or libretas were withheld by employers who wished to bind them to the estate. For example, in March 1863, the jornalero Nicolás Nazario explained to a judge in San Germán that he had been unable to work or to pay a debt of ten pesos to his employer Luis Belgodore because the latter had his libreta and without it he could not work.[23]

Although the judge's ruling is not known, the Nazario case is illustrative of a trend by which the planters in Puerto Rico were attempting to implant the well-known system of "debt-peonage", practiced elsewhere in the Americas for many centuries. In this system, employers generally advanced cash, or provided services the workers needed, and then sought to hold them on the estates until the debts were paid. The fact that many planters paid in vouchers, redeemable only in their own stores, further curtailed the workers' mobility. Underpaid for their work and overcharged for such necessities as food, clothing, shelter and sometimes a subsistence plot (all provided by the estate), many workers spent their lives working to pay off their debts.

In Puerto Rico, however, the oppressive system created by the libreta was gradually challenged not only by the jornaleros, but by peasant farmers and smaller planters. Until the Reglamento was enacted, wrote some planters to the governor, peasant farmers had traditionally offered their labor to the small estates as a way to supplement their income. But since the Reglamento was implemented, they withdrew from the labor market, to avoid having to conform to the regulations of the libreta. They complained also that because the larger planters monopolized the jornalero labor the island's food production had declined and the health and diet of the masses had deteriorated.[24]

Life Among the Jornaleros

Poverty and ill health among the poorer classes became topics of discussion among the intellectuals after the 1860s. They attributed these problems to the seasonal nature of the export crops, which at best provided paid employment for the work force for six to eight months a year. Unemployed the rest of the year, the workers were left to survive by taking odd jobs, or by planting subsistence crops on the lands of relatives or interested hacendados.[25]

Yet, another part of the problem was that the wages the workers received during the months they were employed were inadequate to cover their most basic needs. In the mid-1860s, a day's wages ranged from two reales (one real = eight Spanish centavos) in the haciendas of the interior and three to four reales in those of the coastal area. In Lares, a municipality of the interior, many of the foods imported in 1864 cost more than half of a jornalero's daily wage. A pound of rice, for instance, cost ten centavos; a pound of dried codfish eight centavos; dried beef seven centavos; chocolate twenty centavos; and lard twenty-four centavos. A pound of locally produced sugar cost five centavos.[26]

With imported foods out of their reach, the working classes survived on starchy roots, cornmeal, a few beans and plantains when they could get them. Coffee, which was often given in lieu of cash payment for their labor, was drunk black and generally without sugar. Milk, eggs, and meat were luxuries they rarely consumed. Hunger, some writers believed, was the reason behind the increase in thefts that were reported annually to the authorities during the 1860s.

Barefoot and poorly fed, the majority fell victim to tropical diseases and hookworms. Chronic anemia, tuberculosis, and uncinariasis were common diseases among them. Recurrent epidemics of cholera, yellow fever and smallpox often decimated some communities, while other illnesses forced the workers to lose many days of work.

The meager wages they received also made it difficult for them to clothe themselves. Few could afford more than one outfit, according to a worker from Vega Baja. Having only one set of clothes, he explained, meant the worker could not work Saturdays, since that day was used to wash and iron their clothes, in order to appear presentable at the "patrón's" (employer's) house on Sunday, when they went to pick up their wages.[27]

Peasant huts devastated by a hurricane

The houses occupied by the jornaleros were generally small huts, raised on poles, and thatched with cane husk, or palm leaves. Palm boards were used to cover the floors of the living and sleeping areas, but kitchen floors were made of dirt. The furnishings continued to be the rustic items they could make themselves, as described by George Flinter during the 1830s.[28]

Population and Society

During the first six decades of the nineteenth century, the island's population continued to grow in dramatic fashion (see Table 7.1). Between 1815 and 1830, when the Cédula de Gracias was in effect, the population grew by 102,946 persons, or 46.6 percent. Although the rate of increase dropped to 38.5 percent between 1830 and 1846, and to 30.2 percent during the next fifteen years, the total number of inhabitants grew to more than 600,000 by 1869 (see Table 7.1).

Among the immigrants who settled in Puerto Rico during the first quarter of the century, more than 7,000 were from Venezuela and nearly 3,000 were from Spanish Santo Domingo. As in the past, a large group of the newcomers were Spaniards. But as Spain allowed more of its ports to trade with the colonies, more of its emigrants were as likely to come from Asturias, the Basque provinces, Catalonia and its dependencies (Valencia and the Islands of Mallorca) as from Andalusía and the Canary Islands.[29]

Although most Spanish immigrants were poor and many were also illiterate, they generally fared better economically in Puerto Rico than did the majority of the Creoles. Their connections to the major commercial houses in Spain, for example, enabled the aspiring merchants among them to obtain goods and credit with which to establish businesses in Puerto Rico. In other cases they were sent by the major commercial houses in their provinces to serve as their sole representatives on the island. Many among them started their own shops, or found jobs with Spanish merchants already established on the island.[30] As members of the ruling group, the Spanish immigrants were also more likely than the Creoles, or even other immigrants, to be appointed to the top jobs in the colonial administration, the military, and the church.

Census figures place the number of slaves in Puerto Rico during the first half of the century at 41,818 in 1834 and 51,265 in 1846 (see Table 7.2). Accepted at face value, these figures reveal that between 1834 and 1846 the number of slaves in Puerto Rico rose by 9,447 persons. By 1869, however, this group had lost 12,196 of its members. The reason most often cited for this loss is the cholera epidemic of 1855, which took a total of 30,000 lives. Crowded conditions and lack of medical attention are generally blamed for the fact that 40 percent of the victims of the epidemic were slaves.

TABLE 7.1
Population of Puerto Rico

Year	Population	Increase	Percentage
1800	155,426	—	—
1815	220,892	65,466	42.1
1830	323,838	102,946	46.6
1846	447,914	124,076	38.5
1860	583,308	135,394	30.2

Sources: USDW, 1899, p.40; BHPR 1:169, 2:228; Díaz Soler, *Historia de la esclavitud negra*, pp. 117, 122, Silén, *Historia*, p.57.

During the first half of the nineteenth century the number of free persons of African ancestry also grew substantially. For example, between 1834 and 1846 (see Table 7.2), the free colored group grew more than twice as fast as the white group. The free colored population nearly doubled, from 126,399 in 1834 to 237,710 in 1869, while the number of white inhabitants increased slightly less rapidly, from 188,836 to 323,454 in the same time.

From 1846 to 1869, the free colored population comprised nearly 40 percent of the island's inhabitants. Although many in this group were presumed to be the product of natural reproduction, there is some preliminary evidence that a number of them were immigrants from neighboring Caribbean islands, where a shrinking sugar industry had left thousands of skilled workers unemployed at a time when that industry was expanding in Puerto Rico.[31] The land and tax incentives offered by the Cédula de Gracias lured thousands of free black and mulatto workers from the Caribbean to migrate to Puerto Rico before the 1840s.

As the expansion of the island's sugar industry slowed down during the late 1840s, and the grants of free land once provided by the Cédula de Gracias vanished, there were less incentives for these groups to relocate to Puerto Rico during and after the 1850s. News of black violence in the British and French Antilles during the 1830s also led Puerto Rico's leaders to look to Europe for white immigrants. Fearing that they might be outnumbered, and arguing that the increasing presence of free blacks and mulattoes was unsettling to the slaves, Creoles and Spaniards in government made it clear that white settlers were preferred.

As wars, famines, and other problems began pushing millions to abandon Europe, local officials made it a point to compete for them by pressing Spain to relax the immigration laws. Puerto Rico, however, was only partially successful in attracting the Europeans mainly because there were many other American countries to choose from.

Among those who chose Puerto Rico after 1848 were impoverished Spaniards and oppressed Corsicans. The latter were said to be fleeing the effects of land concentration and political upheaval created by France's imperial policies over their homeland. Once in Puerto Rico, the Spaniards generally became merchants or took government jobs, while the Corsicans devoted themselves to retail commerce throughout the smaller

towns of the western region and/or cultivated coffee and food plots in the
interior highlands.[32]

TABLE 7.2
Population Increases, by Race

	1834	1846	1869
Total Population	**358,836**	**443,139**	**600,233**
White	188,869	216,083	323,454
Increases	—	27,216	107,371
Free Colored	126,399	175,791	237,710
Increases	—	49,392	61,919
Slave	41,818	51,265	39,069
Increases	—	9,447	–12,196

Sources: The 1834 and 1846 figures appear in Henry K. Carrol, *Report on Porto
Rico, with recommendantions, 1899* (U.S.Treasury Dept., Doc. 2118) (Washington,
D.C. Government Printing Office, 1900), p.200. The 1969 figures are from José
Pérez Moris, *Historia de la Insurrección de Lares.* Reprint, Editorial Edil, 1975),
p. 242.

By 1869, more than half, 53.8 percent, of the island's population was
classified as white, nearly 40 percent as free persons of color, and 6.5 percent as slaves (see Table 7.2). Nearly 47 percent of the inhabitants were
under sixteen years of age, and males outnumbered females by about
14,000 persons.

Among the adults in 1869 (those over sixteen years of age) less than a
quarter (22.5 percent) were reported to be married. Probably, the term
refers only to the couples whose weddings were performed by the
Catholic church and ignores those who lived in consensual marriages.
The majority of the "officially" married individuals, 82,319, were classified as white and 52,580 as free persons of color. Among the married
were also 498 slaves. In 1869, the island had 116,252 households, of
which 30.6 percent were classified as "solvent" and 69.4 percent as poor.[33]
Although neither category was defined, the fact remains that poverty was
widespread despite decades of economic growth.

In addition to the economic and white-black divisions, the 1860s society separated its members by a host of other means, including a person's

status (free or slave), color of skin, texture of hair, and other physical attributes.[34] Like other racially mixed societies, the Puerto Rican seemed intent on untangling the racial lines blurred over time by miscegenation. Like them, they subdivided the inhabitants according to degrees of whiteness. Possession of light skin, beauty, straight hair, and other so-called "fine" physical features were considered assets for anyone intent on rising socially and economically. As in the rest of Spanish America, wealth and education also had the power to "whiten" and thus permit a few individuals to elevate their social station, provided these were not seeking such status as a way to marry someone from the upper class.

In such cases, those at the top closed ranks, and barred the aspirant by insisting on proof of racial purity ("limpieza de sangre"). Obtaining such a certificate was a cumbersome, expensive process, which often had to be abandoned to avoid embarrassment and rejection.

Moving up economically for the racially mixed was also no easy task. According to the 1869 census figures, only 10.9 percent in their group owned more than a subsistence plot or a small shop. As peasant farmers and artisans, two of the most marginal occupations in that society, even the property holders among them remained at the bottom rungs of the economic ladder.

Militia service, another avenue by which free blacks and mulattoes had traditionally been able to move up the social ladder, had been gradually closed to them after 1815, when increasing numbers of Spaniards and white foreigners began to settle on the island. By 1869, there were no blacks or mulattoes listed among the military men pensioned by the state.[35]

In Puerto Rico in 1869 there were also 39,069 slaves. Of these more than a third (34.4 percent) worked in the fields, particularly in the sugar estates, and nearly 8 percent worked as domestics and artisans. More than one quarter (25.5 percent) were children and individuals over sixty years of age, and presumably of little work value to the estates. The rest were employed in a variety of jobs.

In Puerto Rico, as in other Spanish colonies, slaves could obtain their freedom by manumission and "coartación." In the former, on rare occasions a slave was given his or her freedom as a gift by the master. In the latter, the slave purchased his or her freedom, or that of a family member, from the master on the installment plan. In these cases, the master stipulated the price of the slave in question, the terms of payment were established, and a document was drafted as evidence of the agreement. Slaves were also emancipated by the state for extraordinary services, including denouncing a conspiracy. Beginning in 1849, the colonial authorities also permitted interested parties to purchase the freedom of infant slaves at the time of baptism, for the sum of twenty-five pesos. The infant, however, remained with the master who owned his/her mother until he/she reached adulthood.

The top of the social pyramid was occupied by the whites, who were also divided along economic lines. Of the three subgroups within this strata (peninsulares, Creoles, and foreign nationals), the penisulares, as stated earlier, controlled the commerce, were awarded the most prestigious jobs, and were extended political considerations rarely extended to the Creoles. Although many of the foreign nationals enjoyed the distinction that came from wealth, socially they occupied an ambiguous place between the peninsulares and the Creoles.

The Political Environment

As long as King Ferdinand remained at the helm there was little possibility of political change. But when he died, in 1833, leaving the throne to his three-year-old daughter Isabel (later Isabel II), the liberals on both sides of the Atlantic began to demand reforms from the Queen Regent María Cristina, the appointed ruler until Isabel could ascend the throne. Yet, for the reformers in Cuba and Puerto Rico, all hopes of reform were soon dashed when the King's brother, Carlos, a pretender to the throne, led the conservative monarchists into war. The battles intermittently fought under his banner kept Spain in turmoil for decades and became known as the "Carlist wars."[36]

Intent on keeping her power, the Queen Regent agreed to a few of the liberals' demands, such as reinstating the Cortes and restoring the constitutional monarchy, although not under the same terms as in 1812. She agreed to rule with a constitution provided that the monarchy maintained the right to initiate legislation and dissolve the Cortes in times of crisis. Her terms were accepted, and the Cortes were established for the third time in the century.

But what about the liberals in the colonies? Would they be extended the same rights and guarantees? At first, it seemed that this would be the case, as both Cuba and Puerto Rico were instructed to send representatives to the Cortes. With the instructions to hold elections, Puerto Rico was notified that it was entitled to send two delegates.[37]

The island elected and sent José de Saint Just and Esteban de Ayala to Madrid, with a list of petitions from the cabildos that varied little from those of earlier periods. These included requests for free trade, tax reform, incentives for the sugar industry, development of the infrastructure, white immigration, and improvements to the educational system. For their part, the delegates also asked the Cortes to grant the island three additional seats at the Cortes. They asked also for the restoration of the provincial deputation, the right to elect the municipal governments and the creation of a free port in San Juan. They got none of these.

With the Carlist wars threatening her government, the Queen Regent and the Cortes became cautious about tampering with the colonial governments. In 1836, they opted to exclude the colonial representatives from the Cortes and to withhold the constitutional guarantees from the colonial subjects. To make the representatives' dismissal more palatable, the Cortes promised that henceforth their homelands would be ruled by "special laws." The request for special laws was first introduced at the Cortes in 1823 by delegates from Cuba and Puerto Rico as a way of attaining more autonomy than was possible as provinces of Spain. Hopeful that all was not lost, the liberals decided to wait.

Meanwhile, life in Puerto Rico continued as before. Governor La Torre, still clinging to his post, declared himself in favor of the Queen, campaigned on her behalf, and even sent her donations he extorted from the colonists. Yet even such tokens of friendship did not save him in the end. In September 1836, he was removed from his job under accusations of having implemented liberal measures not authorized by the monarchy. The governors who succeeded him during the next three decades made sure to err on the opposite side and ruled the island with iron fists no matter which faction governed Spain.

As the reality of exclusion from the Cortes sank in, some in the colonial society began to reconsider their loyalty to Spain. The fact that in 1837 the Madrid government asked the island to pay a war tax of 500,000 pesos fanned the resentment they felt, and probably contributed to their decision to revolt.[38]

In 1838, a number of wealthy hacendados from the area surrounding San Juan, and seventeen members of the armed forces, conspired to depose the colonial government, and declare Puerto Rico an independent republic. Among the leading conspirators were Andrés S. Vizcarrondo, a wealthy hacendado and retired militia officer (appointed by O'Reilly in 1765), his brothers, Juan and Lorenzo, (the latter served as aide to the governor and captain in the Granada Regiment), their brother-in-law Buenaventura Quiñones, a wealthy planter from Trujillo Bajo, and their cousin, José Saint Just, ex-delegate to the Cortes.[39]

The attack, scheduled for July 14, 1838, never took place, as the plans for it were denounced by a member of the group. Eager to make a name for himself, the acting governor, Francisco Moreda Prieto, had most of the suspects arrested and turned over to a military court. The Vizcarrondo brothers, however, were never caught, for they quietly escaped to Venezuela as soon as they heard the news of the aborted plot. But their brother-in-law Buenaventura Quiñones was not so lucky. His body, apparently strangled, was found shortly after his arrest in a cell in El Morro.[40]

Of those tried by the war council, five were summarily executed; others were sentenced to prison terms. Since many of the conspirators were Creoles who served in the Granada Regiment, the governor had that unit dissolved. Reactions to the failed conspiracy ranged from the practical to the ludicrous. The Madrid government, for example, sought to placate the Creoles by ordering the local intendant not to collect the war tax. In the colony, where municipal officials were generally appointed rather than elected, many rushed to congratulate the governor for saving the island from the dangers of revolution.

The right to elect their own governments, given to the municipalities of 1,000 or more inhabitants during the first constitutional period (1812–1814), had been eroded by subsequent decrees and ordinances. Thus, in 1846, only eight municipalities had elected cabildos, although they no longer had the relative autonomy they had once enjoyed. In most cases their meetings were supervised and their activities checked by officers appointed by the governor.[41] Settlements too small to elect their own cabildos had been placed under the jurisdiction of appointed district officials.

Between 1846 and 1856, two other constitutional governments rose and fell in Madrid, without a word to the island about the awaited special laws. In the meantime, the governors continued to rule as they wished. For example, in May 1848, shortly after General Juan Prim became Governor of Puerto Rico, a group of exiles from Martinique, welcomed in San Juan, brought the news that the slave uprising that drove them from that island had already spread to Saint Thomas. Fearful that such violence, if unchecked, might spread to his domain, Governor Prim decreed a series of harsh laws against all members of the black race ("Bando Contra la Raza Africana") known thereafter as the Black Code of 1848.[42]

Article II of the Code, which was published in *La Gaceta*, the government newspaper, stated in essence that: "Any person of the African race, who takes up a weapon against a white person, even if the aggression is justified, shall be shot, if he[she] is a slave, or have the right hand cut off by the executioner, if he[she] is free." Article I of the Code placed all members of the black race under the jurisdiction of the military, while Article V gave the masters power of life and death over their slaves.

Refusing to be intimidated, a group of slaves in Ponce plotted a revolt in July 1848. As in the past, the conspiracy was betrayed, the informer was given his freedom, and the leading conspirators (three in this case) were shot in front of other slaves. Thirteen others were sentenced to ten years in prison and five were flogged, one hundred lashes each.[43]

Worried that the harsh conditions created by the governor might also antagonize the free blacks to revolt, the judges of the local Audiencia appealed to the monarchy to end the Code and recall Prim. In December 1848, Prim was removed from his job and his replacement, Juan de la Pezuela, brought instructions to suspend the Black Code and restore the island to normalcy. In addition to rescinding Prim's Code, Pezuela reduced the number of lashes prescribed to punish the slaves from one hundred to twenty-five, and introduced the measure (discussed earlier) by which infant slaves could be emancipated at the baptismal font.

Yet the same Pezuela issued the harsh libreta system of 1849 and ordered the arrests and deportations of many a Creole. Among those exiled by Pezuela were the journalist, abolitionist Julio L. Vizcarrondo (1830–1889), and the young playwright Alejandro Tapia (1826–1882), a liberal, and critic of the island's educational system. Tapia had apparently antagonized Pezuela when he, along with several compatriots, sought permission to open a secondary school, the Colegio Central, in San Juan. The governor rejected their petition, arguing that education was the reason why "Spain had lost the Americas" and that anyone "who wished to study could do so in Spain." In 1849 Tapia was exiled to Madrid for having challenged an officer of the Spanish army to a duel.[44]

Determined to keep the Creoles from conspiring, Pezuela sought to curtail any activity that permitted them to congregate in large numbers. He prohibited the traditional and very popular horse races held in the capital, private balls and dances, and the annual municipal festivities. The only activities and parties he tolerated were those he authorized or sponsored personally. Anyone who failed to attend his parties or refused his invitation was severely punished. For example, he had a Spaniard arrested, fined 500 pesos, and deported to Spain for the simple reason that he did not attend a party Pezuela gave in honor of the Queen.[45]

His successor, Fernando de Norzagaray, distinguished himself for his zealous vigilance against the circulation of revolutionary ideas and literature. In that quest, he closed down the newspaper *El Ponceño*, in 1852, for publishing part one of a poem titled "Agüeybana el Bravo" (Agüeybana the Brave), by the Creole poet Daniel Rivera. In the poem, the Spaniards were advised by the Indian chief Agüeybana the Brave to return to Spain. The editors, Felipe Conde and his son, were fined 1,000 pesos each and Rivera was placed under surveillance for four years.[46]

In 1859, the governor Fernando Cotoner ordered the exile of two prominent Creole physicians, Ramón Emeterio Betances (1827–1898) and José Francisco Basora (n.a.). The two doctors, with practices in Mayagüez, were accused of organizing a secret abolitionist society. Betances, a mulatto, had become well-known for dispensing medical care, often free of charge, to the poor of Mayagüez, and for his services to the blacks during the cholera epidemic of 1855. Many a Sunday he was seen at the entrance of the church, waiting to purchase the freedom of infant slaves, presumably with funds from the secret abolitionist society he and others had established. Such activities did little to endear him to the authorities.

Basora, a collaborator of Betances in the abolitionist schemes, refused to obey the Governor's orders to exile himself to Madrid and fled to New

York City instead. There, he later helped Betances hatch a revolutionary conspiracy, to free Puerto Rico and emancipate the slaves. By the 1860s, the abolitionist demands were beginning to form part of the larger political struggle that sought to liberate the colonial society from Spain.

The Junta Informativa Raised Hopes

In November 1865, after the liberal monarchists came to power in Spain, they asked Cuba and Puerto Rico to send representatives to the Junta Informativa (an advisory, fact-finding group) scheduled to meet in Madrid the following year. What motivated Spain to recall the colonies to the table after nearly three decades of neglect is not known. Some suspect that she was under pressure from England and local abolitionist groups to end the slave system. In support of this argument, they recall the many times England had forced Spain to address the slave question, and point out that in 1864 the Puerto Rican abolitionist Julio L. Vizcarrondo founded in Madrid the *Sociedad Abolicionista Española* (Spanish Abolitionist Society), to pressure the government into ending slavery.[47]

Exiled from Puerto Rico by Governor Pezuela between 1850 to 1854, Vizcarrondo had spent these years in the United States, where he made contact with other abolitionists. Upon returning to Puerto Rico, he liberated the slaves bequeathed to him by his family, founded a liberal newspaper, *El Mercurio*, and mounted a campaign in favor of abolition. Persecuted by the colonial authorities, he was forced to move to Madrid in the late 1850s. In Madrid, he continued his campaign on behalf of abolition, publishing articles in several newspapers in New York and London. He also founded two journals, *El Abolicionista Español* and *La Revista Hispanoamericana*, as vehicles for the abolitionists and reformers to express their views.[48]

Others believe that Spain's invitation to the colonies was spurred by fear that the expansionist mood displayed earlier by the United States would continue once the Civil War ended. Between 1836 and 1848, the United States had despoiled Mexico of nearly half of its territory, first by the annexation of Texas (1845) and then by the acquisition of present-day California and much of the southwest in the Anglo-Mexican War of 1845-1848. Already during the 1850s the United States had made evident its desire to acquire territory in the Caribbean, when it offered to purchase

Cuba.[49] Since the United States had emancipated its own slaves, it was also presumed that slaves, abolitionists, and other disgruntled Creoles might revolt in Cuba or Puerto Rico, especially if they felt they could obtain support from either the American government or the American troops recently demobilized.

Regardless of Spain's motives, the Cuban and Puerto Rican delegates welcomed the opportunity to represent their homelands in Madrid. Three of the six seats assigned to Puerto Rico were occupied by reform liberals, despite the efforts of the colonial authorities to curtail their voting rights by the imposition of a poll tax most Creoles could not pay. Because two of the three conservatives elected failed to attend the Junta sessions (1866–67), the liberals became the majority within the Puerto Rican delegation. The group of attendees included the liberal abolitionists José Julián Acosta (1825–1889), from San Juan; Segundo Ruiz Belvis (1829–1867), from Mayagüez; Francisco Mariano Quiñones (1830–1908), from San Germán; and the conservative Manuel de Jesús Zeno Correa (n.a.), from Arecibo.[50]

Aware of their limited roles as advisors, the Cubans and Puerto Ricans sought to influence the metropolitan government to deliver on the awaited special laws. In this quest, they worked on behalf of three proposals. One of them, drafted and introduced by the Cuban José Morales Lemus, called for political reforms for the colonies. These included a request for proportional representation at the Cortes (one delegate for every 45,000 inhabitants), decentralization of the colonial administration, Creole participation in government, extension of the constitutional guarantees (enjoyed by Spaniards in the peninsula) to the citizens in the colonies, and uniformity in the electoral law, to extend the right to vote to any adult male (twenty-five years old and older) who paid twenty-five pesos in taxes annually. The proposal also reiterated the demand that both islands be ruled by special laws.[51]

The other proposal the Puerto Rican liberals supported was an economic plan presented by the Spanish representative, Luis María Pastor, which called for reciprocal free trade between the islands and Spain, free registration of all foreign ships, and reduction or abolition of tariffs and customs duties for many trade items. It called for a tax reform in which indirect taxes were replaced by a tax on income.[52]

The third project was drafted and introduced by Segundo Ruíz Belvis, a member of the Puerto Rican delegation. It called for the immediate abolition of slavery, with or without compensation to the slave owners.[53] Little support was obtained from either the Spaniards or the Cubans at the Junta, who favored a gradual solution to the slave question.

Intent on making their case, the abolitionists in the Puerto Rican delegation presented a series of reasons why slavery should be abolished at once in their homeland. They explained that Puerto Rico, unlike Cuba, depended almost entirely on its free labor force for its agricultural production. Citing figures from the 1860 population census, they claimed that the number of adult free workers employed by Puerto Rico's productive sector was "seven times greater (70,000) than that of slave workers (10,000)." They stated that although Puerto Rico had 41,000 slaves at the time, close to one half (approximately 20,000) were women, children and old persons, of little value to the productive sector. They argued that of the 20,000 active slave workers one half worked as domestics, and artisans, or performed jobs unrelated to commercial agriculture (government figures listed 3,000 in these occupations). They highlighted the fact that productivity in Puerto Rico had risen, even though the number of slaves had been declining for some time, and concluded that free labor was cheaper and more efficient than slave labor.[54]

In April 1867, the Junta ended its sessions without granting any concessions. The representatives were sent home with only a vague promise that the special laws would be forthcoming. Another coup in Spain, however, put an end to that promise. Frustrated with Spain's inability to address their grievances, some in Cuba and Puerto Rico returned to conspiring against her. In Puerto Rico, the conspirators had come to agree with Betances that "Spain cannot give us what she herself does not possess."

Suggested Readings

Abadía, Jesús Lalinde. *La administración española en el siglo XIX puertorriqueño* (Sevilla, España: Escuela de Estudios Hispano-Americanos, Universidad de Sevilla, 1980).
Baralt, Guillermo. *Esclavos Rebeldes: conspiraciones y sublevaciones de*

esclavos en Puerto Rico, 1795–1873 (Río Piedras: Ediciones Huracán, 1982).

Cruz Monclova, Lidio. *Historia de Puerto Rico: Siglo XIX*, Vol. I (1808–1868) (Río Piedras: Editorial Universidad de Puerto Rico, 1970).

Córdova, Pedro Tomás de. *Memorias geográficas, históricas, económicas y estadísticas de la isla de Puerto Rico*. 6 vols. (San Juan: Imprenta del Gobierno, 1831–1833), vol. 2.

Curet, José, "De la esclavitud a la abolición: transiciones económicas en las haciendas azucareras de Ponce, 1845-1873," in Andrés Ramos Mattei, Editor. *Azucar y esclavitud* (San Juan: n.p. 1982).

Dietz, James. *Economic History of Puerto Rico: Institutional Change and Capitalist Development* (Princeton, NJ: Princeton University Press, 1986).

Flinter, George. *Examen del estado actual de los esclavos de la Isla de Puerto Rico bajo el gobierno español*. Reprint of 1832 edition (San Juan: Instituto de Cultura Puertorriqueña, 1976).

Gómez Acevedo, Labor. *Organización y reglamentación del trabajo en el Puerto Rico del siglo XIX* (San Juan: Instituto de Cultura Puertorriqueña, 1970).

Morales Carrión, Arturo. *Auge y decadencia de la trata negrera en Puerto Rico (1820-1860)* (San Juan: Centro de Estudios Avanzados de Puerto Rico y el Caribe and the Instituto de Cultura Puertorriqueña, 1978).

————. "Orígenes de las relaciones entre los Estados Unidos y Puerto Rico, 1700–1815," *Albores históricos del capitalismo en Puerto Rico* (Río Piedras: Editorial de la Universidad de Puerto Rico, 1972).

Moreno Fraginals, Manuel. *The Sugarmill: The Socio-economic Complex of Sugar in Cuba, 1760–1860*, trans. by Cedric Belfrage (New York: Monthly Review Press, 1976).

Nistal-Moret, Benjamín. *Esclavos Prófugos y Cimarrones: Puerto Rico 1770–1870* (Río Piedras: Editorial de la Universidad de Puerto Rico, 1984).

Ormachea, Darío. "Memoria acerca de la agricultura, el comercio, y las rentas interiores de la isla de Puerto Rico," (1847) in Cayetano Coll y Toste, Editor. *Boletín Histórico de Puerto Rico*. 14 vols., San Juan: Tipografía Cantero Fernández, 1914–1927), II.

Picó, Fernando. *Libertad y servidumbre en el Puerto Rico del siglo XIX: los jornaleros utuadeños en vísperas del auge del café* (Río Piedras: Ediciones Huracán, 1979).

Quintero Rivera, Angel. *Conflictos de clase y política en Puerto Rico* (Río Piedras: Ediciones Huracán, 1976).

Ramos Mattei, Andrés, *La Hacienda Azucarera: su crecimiento y crisis en Puerto Rico (Siglo XIX)* (San Juan: CEREP, 1981).

Ruíz Belvis, Segundo, et. al., *Proyecto para la Abolición de la Esclavitud en Puerto Rico* (1865) (San Juan: Instituto de Cultura Puertorriqueña, 1959).

Toro, Fernando Bayron, *Elecciones y Partidos Políticos de Puerto Rico, 1809–1976* (Mayagüez, Puerto Rico, Editorial Isla, Inc., 1977).

Vizcarrondo, Julio. *Elementos de Historia y Geografía de la Isla de Puerto Rico* (San Juan: Imprenta Militar de J. González, 1863).

Ramón Emeterio Betances

CHAPTER EIGHT

From the Lares Uprising to Autonomy, 1868–1897

Before the last representative returned home, the colonial governor, José María Marchesi, had been looking for a pretext to dissuade the metropolitan government from extending political reforms to Puerto Rico. He found one in June 1867, when the artillery garrison stationed in San Juan mutinied in their barracks. The rebellion had been in response to a metropolitan decree that excluded the overseas troops from the benefits conferred on the peninsular soldiers. Intent on making the point that Puerto Rico was a security risk, he seized the mutiny as a pretext to charge, arrest, and deport nearly a dozen Creole liberals, charging them with being the forces behind the mutiny.[1]

The War Council he appointed to investigate the case disagreed, reporting that the riot was an isolated incident which should be shelved, with no more than a reprimand to the leaders. Dissatisfied with these recommendations, Governor Marchesi persuaded the Council to issue a death sentence against the leading rebel, Benito Montero. He promised that he would pardon Montero and keep the sentence from being carried out. The tribunal did as he instructed, but Marchesi did not keep his promise and Montero was executed.[2]

Next, he ordered the arrest and immediate deportation of eleven Creoles, among whom were: the abolitionists Ramón Emeterio Betances, and Segundo Ruíz Belvis, the liberals Calixto Romero-Togores, Pedro Gerónimo Goico, Julián Blanco, Jose Celis Aguilera, Rufino Goenaga, Vicente María Quiñones (mistaken for his cousin, Francisco Mariano), Carlos Elio Lacroix, Felix del Monte, and a Cuban, Luis de Leiras. Omitted from the list, possibly because he was still in Spain, was José Julián Acosta.[3]

Ramón Emeterio
Betances (1827–1898),
leader of the Lares
Conspiracy

Segundo Ruiz Belvis
(1829–1867),
conspirator with
Betances

Ana Maria (Mariana)
Bracetti Cuevas
(1825–1903), sewed the
revolutionary flag

Except for Betances and Ruíz Belvis, who escaped to Santo Domingo in July 1867, the rest obeyed the governor's orders and exiled themselves to Madrid. From Santo Domingo, Betances and Ruíz Belvis made their way one month later to New York City. There, they joined the *Sociedad Republicana de Cuba y Puerto Rico*, cofounded by the exiled Mayagüez physician, José Francisco Basora, and met with several Cuban exiles, who like them, were working for the liberation of their homeland. They also met the Chilean Benjamín Vicuña Mackenna, whose homeland was then at war with Spain, and was thus eager to encourage any group willing to take up arms against her.[4] After a month's stay in New York and many discussions among the Cuban and Puerto Rican exiles, it was apparently decided that Puerto Rico should strike first.

Among the many motives they listed as the reasons to break with Spain were the metropolis' latest refusal to deliver on the promised special laws and the never-ending arbitrary rule of the colonial governors. They complained also that in recent years the colonial treasury had been seizing the municipalities' savings, under the guise of loans. These were then used to pay the salaries of local officials, and in other instances were either sent to Madrid, or squandered on foreign military campaigns that had nothing to do with Puerto Rico.[5]

By the early 1860s, the loans, euphemistically called "voluntary contributions", had become a means by which district officials also periodically raided the municipal treasuries under their jurisdiction. Between August 1864 and January 1865, for example, seven municipal coffers were deprived of sums ranging from 12,000 to 50,000 pesos. In July 1865, one such "loan" extracted by the governor from the cabildo of San Juan deprived the city of 103,000 pesos it had earmarked for the construction of an aqueduct system.[6] The money, which was never repaid, was used instead to pay the salaries of civil and military officials.

A military edict, in effect since 1817, divided the island into seven military districts or "comandancias" and required all males sixteen years old and older to serve in the local militia. From these units local men were periodically recruited and dispatched to other islands in the Caribbean where Spain was directly or indirectly involved in squashing political or slave uprisings. The most recent of these military sojourns had been to Santo Domingo, where the Spaniards had been fighting a restoration war (1861–64). That call for fighting men to supplement the veteran forces had forced Puerto Rico to create five additional militia units.

Such demands and the island's own military expansion placed a strain on the colonial budget, which in 1865 consumed nearly 43 percent of the total. Military appropriations for the troops stationed on the island had risen from 100,000 pesos in 1815 to more than 1.5 million pesos in 1865. But even this sum was apparently not sufficient since every year the soldiers' salaries went unpaid for months.

In addition to the cost of supporting the local troops, Spain periodically asked Puerto Rico and Cuba to contribute to its war chest. The demands for such subsidies from Puerto Rico had also increased from the relatively small sum of 12,000 pesos in 1821, to nearly one million pesos by the early 1860s.[7] Most of the latter sum had been spent by Spain to finance its wars against Santo Domingo and Morocco. In the case of the Spanish-Dominican war, Puerto Rico also contributed men and medical supplies.

Besides the war contributions, Puerto Rico, as well as Cuba, was from time to time asked to pay some portion of Spain's debts. This was the case in October 1865, when the metropolitan government advised both colonies that beginning in 1866 they would be expected to pay the interest on Spain's public debt.[8]

Angered by the unjust demands for men and funds for Spain's benefit,

Betances and other disgruntled Puerto Rican leaders issued a series of proclamations in which they outlined the history of their oppression and urged the inhabitants to rise against such a tyrannical system.

In one of these proclamations, Betances outlined the creoles' demands in his famous "Ten Commandments of Free Men", *Los Diez Mandamientos de Hombres Libres*. These were: (1) abolition of slavery; (2) the right to fix taxes; (3) freedom of worship; (4) freedom of speech; (5) freedom of the press; (6) freedom of trade; (7) freedom of assembly; (8) the right to bear arms; (9) inviolability of the citizen; (10) the right to elect one's officials.

"If Spain grants us these liberties", he concluded, "we will remain loyal to her." But entertaining no such illusions, he went ahead with the plan to revolt. From exile, he issued another proclamation, later circulated among the rebel cells, in which he summarized the major grievances of the Creoles. It said in part:

> We must conspire, because of the five million pesos
> that we pay in taxes annually, more than half finds its
> way to Spain, to never return, under the pretext of
> surplus, or savings belonging to the [peninsular]
> employees. The other half is squandered in an un-
> necessary military force, in a ravenous public treasury,
> in an immoral administration, in faulty public works,
> and in a secret police [that spreads terror everywhere].[9]

Later pamphlets also portrayed the colonial government as disinterested in the plight of the people. They pointed out how the government had done nothing to help the municipalities devastated by the October 1867 hurricane and the tremors that shook the island from November 1867 to January 1868. The fact that thousands had lost their lives and others their homes, their crops, and their animals, the rebel literature said, was of little concern to the treasury officials. These, they reminded the public, not only failed to help, but insisted on demanding prompt payment of taxes and subsidies. What was worse, according to the syndic of Mayagüez, Manuel María Mangual, was that the treasury demanded at least two-thirds of the tax revenues in advance, knowing full well that the crops' yield after the hurricane "was barely enough to allow the planters to pay the loans they owed to the merchants."[10] The government's insensitivity was also reflected in its warning to the taxpayers that taxes would probably have to be increased if the sums collected were insufficient to cover the projected budget. Dismayed by what was viewed as a cynical posture, another proclamation warned the islanders:

> "Puerto Ricans: The hand of the government is forever
> in our pockets. The right to own property [here] is an
> illusion, for no one can be said to own what another
> has the right to take away."

They described the announcement of rising taxes, for a people already saddled with a long list of obligations, as an unwelcome prospect during the best of times, but especially in times of economic crisis, as was the case in 1867. A tax increase in such circumstances, they argued, would force many of the property holders into bankruptcy and further impoverish the poorer classes.

Among the most common levies the islanders paid in 1865 were the "subsidio" (a tax on gross income), the "culto y clero" (church tax), the stamp tax, the "primicias" (a tax levied for special projects), and the consumers tax, paid by everyone. They were also periodically required to make "voluntary contributions" to cover the so-called extraordinary expenses the government incurred in the construction and/or repair of roads and other public projects. Such "voluntary contributions" were usually satisfied in one of two ways. The wealthier residents met the requirement by hiring laborers to perform the tasks assigned to them, while those in the poorer classes paid in services. In 1865, the value of these "voluntary" contributions was estimated at 600,000 pesos for the property holders and the equivalent of 300,000 pesos in in-kind services by the poorer sectors.[11]

Spain's indifference, rising taxes, colonial repression, and the ongoing economic crisis were among the many grievances that fed the Creole leaders' resentment against Spain. The arguments they articulated about how the people were exploited and abused were translated into simpler messages by the rebels who took up arms against the government in September 1868. For them, the culprits of their suffering were the Spaniards in the colony, the civil and military officials, who regulated their existence, and the merchants in their neighborhoods, who underpaid them for their work and crops and overcharged them for goods. The culprits were also those who deprived them of access to the land and forced them to remain perpetually in debt.

The notarial records of three municipalities that took part in the Lares uprising reveal in part many of the reasons for the growing sources of tension between the Creoles and the Spanish merchants. For example, of the four commercial houses established in Lares between 1844 and 1863, one belonged to the pioneer merchant Juan Marquez. A native of Mallorca, one of the Balearic Islands, Marquez had reached Lares in the early 1840s, and within four years had accumulated sufficient funds to open his store, Casa Marquez. Apparently he amassed this sum by lending out the salary he earned at the estate of Dona María de Soto at high interest rates.[12]

A literate man among a mass of illiterates, Marquez had also parlayed his skills into a municipal post in 1844, the year he opened his store. As alderman of the municipality, he earned a certain prestige which further helped him in his business dealings. The economic prosperity that resulted from these dealings, in turn, ensured his rise to the post of acting mayor of Lares a few years later.

Determined to expand his business, Juan Marquez sent for his four brothers, and with their help transformed his initial store into the largest commercial establishment in the area, the Casa Marquez & Compañía. In 1863, when Juan Marquez returned home to enjoy the "fruits of his labors", he left an impressive business to his brothers. They, in turn, invested another 38,149 pesos in Casa Marquez & Compañía, a sum they more than doubled within two years.

In 1868, the Marquez brothers took in two other Spaniards as partners, who invested a total of 35,589 pesos. At the end of 1868, the firm had approximately 31,483 pesos in accounts receivable and the estimated value of the establishment was 128,288 pesos.[13]

The Casa Marquez & Compañía, however, was not without competition. Yet, as pioneers in the town's commerce, the Marquez brothers not only had set the standards for the industry, but generally had first claims on the major crops and estates in the region. They also fulfilled many of the town's needs. As importers of foodstuffs, manufactured products, farm tools, and textiles, they supplied the consumers, almost always on credit, with a broad range of consumer goods. As exporters of the region's crops, they provided financing, warehouses, and linkages with the outside market. To compensate for the risks each of these transactions entailed, they usually underpaid for the commodities they bought and overcharged for the services they rendered.[14]

In a society deprived of banks and financial institutions, the merchants were also called upon to provide credit and loans to planters and other producers. As guarantees for these sums, they usually demanded exclusive rights over the debtors' major crops or held the titles to their properties as collateral. If the debt stemmed from cash loans, they charged (during the late 1860s) an interest rate of 2 to 3 percent a month.[15] Such debts could be repaid either in cash or in crops, but had to be repaid within two years. If the debt was the result of accumulated purchases on credit, or some other transactions, the interest rate remained fixed and the time of payment was extended over a longer period, provided the debtor had the proper collateral. In cases where debtors delayed or failed to pay, the creditors were free to foreclose or to renegotiate the debt.[16]

A few examples from the many listed by the notarial records demonstrate that most of the rebels who converged on Lares in 1868 had fallen on hard times. Almost all of them were in debt to the Spanish merchants and many had either already lost, or were on the verge of losing, their properties to foreclosure.

One of those caught in the debt-foreclosure cycle was Manuel Rojas, president of the revolutionary cell, *Centro Bravo No. 2*, and the military leader who led the rebel troops into battle. The story of Rojas' economic woes began in 1862, when he purchased a coffee estancia of 569 cuerdas from Amell, Juliá & Co., a Spanish commercial establishment in Aguadilla. The selling price of this property was 23,000 pesos (56,000 escudos). Since Rojas had only part of the money, the sellers extended the balance on credit. They also advanced him a cash loan of 3,800 pesos to finance the cost of operating the hacienda until the next harvest.[17]

When time came to pay Amell, Juliá & Co. the following year, Rojas did not have the funds and mortgaged the hacienda to a Spanish commercial establishment in Lares, owned by Francisco Ferret y Hermanos, for the sum of 14,250 pesos (28,510 escudos). Four years later (1866),

Rojas declared before the notary, Evaristo Vélez, that he still owed Ferret y Hermanos most of that money, even though he had paid them regularly in cash and crops every year.[18]

Between 1862 and 1868 Rojas bought and mortgaged a few more estancias in the Lares area, digging himself deeper into debt with Ferret & Hermanos. Forced to pay his debts, on May 7, 1868, Rojas mortgaged everything he owned for the sum of 25,689 pesos (51,378 escudos). To pay Evaristo Vélez the notarial fees of approximately 900 pesos (1,862 escudos), Rojas ceded him a farm of 15 cuerdas he owned in barrio Mirasol, Lares.

Still in need of money, Rojas borrowed 3,451 pesos (7,903 escudos) on May 26 from the Creole merchants Vivó Méndez & Co. The loan was approved on condition that he repay it in "good quality coffee and other products still unclaimed by Ferret y Hermanos."[19]

It is hard to say whether he repaid this loan since the story of Rojas, the hacendado, ends abruptly on April 12, 1869, when Ferret y Hermanos foreclosed on his property. All he managed to salvage from this creditor was a plot of 11 cuerdas, which he sold seven days later for the meager sum of 200 pesos (400 escudos).

Like Rojas, at least twelve others in his rebel cell, *Centro Bravo No. 2* were in difficult economic straits. Among them was Francisco Ramírez, president of the republic that was born in Lares. In Ramírez' case the economic problems stemmed from debts he had incurred to keep afloat a small store ("pulpería") he owned in barrio Bartolo, Lares. Unable to pay his debts, Ramírez eventually lost the store, as well as a horse, a cow, and all his accounts receivable to Ferret y Hermanos in March 1869.

The stories of Rojas and Ramírez are just two of the hundreds of cases I uncovered in my research on El Grito de Lares. They reflect an aspect of the tensions that permeated the relations between the Spanish merchants and the Creoles in rural Puerto Rico.

Another visible source of tension between the two groups was racism. On January 15, 1863, José G. Coca, the mayor of Pepino (San Sebastián), asked the governor to fire Pascasio Lamourt, a mulatto auxiliary scribe, from his municipal post. He explained his intent on the basis that "his mere presence is distasteful to my visitors."[20]

At first, the governor played the role of impartial judge and asked for a report of Lamourt's conduct, skills, and work. In the meantime, the mayor pressured Lamourt to resign. Lamourt refused and instead obtained a favorable evaluation of his work from the municipal commission. Determined to be rid of Lamourt, Mayor Coca pressed the governor again on July 26 and on August 12 Lamourt was fired. Lamourt, too, was among the rebels who stormed Lares in 1868.[21]

Five years earlier the mulatto Bernabé Pol had been barred from working at Lares' City Hall by the mayor Enrique O'Neill. In 1858, Pol had requested authorization from the governor to remain at his post as secretary of the municipality. The governor referred the petition to Mayor O'Neill and asked for a full report on Pol. The mayor replied that while there were "no obvious faults with either the man or his work", he did not recommend him for the position "because of the color of his skin."[22] In September 1868, Pol not only joined the men who stormed Lares, but was the one they appointed secretary of the newborn republic.

In sum, the rebels who took up arms in Lares had many reasons to revolt. Most were victims of a predatory economic system which benefited a select minority. The racially mixed among them were excluded from all but the most marginal jobs, while others were still suffering under the yoke of slavery or the restrictions imposed by the libreta. Although most were aware that not all the oppressors were Spaniards, they recognized that their lives would not improve as long as the colonial system continued.

Staging the Uprising

Intent on ending that colonial rule, Betances and Ruíz Belvis returned to Santo Domingo in September 1867 to plan a revolution. Their presence in the nearby island permitted them to communicate with those of similar views in Puerto Rico, to reach out to the other exiled compatriots, and to have access to the port of Saint Thomas, where they could purchase weapons and war matériel and enlist mercenary troops.[23] The initial group of conspirators was rather small at first. It included, in addition to Betances and Ruíz Belvis, Carlos Elio Lacroix and José Celis Aguilera, also exiled by the governor in 1867, Mariano Ruíz (Segundo's brother), and Fernando Merino, a Dominican priest. The four in Santo Domingo formed a revolutionary committee, the *Comité Revolucionario de Puerto*

Rico and assigned Ruíz Belvis the task of soliciting help for their cause from the republic of Chile.

Ruíz Belvis' mission was aborted by his sudden death. On November 3, 1867, four days after he docked at the port of Valparaíso, Chile his body was discovered at the Hotel Aubrey. At first, Betances and his followers feared that Ruíz Belvis had been murdered by order of the Spaniards, but it was eventually learned that his death was caused by natural causes.[24]

Deeply saddened by the loss of his loyal friend and fellow revolutionary, Betances issued a series of proclamations in which he declared Ruíz Belvis "a martyr, who gave his life for the cause of liberty" and urged the islanders "not to let him die in vain". The way to do justice to Ruiz Belvis, he exhorted his compatriots, was "to make war on the Iberians."[25]

Determined to block all rebel attacks, Governor Marchesi ordered Lieutenant Colonel Sabino Gamir y Maladeñ to devise two defense strategies: one in case the invasion was launched from outside the island; the other in the eventuality that the attack came from within, with support of the local military troops.[26] But, suspecting that Saint Thomas and Santo Domingo were the most likely launching pads, he secured promises from both governments that they would arrest and deport Betances and his followers as soon as they were found.

Protected by friends in these places, Betances and the other members of the rebel committee were able to escape their pursuers long enough to plan the invasion, recruit willing fighters, collect funds, and purchase a ship and a variety of weapons.

To guide the revolutionary process in Puerto Rico, the Comité drafted a constitution in early January 1868, while its members were still in Santo Domingo. The document assigned a guiding and supervisory role to the Comité in exile and left the day-to-day details of recruiting, training, and sending funds to the Comité to the chapter leaders in Puerto Rico.

As linkages between the Puerto Rico chapters and the Comité, the constitution provided for the appointment of agents and delegates. The primary functions of these individuals were to recruit chapter leaders, to help them establish secret societies or cells, and to serve as conduits for funds, weapons, and propaganda between the groups.[27]

By the end of January 1868, the conspirators had in place a revolutionary plan, an intellectual rationale for their decision to break with

Spain, and an organizational structure capable of staging the attack. During the next eight months the chapter leaders focused on recruiting followers, while the members of the Comité sought to enlist foreign volunteers, and organize the invasion. The date for the invasion was set for September 29 and the place chosen to lead the attack was Camuy.

Lares Takes the Glory

The plan of attack was moving ahead quite well until the morning of September 20, when a recruit turned informer and alerted the colonial authorities. His disclosure led the military commander of Arecibo to order a search of the home of Manuel María González, president of *Lanzador del Norte*, the rebel cell of Camuy. Incriminating evidence was found and González was arrested and sent to the district jail of Arecibo.[28]

News of González's arrest, the morning of the 21st, forced the members of Lanzador del Norte to join forces with their counterparts in Lares and Pepino (San Sebastián) and to accept orders from Manuel Rojas, the president of Lares' *Centro Bravo*. After many discussions with the rebels of Lares and several exchanges between Rojas and Matías Brugman, president of Mayagüez' *Capá Prieto*, the decision was reached that Lares, rather than Camuy would launch the war on September 23, six days before the originally scheduled date. Lares, like Camuy, was also far from the military headquarters in San Juan and its mountains offered a degree of cover to the rebels should they be forced to fight a guerrilla war.

The night before the attack was spent notifying members of other cells about the change of plans. On the morning of the 23rd, Rojas stationed some of his men along the paths leading to town, to guide arriving rebels to his place, and to keep informers from leaving the area. Others were left at his hacienda ironing out last minute details, such as rounding up horses and weapons and preparing food for the incoming troops.[29]

By early evening 600 men had congregated at his estate, although few of them had horses and fire arms. The majority were on foot and carried only machetes and knives. The group was racially and socially very diverse. It included hacendados, peasant farmers, jornaleros, artisans and slaves.[30] Although women were involved in the conspiracy, they did not form part of the fighting force.

After a fiery speech by Rojas, in which he recounted the abuses and injustices that had brought them there, he issued a call to arms, and gave the order to march on Lares. He reminded those present that, under the republican government they were about to create, taxes would be abolished, debts would be canceled, and the oppressive system of the libretas would end. To show his commitment to the jornaleros, he urged them to destroy their libretas at once. Within minutes hundreds of libretas were shredded and set on fire.

With cries of "Death to Spain, Long Live Liberty, Long Live Free Puerto Rico, Liberty or Death" the men followed Rojas and the other military leaders into Lares. They stopped along the way to arrest nearly two dozen leading Spaniards and ransack their properties.[31]

Upon reaching the town of Lares, the rebel leaders arrested and jailed the mayor and his assistant. They then occupied City Hall, removed the portrait of the Queen, and declared Puerto Rico a free republic. Between midnight and dawn, they organized a provisional republican government, in which Bernabé Pol, the mulatto previously barred from a civilian job, occupied the post of secretary of state.[32]

Once the officials of government were installed, Rojas instructed them to protect the town, keep the prisoners behind bars, and secure horses and supplies for the war while he and the others prepared an attack against the neighboring town of Pepino. The attack on Pepino, however, was delayed on account of the rebels' decision to celebrate a *Te Deum* mass.[33] By the time they reached the outskirts of Pepino that morning they had lost the cover of night and the element of surprise, both of which had been instrumental in the occupation of Lares.

The mayor of Pepino, meanwhile, had organized a counter offensive and had asked the military commander of Aguadilla to send reinforcements. Informed that the rebels intended to seize the weapons stored in the militia headquarters, and that some militiamen sympathized with the rebel cause, he also took the precaution of sending the suspects to prison and placing men of unquestioned loyalty to guard the weapons.[34]

As a result of these simple measures, the rebel troops were unable to take the plaza despite repeated attempts. With each charge against the plaza many rebels were either wounded or captured by the enemy. After hours of this futile struggle Rojas conferred with the others and gave the order to retreat. By then the military troops of Aguadilla were on their way to Lares and Pepino.

Short of fire arms and ammunition, they sought cover in the nearby mountains until Betances launched the scheduled invasion on the 29th. They had no way of knowing that Betances, too, was on the run. After Manuel María González was arrested in Camuy, the governor had instructed the Danish authorities in Saint Thomas, to arrest Betances and his followers and confiscate the vessel and war equipment the rebels had at that island's ports. Betances and his collaborators escaped, but the ship and war matériel so painfully obtained were lost.[35]

Left to their own devices, poorly armed, and unable to flee the island for lack of ships, the rebels were quickly rounded up by the Spanish military. By December, 523 had been captured, eight had died as a result of battle wounds, two (Matías Brugman and his companion, the Dominican, Baldomero Baurén [Bauring]) had been executed by the troops sent to arrest them, and only 20 had managed to escape.[36] Three of the 545 persons charged in connection to the uprising were women. Two of them— Eduviges Beauchamp, member of the Mayagüez rebel cell, and Mariana Bracetti, the Lares housewife who sewed the revolutionary flag—were involved in the conspiracy from the start, but of the two only Mariana, also known as "Brazo de Oro" (Golden Arm), was sent to prison. The other woman to suffer prison was Francisca Brignoni, a free mulatta from Ponce, who was charged with inciting others to revolt when she heard the news of the uprising.[37]

Of the 545 taken into custody, seven were sentenced to death by a military court and eighty died in prison, victims of yellow fever, before they were tried or sentenced. The death sentences, were shortly after commuted by the governor. They were instead sent to Spain to serve out prison sentences. All rebel prisoners, however, were freed in January 1869 by virtue of a general amnesty[38] decreed by the latest liberal government that seized power in Madrid after deposing Queen Isabel on September 17, 1868.

The unprecedented generosity of the new government was probably due in part to the fact that Cuba, too, had revolted on October 10, 1868. Unable to determine how long the Cuban war might last, the metropolitan government resorted to the two-pronged strategy of pardoning the Puerto Ricans and concentrating their punitive energies against the

Cubans. Neutralizing Puerto Rico not only avoided having to send troops to two fronts at once, but allowed the Spanish government to use the smaller island, as it had in the past, as a base of operations from which to dispatch troops and weapons against Cuba whose war against Spain lasted another ten years.

In Puerto Rico, meanwhile, the olive branch approach paid off. As in 1838, numerous persons from diverse sectors of the society came forth to congratulate the governor for the intelligent manner in which he had handled the Lares affair. The more conservative among them pledged their lives and estates in case of further disturbances. Some of the liberals, too, thanked the government for the generous amnesty and denounced Betances and the Lares rebels as "fools and madmen", whose actions, they insisted, lacked support within the society at large.[39]

By distancing themselves from the separatists, the Creole liberals hoped to capitalize on what they perceived to be the beginning of a new reform era in Spain. Eager to obtain the constitutional benefits already in effect in Spain, the Puerto Rican liberals adopted an assimilationist stance during the next two decades. They seemed to ignore the fact that, had it not been for the Lares uprising and the ongoing war in Cuba, Spain would have had little reason to consider their petitions.

The Lares' Aftermath

As noted elsewhere, the Spanish Queen Isabel II was dethroned by a military coup on September 17, 1868, six days before the Lares uprising erupted in Puerto Rico. Her removal as head of state led the rebels to esbablish an interim liberal government while they searched for a new monarch who would agree to share power with the Cortes and the provincial assemblies. The 1868 rebels wanted a return to the liberal, constitutional form of government Spain had known several times since 1812.[40] As in the previous constitutional periods, they were inclined to extend limited representation to the colonies and thus invited them to send delegates to the metropolitan Cortes, scheduled to convene in early 1869.

Deprived of access to the Cortes since 1837, the island's inhabitants were surprised when they were instructed by the Spanish government to send eleven delegates to represent them. The call for delegates came accompanied with instructions to the governor to lift restrictions on speech, press, assembly and association, to ensure that the voters ex-pressed their wishes freely.

But, as it often happened in the colonies, the governors had the power to interpret the metropolitan mandates and to adjust them according to their wishes. In this case, the authoritarian José Laureano Sanz imposed a gag rule of sorts by prohibiting all discussions of the slave question, a topic he knew to be of great interest to Puerto Rico's liberals and aboli-tionists. He also resorted to the standard conservative practice of limiting the right to vote to literate, tax-paying males only, and announced that he would supervise the outcome of the elections personally.

These constraints, and his obvious support for the conservative, most-ly Spanish candidates, tipped the elections in their favor. As a result, their camp won eight of the eleven seats contested. The Creole liberals won only three seats, even though they represented the largest sector of the population.[41]

The Delegates's Work in Madrid

To shore up the liberal delegates at the Cortes, two well-known Creole liberals, José Julián Acosta and Román Baldorioty de Castro accompa-nied the delegation to Madrid. Their idea was to organize a press cam-paign, to alert the Spanish citizens as to the island's wishes. It wanted equal status with the peninsular provinces, proportional representation at the Cortes and at home, extension of the guarantees provided by the 1869 Constitution, and the immediate abolition of slavery. To keep alive the issues that mattered to most islanders, they also founded the magazine *Asuntos de Puerto Rico* (Puerto Rico Affairs).[42]

The liberals in the Puerto Rican delegation, however, were only par-tially successful. Their demand for the immediate abolition of slavery found only minor support among the Spanish delegates. Still insisting that abolition should be gradual rather than immediate, the Cortes approved a bill introduced by the Spanish minister Segismundo Moret. The bill, approved in 1869 as "Moret's Law", provided for the emancipation of only the state-owned slaves, those over sixty years of age, and slave chil-dren, who were born on or after September 17, 1868.

The demand to make Puerto Rico a province of Spain, with equal rights and duties as the other peninular provinces, found no immediate support. Insisting that they wanted to treat Cuba and Puerto Rico alike, the Spanish delegates advised that all demands for political reforms be postponed until Cuba put down its arms.[43]

The Cortes, however, extended the right to limited representation at home and at the Cortes, and as in previous constitutional periods, authorized the governor to establish a Provincial Deputation (Diputación Provincial), a sort of advisory cabinet to the governor. To protect the islanders' political concessions and safeguard their civil and human rights, the Cortes extended title I of the 1869 Constitution.[44]

Governor Sanz, nonetheless, continued to harass the liberal Creoles, removing them from public posts, accusing them of harboring ill feelings toward Spain. Determined to reduce what he perceived to be a growing disaffection towards Spain, he dissolved the colonial militia and replaced it with a Civil Guard, staffed mainly with conservative Spaniards. He organized an islandwide spy network and ordered that its members report their suspicions to the military commanders of their districts.

The creole liberals deluged the Madrid government with complaints about Sanz. In 1870, the metropolis replaced Sanz with the much more amiable Gabriel Baldrich, a liberal constitutionalist, who became the first of three governors to implement the political reforms provided by Title I of the 1869 Constitution.

The Third Constitutional Period (1870–1873)

Baldrich's term in Puerto Rico (1870–71) was short-lived, in part because of the rapid succession of changes that were taking place in Spain. Between 1870 and 1873, for example, Amadeus of Savoy accepted and briefly held the Spanish crown before abdicating it for himself and his descendants. His resignation in turn led to the creation of the first Spanish Republic. That government, however, was deposed by a military coup a year later, as the loyal monarchists restored the Bourbons to power. Meanwhile, in Puerto Rico, Baldrich and his two successors implemented in piecemeal fashion the reforms granted in 1869 by the metropolis. Baldrich, for example, stripped the governor's office of the absolute powers which since 1825 had permitted its occupants to rule with iron fists. He reinstated the Sociedad Económica Amigos del País, abolished by Sanz the previous year, and provided a financial subsidy for the Sociedad's educational courses. He enforced the Moret Law, and thus made possible the emancipation of approximately 10,000 slaves. He abolished the spy network created by Sanz, promulgated the constitutional guarantees extended by the Cortes in 1869, and lifted the prevailing restrictions on speech, press, and association. Yet, he kept the hated Civil Guard, claiming that it was necessary to patrol the rural area. He did, however, instruct the guards to refrain from harassing the peasantry.

In October 1870, he established the Provincial Deputation, comprised of twenty-five elected district representatives, in which he served as ex-officio president. In November, he authorized the creation of the first political parties in Puerto Rico, but did not change the literacy and tax requirements which limited the right to vote to a privileged minority.[45]

Within these limited parameters, the group with the largest following was the Liberal Reform Party (LRP), a vehicle used mainly by the Creoles. The Conservative Party (CP), a much smaller group, primarily represented the interests of the peninsulares on the island.

Protected by the civil guarantees extended by the 1869 Constitution, both groups campaigned relatively openly in search of adherents to their programs. The Liberal Reformers, for their part, argued for the abolition of slavery, both on economic and humanitarian grounds. The economic arguments eventually convinced a sector of the hacendados that free labor was cheaper and more efficient than slave labor. The same arguments apparently also swayed the government, since it organized several labor contests among slaves in which the winners were rewarded with certificates of freedom.

Until the 1870s, the quest for abolition in Puerto Rico had been the task of a handful of Creole professionals who, having spent time abroad, were appalled by the cruelty of the slave system that still prevailed at home. At first, their message had not reached beyond their immediate circles, in part because of the repressive political climate in Puerto Rico, and partly because their arguments had focused on moral and humanitarian issues. With the establishment of the new constitutional period, they were able to revise their strategies and to articulate the more convincing argument that the continuation of slavery represented a stumbling block for the island's modernization and economic progress. For some in their camp, as had been the case with the Lares rebels, the abolition of slavery was also viewed as a step in the larger struggle of the emancipation of Puerto Rico.

Meanwhile, the Spanish Republican government that came to power after the abdication of the throne by Amadeus of Savoy took an unprecedented step: on March 23, 1873 it opted to abolish slavery in Puerto Rico. The decree detailing the terms of the abolition, however, had its limitations.[46]

The emancipation of the slaves, for instance, was not immediate. The 30,000 slaves still working on the island were required to serve a three-year apprenticeship period. Until the apprenticeship was served, what they had in essence was the opportunity to change employer and place of residence, if they so desired. Few took advantage of that incentive, in part because it made little sense to uproot themselves if they were to continue performing the same tasks. The fact that the decree made no provisions to assist them was probably another consideration in the freedmen's decision to remain in close proximity to the hacendados who knew them and who might offer them paid employment and subsistence plots when the apprenticeship ended. As a result, only a few hundred skilled artisans and domestics abandoned the haciendas for the urban centers.[47]

For the slave owners also, the decree turned out to be less than they had anticipated, as the indemnization they received was paid out over a ten-year period, rather than in a lump sum. Fixed yearly sums were better than nothing, but they were often not enough to cover the wages of the freedmen the planters had to hire.

Yet for most Creoles and the freedmen the abolition was a welcome development. For the latter abolition represented the realization of an old cherished dream, as well as an opportunity to take charge of their own lives. For the former, it represented an important precedent upon which they hoped to build future arguments for the changes they envisioned for the colony.

The abolition decree was followed by other social measures. In July 1873, Baldrich's successor, Rafael Primo de Rivera, abolished the hated libreta system, which since 1849 had kept the free laboring classes in a state of virtual bondage. Two months later he expanded the political rights of the islanders, by enforcing the municipal electoral law and enabling the towns to elect their own governments and to regain the fiscal powers they had lost during the 1830s.

These reforms, and the visible strength of their numerical superiority, encouraged the leaders of the Liberal Reform Party to demand provincial status for the island, with equal rights and obligations equal to those accorded to the rest of the provinces of Spain.[48] That petition was immediately opposed by the local Conservatives who feared that any change in the colonial status would jeopardize their privileged positions on the island. Adamant about protecting their interests, they mounted an obstructionist campaign on two fronts.

In Puerto Rico, they persuaded the governor to erect new electoral barriers against the Liberals, and through the press sought to discredit the Liberals' plan and candidates. When these efforts failed, and Liberal delegates took their seats at the Cortes, the local Conservatives worked through their counterparts in Spain to characterize their plans as major threats to Spain's interests. The perennial Creole demand for relaxation of the trade, for instance, was interpreted as detrimental to Spain, in that it would result in further penetration of the island's economy by the United States. Changes in the colonial administration, they argued, would serve only to empower individuals whose loyalty to Spain was at best questionable. Convinced that the changes introduced by the Spanish Republic had only resulted in "chaos and licentiousness", the Conservatives on both sides of the Atlantic agreed it was best to depose it and restore the monarchy. With the restoration of the Bourbons to the Spanish throne in 1874, the third constitutional period in Puerto Rico ended, and the Conservatives regained much of their lost ground, even though the monarchy, in one of those ironic twists of politics, declared Puerto Rico a province of Spain.[49]

Provincial Status and Despotic Rule

In theory, provincial status entitled Puerto Rico's inhabitants to representation at home and at the Cortes. In reality, the monarchy failed to deliver on that promise when it appointed as governor, for the second time, the hated José Laureano Sanz.

As soon as Sanz arrived in Puerto Rico, he suspended all constitutional guarantees, banned discussions of reforms, and made known his preference for the most conservative social elements. His policies barring voters from the polls were so effective that in 1879 only 3,000 of the more than 20,000 eligible voters (according to the 1871 electoral rules) cast their votes. One unexpected, but damaging, result of the provincial status was, that any Spaniard who wished to represent Puerto Rico at the Cortes could do so, even if he had never set foot on the island.[50] This representation by proxy, known locally as "cunerismo", in effect denied the Liberals the very opportunity to represent themselves at the Cortes, which was the major reason why they had petitioned for provincial status in the first place.

Provincial status, at least formally, required also that the governor share his power with an elected Provincial Deputation. But since such a notion ran counter to Sanz' authoritarian style, he replaced the Deputation's elected members with his own appointees. He then purged the administration of the few Creoles who held posts, claiming that they could not be trusted. Charging also that the waning love for Spain in the colony was the work of the local teachers, especially those at the secondary schools, he fired them, closed down the teaching institutions, and forbade the establishment of other educational facilities without his authorization. To silence the teachers and intimidate other potential dissenters, he strengthened the Civil Guard.[51]

Although Sanz' second term on the island lasted less than two years, his style and arbitrary rules were continued by his successors for nearly two decades. Segundo de la Portilla, his immediate successor, sought to intimidate the jornaleros and the recently emancipated blacks by issuing a law against vagrancy that prescribed stiff fines, prison sentences, and hard labor for anyone who avoided or refused paid employment.

The realization that provincial status had not yielded the reforms or benefits they had envisioned was probably a major motivation for many in the Liberal Party leadership to abandon the assimilationist quest and opt in favor of self-government.

The Tortuous Road to Autonomy

One of the first Liberal Reformers to favor autonomy for Puerto Rico was Román Baldorioty de Castro. Dismissed from his teaching post shortly after Sanz returned to Puerto Rico, Baldorioty moved from San Juan to Ponce, and attempted to earn a living as editor of the newspaper *El Derecho*. Harassed by the colonial authorities, in 1874 Baldorioty exiled himself to the Dominican Republic, where he remained until 1878, when he was permitted to return home.[52]

Still barred from teaching or opening a school, Baldorioty turned to journalism, founding the newspaper *La Crónica*. Convinced it was time for change in the life of the colony, he used La Crónica to propagate the idea of demanding "home government" from Spain. The model of self-rule he had in mind resembled that which Canada had obtained from England in 1867.

Such a government, he explained, would grant the island its own constitution and bicameral legislature, in which the members of the upper house, or Senate would be appointed for life by the governor-general, and those of the lower house, or Chamber of Representatives, would be elected every five years. It would also provide for elective municipal governments.

Although under this formula the governor and his cabinet would continue to be appointed, the power of the executive branch would be shared by the legislature, and the governor's actions would be checked by the Chamber of Representatives.

The constitution he envisioned would ensure the political rights of the island's citizens, and protect their property and their persons from unlawful assaults and seizures. In addition to these powers and guarantees, Baldorioty recommended asking for fiscal autonomy, a condition he viewed as necessary if the island was to take charge of its own destiny. Fiscal autonomy, he reasoned, would allow them to fix the island's budget, to levy and collect the taxes, and to determine priorities. As part of that economic autonomy, he believed, Spain should also authorize Puerto Rico to negotiate its own trade treaties and fix its own tariffs.[53]

Although many in the Liberal Reform party agreed in principle with Baldorioty, few shared his conviction that Spain could be forced to grant autonomy to Puerto Rico. One of his earliest critics, the moderate Liberal José Pablo Morales, expressed the view, in the newspaper *El Agente*, that Baldorioty's proposal would not succeed because it was "too radical". Meanwhile, those who favored independence rather than autonomy criticized his proposal as not being "radical enough." In between these two views others offered a wide range of opinions.

Even among those who supported his formula there was a great deal of disagreement regarding the methods and personalities best qualified to achieve it. Lack of consensus on these matters, personal jealousies, and factional rivalries nearly doomed the autonomist movement from the start. Thus divided by internal strife, the Liberals lost the 1884 elections and disbanded their party. Ironically, the party's demise in 1884 and a ruling from the Spanish Supreme Court, which held that "discussions of autonomy were not illegal," led the Liberals to create a new political party three years later.

Many in the now defunct LRP embraced the idea of regrouping under the autonomist banner, despite their doubts about the probability that they could achieve that goal. The more moderate elements among them turned their attention to their counterparts in Cuba who, after negotiating a truce with Spain (the Pact of Zanjón of 1878), had founded a moderate autonomous party, the Partido Autonómico Cubano (PAC). They were interested in the fact that the founders of the PAC had agreed to ally their party with any political group in Spain that promised to grant autonomy to Cuba.[54]

But even among those willing to follow the Cuban Autonomists' example there were differences of opinion in terms of which political group in Spain constituted the best option for Puerto Rico. Some were decidedly in favor of linking their fate to the Spanish Republicans, while others argued that any liberal group would do, provided it committed itself to granting autonomy to Puerto Rico. The latter faction believed that Puerto Rico would strengthen its position if it formed an alliance with the Cuban autonomists and allowed them to negotiate with Spain the same kind of government for both islands. Baldorioty and his followers disapproved of both suggestions, explaining that Puerto Rico ought to do its own bidding, independently of the Cubans and of the Spanish political parties.

Thus, by the time the delegates of the defunct LRP met in Ponce, in February 1887, the lines between the various factions had been drawn. Yet the discussions at that forum were sufficiently encouraging as to merit a second meeting the following March. The purpose of the second Ponce meeting, attended by 295 party delegates, was to review Baldorioty's draft of the new party's platform. After numerous debates and lengthy rebuttals, the moderates had their way, and the party that finally emerged,

the Partido Autonomista Puertorriqueño (PAP) was a stripped down version of the formula Baldorioty had proposed. Gone from its platform
were the principles demanding fiscal autonomy, constitutional guarantees, and a local legislature. Contrary to the wishes of Baldorioty and others, the moderates accepted the idea of allying the PAP with a party in
Spain, although the question of that party's ideology (liberal or republican) was left unsaid. They also resolved to ally their party with Cuba's
Autonomous Party and to let its representatives negotiate for them in
Madrid.[55]

Whatever his disappointment, Baldorioty abided by the moderates'
wishes and even accepted the presidency of the party. Others in his camp
were not so conciliatory. Many of them abstained from voting, while others left the movement altogether. Of the latter group at least 200 moved
to New York City, to collaborate with their Cuban counterparts in exile in
a war of liberation.

Baldorioty and other leaders of the PAP began preparations for the
elections of 1887, in which they would face the Conservatives who, reen-
ergized by the activities of the Autonomists, had recast their own party
into the Partido Español Sin Condiciones, known as the Incondicionales.
As the campaign got under way, both sides resorted to the typical strategies of discrediting each other's candidates in the press. But when the
PAP began to take the lead in the municipalities, the Incondicionales
turned to violence, physically attacking PAP candidates and destroying
their property. The Autonomists retaliated by organizing a boycott of the
Spanish commercial establishments. Grouped under the secret societies
of "La Torre del Viejo" and "Los Secos" (an allusion to those born in
Puerto Rico), the Autonomists inflicted economic damage upon their
rivals and their supporters.[56]

Stung by the boycott, Spanish distributors responded by refusing to
supply the Creole-owned stores and by calling in their debts. When the
boycott continued, the leading citizens in the Spanish circle demanded
that the incoming governor, Romualdo Palacio, punish the Autonomists,
believed to be the force behind the boycott.

In response to their demands, Palacio strengthened the Civil Guard and
distributed numerous rounds of ammunition among the military troops.[57]
As might be expected, his actions did little to stop the escalating violence.

In fact, during the first three weeks of August 1887 dozens of Spanish and Creole businesses were destroyed by mysterious fires, and candidates from both camps continued to clash in physical confrontations.

Convinced that the Autonomists were the culprits, Palacio ordered the arrest of eighty of PAP's members, including Baldorioty and fifteen other well-known leaders. Treating such crimes as if they had been attacks against the state, he assigned their cases to the Military Court and allowed some of the prisoners to be tortured, in an effort to get them to disclose the names of the boycott organizers.

News of the tortures and rumors that Baldorioty and other party leaders were to be transferred from the jails of Ponce and Juana Díaz to the dungeons of El Morro caused misgivings among their followers. Fearing that the prisoners were being moved so they might be sentenced to death by the Military Court, the Autonomist press mounted a campaign on their behalf and cabled Madrid to recall the governor. Incensed by these actions, Palacio retaliated by increasing the pace of arrests.[58]

Fortunately for all concerned, Madrid removed Palacio from his post in November and in his place appointed an interim governor. The new governor, Juan Contreras, was instructed to put a stop to the violence and to make sure that the prisoners' rights were respected. Recognition of the prisoners' right to legal counsel and bail made it possible for them to return home by Christmas. Yet the problem of the violence continued unabated in part because Contreras[59] failed to punish the major offenders. All he did in this regard was to fire two of the guards, identified as the torturers. Convinced that the system was stacked against them, many in the Autonomist camp continued to take justice into their own hands. As a result, the remainder of the century was characterized by intermittent violence.

Within the Autonomist Party, the arrests and tortures of their members provoked heated discussions and recriminations from those who opposed the boycott. The time spent in prison also aggravated Baldorioty's poor health, and once released he decided to resign the presidency of the party. His resignation in turn created a power vacuum, which leaders of the various factions sought to fill. In addition to the old rivalries and personal animosities, the aspirants to the presidency also had to contend with two immediate issues: (1) whether to continue or to end the boycott against the Spanish merchants; (2) with what political party in Spain should the PAP negotiate Puerto Rico's self-government.

One faction, led by Salvador Brau, favored ending the boycott and reaching an amicable agreement with the Spanish merchants. Regarding the pending negotiations with Madrid, this group appeared willing to let the Cuban representative, Rafael María de Labra, negotiate Puerto Rico's autonomy..

Another faction, led by Luis Muñoz Rivera, wanted no accommodation with the local Spaniards, but was willing to collaborate with any metropolitan party (monarchist or republican) so long as it promised to grant autonomy to Puerto Rico. The one group in Spain that seemed willing to accommodate Puerto Rico was the monarchist Liberal Fusionist Party, headed by Práxedes Mateo Sagasta. That group, however, was unacceptable to the Puerto Rican faction of the Autonomist party headed by the black physician José Celso Barbosa, which insisted on negotiating only with Spanish republicans.[60]

Hoping to resolve the impasse, the Autonomist party leadership called a meeting in Mayagüez in 1891. The meeting was a waste of time, since few of Barbosa's followers bothered to attend it. With only sixty-two party delegates present, the faction led by Muñoz-Rivera prevailed, approving the plan to establish a commission which was to go to Madrid to negotiate the terms of the island's self-government with the Liberal Fusionists.

Determined not to be upstaged, Barbosa declared those in his camp to be the only true autonomists, and renamed his faction the Partido Autonomista Ortodoxo, the Orthodox Autonomist Party (PAO). Muñoz-Rivera in turn renamed the remnant of the party the Partido Liberal Fusionista Puertorriqueño (PLFP), known thereafter as the Liberal Party.[61]

In the summer of 1897, the incumbent Prime Minister Antonio Cánovas del Castillo was assassinated and his death led to the appointment of Práxedes Mateo Sagasta to the post, for the fourth time in his career. Sagasta's rise to power and the fact that in 1895 Cuba had once again declared war against Spain, benefited the Puerto Rican autonomist commission. The fact also that hundreds of Puerto Ricans, like the Cubans, had been making plans to liberate Puerto Rico probably helped Sagasta to see the wisdom of accepting the more moderate demands of

The First Autonomic Cabinet (Seated from left: Luis Muñoz-Rivera, Francisco Mariano-Quiñones, Manuel Fernández–Juncos; Standing from left: Juan Hernández-López, Jose S. Quiñones, Manuel F. Rosey)

the Puerto Rican Liberal Fusionists. Thus, on November 25, 1897, Sagasta authorized an autonomous government for Puerto Rico.

Puerto Rico Becomes Autonomous

The Autonomic Charter granted in 1897 allowed Puerto Rico proportional representation at the Cortes and at home. It provided for a bicameral legislature, with an upper chamber, or Council of Administration, consisting of fifteen members, partly elected and partly appointed, and a lower house, or Chamber of Representatives, consisting of thirty-two elected members. The executive was comprised by a governor, appointed by Spain, and a cabinet he appointed. The executive governed with the cooperation and consent of the legislature. The governor remained the military chief of the island's armed forces, and Spain continued to represent the island in the international community. The legal system of the island remained unchanged, but economically the autonomist government was authorized to negotiate commercial treaties with foreign nations and to set its own tariff rates.[62]

The first autonomous cabinet was formed in February 1898 and the first legislative elections were held the following March. The Liberal Fusionist Party captured twenty-five of the thirty-two seats in the Chamber of Representatives and thus gained control of the lower chamber. The legislative sessions, however, had to be postponed until mid-July, as the governor declared a state of emergency in April 1898, when the United States first declared war against Spain. As a result of the war, the municipal elections were never held, and the legislative deliberations were abruptly ended on July 25, when the United States invaded Puerto Rico. The motives, events, and repercussions of the U.S. invasion will be the subject of a separate chapter.

Coffee and the Economy

Until the 1860s the coffee industry in Puerto Rico had grown slowly in comparison with sugar. The pace of growth in this industry began to accelerate in the 1870s and by the 1880s its export revenues already surpassed those earned by sugar.

Sugar, meanwhile, had been experiencing an erratic pattern of growth. Between 1851 and 1868, for example, the value of its exports declined from 3.91 to 3.70 million pesos. Its production in 1879, after a brief period of recovery, averaged 340.6 million pounds, but by 1885 had dropped to 184 million pounds.[63]

The coffee industry, on the other hand, had begun to reap the benefits of a series of fortuitous events. World market coffee prices, which had been rising steadily since the 1860s, increased rapidly after 1876 and remained so until the end of the century. As a result, the 15.9 million pounds of coffee exported by Puerto Rico in 1860 sold in the world market for between eight to ten pesos a "quintal" (one hundred lb. measure). A decade later the same quintal sold for fourteen to twenty pesos. By 1879, the year of sugar's temporary recovery, the revenues earned by the coffee exports (519 million pesos) surpassed those of sugar by 54 million pesos.[64]

Another factor in coffee's favor was the government's decision to award land grants to prospective coffee growers in the interior highlands, where the soil and climate were conducive to this particular crop. Property laws, gradually implemented since the late eighteenth century, not only protected private ownership, but encouraged commercial agriculture and land consolidation. The rising population also played a role in the expansion of the coffee industry, as it increased the potential labor pool.

One additional incentive to the industry was the establishment of Spanish and Corsican merchants in the towns of the interior. Lured by the demand and rising prices for coffee in Europe, merchants representing commercial establishments in Spain, Danish Saint Thomas, and coastal cities in Puerto Rico provided linkages to the world market and much of the finance capital needed for the island's coffee industry. They bought and sold the island's coffee, imported the tools, machines, and consumer goods for planters and workers, and acted as creditors and bankers for the coffee region.[65] And when the planters defaulted on their debts, the merchants took over the farms and often engaged directly in coffee cultivation. The optimism generated by the rising coffee prices in turn pushed the government to take its first steps towards building an infrastructure to link the highlands to the coastal ports. In its construction of roads and bridges the government was assisted by the local merchants, producers and laborers.[66]

Immigrants, whether foreign-born or Spaniards, were more likely than Creoles to own the larger coffee haciendas in part because the new arrivals were familiar with the latest methods of production, had larger sums to invest, and had links to the world market. Limited by the lack of financial institutions and a shortage of credit lines, the Creoles's economic mobility was circumscribed by the discriminatory strategies of the colonial administration, which sought to benefit the peninsulares.[67]

The expansion of the coffee industry, like that of sugar after the 1820s, also benefited some regions more than others. For example, as coffee cultivation expanded from the western to the southwestern region in the 1870s, the port and city of Ponce grew in importance. In 1874, the ports of Aguadilla and Mayagüez handled nearly two thirds (64.9 percent) of the island's coffee exports, while Ponce handled 20.3 percent. But during the next decade, the combined share of Aguadilla and Mayagüez' coffee export trade declined to 35.8 percent in 1885, while that of Ponce increased to 35.6 percent.[68]

The period between 1885 and 1897 was characterized by rising world market prices and the expansion of coffee farms and production in Puerto Rico. During the decade 1886–1896, for example, the value of the island's exports nearly doubled, from 9.5 million pesos to 18 million. A review of those figures discloses that nearly one half (49.4 percent) of the export revenues garnered in 1886 and more than three quarters (76.9 percent) of those of 1896 were due to coffee.[69]

Rising coffee prices helped to expand the industry's credit lines, making it possible for the large producers to invest in coffee machinery to hull, dry, and process the coffee beans. The introduction of machinery modernized the haciendas' operations and helped paved the way for the division and specialization of labor. The rising revenues from the industry also led the government to improve transportation between the ports and the coffee regions.

These changes, in turn, allowed Puerto Rico to compete favorably with other coffee-growing nations in the Caribbean and Latin America. By the late 1880s Puerto Rico became the third largest coffee producer in the region, after Brazil and Venezuela. Its annual averages between 1884 and 1889 were 41.8 million pounds.[70]

The continual push to expand production, however, had some detrimental effects for the poorer rural classes. The rush for the best arable lands along the foothills and highlands of the interior caused the price of land to rise beyond the reach of the poorer competitors. As the quest for land in the interior accelerated during the last two decades of the century, family plots were progressively subdivided among members of the family, or were purchased or annexed by the larger holders.

In 1897, coffee acreage represented 41 percent of the cultivated land while 56 percent of all farms grew some coffee. Due to the constant subdivision of the farms, the average plot in the coffee regions ranged from four to eleven cuerdas. The acreage occupied by sugar in 1897 represented 15 percent of the cultivated land, while 6 percent of the farms planted sugarcane. The average size of the farms in the sugar-growing areas was about 31 cuerdas.[71]

Although in the 1890s the island's economy still revolved around commercial agriculture, it also had an incipient manufacturing sector. In addition to the sugar-processing mills, the island had several distilleries and breweries. It had also a few factories for the production of matches, soap, shoes and furniture. Some produced ice and others processed chocolate and made candy in great quantities for the local market.[72] Yet the most important processing centers in Puerto Rico in the late 1890s were the cigar factories.

Workers in the tobacco industry were better paid than workers in the farms. They also enjoyed a unique privilege of learning about the world while they worked, as it was a common practice for the cigar factories to allow an individual to read to them during the day. The "reader", as this individual was known, generally read the local newspapers in the morning and novels and other recreational literature in the afternoon. The news about workers' demands and struggles elsewhere gave the cigar makers an edge over other workers on the island. That advantage, in turn, proved useful when the workers began to organize themselves during the last decade of the century.[73]

Suggested Readings

Barbosa de Rosario, Pilar, *De Baldorioty a Barbosa: Historia del Autonomismo Puertorriqueño* (San Juan: n.p., 1974).

Bergad, Laird, W., *Coffee and the Growth of Agrarian Capitalism in Nineteenth-Century Puerto Rico* (Princeton: Princeton Univeristy Press, 1983).

———. "Towards Puerto Rico's Grito de Lares: Coffee, Social Stratification, and Class Conflicts, 1828–1868," in *Hispanic American Historical Review* 60, no. 4 (November 1980).

Bonafoux, Luis, *Betances* (San Juan: Instituto de Cultura Puertorriqueña, 1970).

Buitrago Ortiz, Carlos, *Haciendas Cafetaleras y Clases Terratenientes en el Puerto Rico Décimonónico* (Editorial Universidad de Puerto Rico, 1882).

Camuñas, Ricardo. *Hacendados y Comerciantes en Puerto Rico en Torno a la Década Revolucionaria de 1860* (Mayagüez, Puerto Rico: n.p., 2nd. Edition, 1994).

Coll y Toste, Cayetano, *Boletín Histórico de Puerto Rico*, 14 vols. (San Juan: Cantero, Fernández & Co., 1914–1927), vol. 2.

Cruz Monclova, Lidio, *Historia de Puerto Rico (Siglo XIX)*, Vols. 3-6 (1868–1898) (Río Piedras: Editorial Universidad de Puerto Rico, 1970).

Delgado Pasapera, Germán, *Puerto Rico: sus luchas emancipadoras* (Río Piedras: Editorial Cultural, 19884).

Dietz, James L., *Economic History of Puerto Rico: Institutional Change and Capitalist Development* (Princeton: Princeton University Press, 1986).

Fernández Almagro, Melchor, *Historia Política de la España Contemporanea* 3 vols. (Madrid: Alianza Editorial, 1969), vol. 1.

Figueroa, Loida, *History of Puerto Rico* (New York: Anaya Book Company, Inc., 1974).

García Ochoa, María A., *La política española en Puerto Rico durante el siglo xix* (Río Piedras: Editorial Universidad de Puerto Rico, 1982).

Gómez Acevedo, Labor, *Sanz, promotor de la conciencia separatista en Puerto Rico* (Río Piedras: Editorial Universidad de Puerto Rico, 1974).

Jiménez de Wagenheim, Olga, *Puerto Rico's Revolt for Independence: El Grito de Lares* (Princeton: Markus Wiener Pub., 1993).

Lares, "Protocolos Notariales, 1844–1846," Caja 1430, Municipalidades, Archivo General de Puerto Rico, San Juan.Documentos Municipales, Mayagüez, "Asuntos Varios" (Bound Documents), Vols. 1 & 2 (1866, 1867, 1869)."Diario de la Casa Marquez, No. 4," Colección Emiliano Pol (Lares 1864–1871), Audiencia Territorial, Tribunal Pleno, Caja 7, Pieza 1, Archivo General de Puerto Rico, San Juan (AGPR) "Protocolos Notariales, Camuy, 1866–69," Caja 1702.

Miles, Galvin, *The Organized Labor Movement in Puerto Rico* (Madison, NJ: Fairleigh Dickinson Univ. Press, 1979).

Pérez Moris, José, *Historia de la Insurrección de Lares*. Reprint of 1872 edition (Río Piedras: Editorial Edil, 1975).

Picó, Fernando, *Amargo Café* (Río Piedras: Ediciones Huracán, 1981).

Scarano, Francisco A., *Puerto Rico: Cinco Siglos de Historia* (Mexico: McGraw Hill, 1993)

Toro, Fernando Bayron, *Elecciones y Partidos Políticos de Puerto Rico, 1809–1976* (Mayagüez, Editorial Isla, 1977).

U.S. Department of the Census, "Census Report on Puerto Rico, 1899" (Washington, D.C.: Government Printing Press, 1900).

White, Trumbull, *Our New Possessions* (New York: n. p., 1898).

CHAPTER NINE

Invasion and Occupation by the United States, 1898–1900

On July 25, 1898, the United States invaded Puerto Rico and within the next few months gained control of the island. The acquisition of Puerto Rico was at once the culmination of an old American dream to gain a foothold in the Spanish Caribbean, and a result of the Cuban-Spanish-American War.

Among the first Americans to articulate his nation's dream was President Thomas Jefferson (1801–1809), when he observed that the Greater Antilles "were destined" to become part of the United States.[1] Years later, President James Monroe (1817–1824), fearing a joint effort by Spain and France to reconquer their lost colonies in the Americas, issued the Monroe Doctrine (1823) as a warning to the European powers against intervening in the Western Hemisphere.

In the 1850s, the United States sought to purchase the Bay of Samaná from the Dominican Republic, with the intention of building a coaling station for its ships. During the same decade it supported Narciso López' invasion of Cuba, and later sought to purchase the island from Spain.[2] But the outbreak of the Civil War during the 1860s between the north and the south forced the expansionists within the United States government to focus their attention inward.

Following the Civil War, the United States abolished slavery, consolidated its hold over the western territory, built extensive railway networks, to connect its Atlantic and Pacific coasts, and became an industrial and financial center. These accomplishments in turn led the advocates of expansion to assert that it was the United States' "destiny" to become a world power. To do so, argued Alfred T. Mahan, Captain of the U.S. Navy,

"Americans [must] begin to look outward" and to expand the country's naval operations. A student of "sea power", Mahan reminded his compatriots that the most powerful nations in history had been those that possessed powerful navies.[3]

In the business sector also, capitalists and industrialists pressured the State Department to expand the United States' access to the markets and sources of raw materials in Africa Asia, and Latin America. They felt entitled to a portion of the trade and the productive sectors in these areas, which at the time were controlled by the British, the Germans and other Europeans.

Spurred by a desire for U.S. world hegemony, academics, clergymen and politicians alike presented secular and divine arguments to justify the need for American expansion. Professor John W. Burgess, of Columbia University, observed that "Teutonic nations are peculiarly endowed with the capacity for establishing national states." He explained that this quality made them "especially called to that work...[and to be] entrusted... with the mission of conducting the political civilization of the modern world."[4]

More to the point, Reverend J.F. Carson told his congregation at the Central Presbyterian Church of Brooklyn that, "the high, the supreme business of this Republic is to end Spanish rule in America, and if to do that it is necessary to plant the Stars and Stripes on Cuba, Puerto Rico, the Philippines, or Spain itself, America will do it."[5] Another clergyman, the Reverend Robert McKenzie told his flock at New York's Fifth Avenue Presbyterian Church, "God is calling a new power to the front. The race of which this nation is the crown...is now divinely thrust out to take its place as a world power."[6]

On the eve of the Spanish American War, *The Washington Post* summarized the expansionist mood of the country when it said, "...a consciousness of strength seems to have come upon us and with it a new appetite, the yearning to show our strength... The taste of Empire is in the mouth of the people..."[7]

That yearning to control the Americas was succinctly expressed by Senator Henry Cabot Lodge when he asserted, "From the Rio Grande to the Arctic Ocean there should be one flag and one country." Convinced that England's presence in the West Indies was "a standing menace to our

Atlantic seaboard," Senator Lodge advised his government to build "at least one strong naval station" in the area. Aware also that a French company had signed a treaty with Colombia, to build an interoceanic canal through Panamá, Cabot Lodge suggested that the United States "build the Nicaraguan canal". He explained that, "when the Nicaraguan canal is built, the island of Cuba... will become a necessity."[8] But in 1898, as Cuba's independence seemed imminent, the expansionists turned their attention toward Puerto Rico.

Reflecting on the United States need of foreign markets, Senator Albert J. Beveridge told the members of Boston's exclusive Middlesex Club in April 1898 that "American factories are making more than the American people can use... [and] to export these we will establish trading posts throughout the world as distributing points for American products."[9]

One of those trading posts, the *New York Journal of Commerce* editorialized on May 11, 1898, would necessarily be Cuba or Puerto Rico. Puerto Rico, wrote some American businessmen to the State Department, was an ideal "garden spot" to boost American commerce and should therefore be annexed. In the 1880s Puerto Rico represented the tenth largest market for American goods in the hemisphere and yielded the United States a favorable annual trade balance of nearly 2.5 million dollars.[10]

More importantly, from Captain Mahan's perspective, the island was a good strategic point for the United States defense network. "Puerto Rico", observed Mahan, "is to Cuba, to the future of the isthmian canal, and to our Pacific coast, what Malta is, or may be, to Egypt and the beyond..." He explained that "just as it would be extremely difficult for a European state to sustain operations in the eastern Mediterranean with a British fleet at Malta...it would be... for a transatlantic state to maintain operations in the Western Caribbean with a United States fleet based upon Puerto Rico and the adjacent islands."[11] A *New York Times* op-ed writer (July 11, 1898) concurred with the expansionists' views that Puerto Rico was "the real gem of the Antilles", which would make "a fine naval station with a commanding position between two continents." Once taken, the writer continued, "it should be kept for all time" because unlike Cuba, it had done "nothing to win its independence".

Two months earlier, after Admiral George Dewey defeated the Spanish forces at Manila Bay, the press reported a rumor that President McKinley intended to establish a permanent colony in Puerto Rico as a "salve to the imperialists."

Puerto Ricans in New York Seek American Help

During the mid-1890s, when José Martí—one of Cuba's greatest revolutionary leaders—and other members of the *Cuban Revolutionary Party* (CRP) in New York organized a military campaign against Spain, many in the Puerto Rican community came to their aid, founding political clubs and raising funds for their cause. Grateful for the gesture, the CRP members pledged their support to the members of the *Borínquen Club*, a Puerto Rican pro-independence group which had been established in New York city in 1892. From Paris, Ramón Emeterio Betances, the old leader of Puerto Rico's Lares uprising, offered his help to the revolutionary struggle and was appointed Delegate General of the CRP.[12]

Cooperation between the Cubans and Puerto Rican exiles led the Borínquen Club to change its name to the *Puerto Rico Section* (PRS) and to join the CRP in 1895. That decision, however, was not accepted by all of the members of the Borínquen Club. Claiming they would lose autonomy, some members abandoned the organization altogether. Their departure, in turn, led some of the more moderate members to assume roles of leadership.

One of those who benefited from the change was the physician José Julio Henna, a long-time resident of New York City and an ardent admirer of the American government, who became president of the PRS. Roberto H. Todd, also a great admirer of the United States, became the PRS' secretary.[13]

Shortly after the PRS-CRP merger, leaders of the two revolutionary groups convened on twenty-fifth Street in Manhattan to design the flags of Cuba and Puerto Rico. The model they finally adopted was a rectangle, divided into five stripes, and a triangle, dotted by a single white star in its center. To differentiate one flag from the other, they simply inverted the colors. Puerto Rico's flag displayed a blue triangle as the backdrop to its white star, and alternating red and white stripes. Cuba's flag settled for a red triangle with a white star at its center and alternating blue and white stripes.[14]

With flag in hand, and a commitment of support from the CRP, the Puerto Ricans began planning their own military expedition against the Spaniards. To head the expedition, they enlisted the Puerto Rican veteran of the 1868–1878 Cuban war, Juan Rius-Rivera, also known for his participation in Puerto Rico's Lares uprising. Rius-Rivera's military experience and contacts in Cuba and Puerto Rico made him, in the PRS' eyes, the best candidate to lead the island's revolutionary mission.[15]

However, in the thirty years since the uprising of Lares, the political leadership in Puerto Rico had become more concerned with obtaining reforms from Spain than in fighting for independence. Some, like Luis Muñoz-Rivera, leader of the Autonomist party, rejected the PRS's revolutionary plan, for fear that Spain's departure would act as an invitation to the United States to intervene in the island's affairs. Muñoz-Rivera and others in his party preferred to negotiate with Spain for local self-government, a formula that would permit them to take charge of their own destiny without the need of war. Rebuffed by the Puerto Rican leaders, Rius-Rivera and dozens of his compatriots abandoned the Puerto Rico project and joined the Cuban front instead.[16]

Unwilling to accept defeat, the PRS leaders in New York turned to the United States government for help in evicting Spain from Puerto Rico. In March 1898, PRS president José Julio Henna and secretary Roberto H. Todd, paid a visit to Senator Henry Cabot Lodge, then a member of the Senate's Foreign Relations Committee. Senator Lodge was receptive to their request and promised to bring up the case of Puerto Rico to the Senate. Meanwhile, he requested that Todd and Henna send him a detailed account of the island's military readiness. He also gave them a letter of introduction to Theodore Roosevelt, then Assistant Secretary of the U.S. Navy, and one of the men in charge of war preparations.[17]

Roosevelt was also receptive, and the PRS leaders delivered the promised report shortly after returning to New York. In addition to the military information requested by Lodge, the report included maps and numerous details about the island's ports and topography. In effect, the report they sent contained nothing American naval officers did not already know. That sort of information had been periodically gathered since 1815 by the American consuls stationed in Puerto Rico.[18] Yet, having the PRS leaders send these details had potential propaganda value for the Americans when the time came to invade the island. Their involvement also meant they could be counted on to provide support.

Whether Henna and Todd were aware of the extent of the expansionist plans when they visited Lodge and Roosevelt in March is not known. Yet a letter from Secretary Roosevelt to Captain Mahan in November 1897 makes the point that entering the Cuban-Spanish War "on behalf of the Cuban rebels", would be good a step to rid the area of "European dominion" once and for all.[19] The following May, with the United States already at war with Spain, Roosevelt wrote to Senator Lodge to "keep the war going until we get Puerto Rico,... Cuba is made independent and the Philippines at any rate taken from Spain." He further advised the Senator that in Cuba's case, "it would be best if it did not seem that we are engaged merely in a land-grabbing war."[20] With respect to Puerto Rico, Senator Lodge replied on May 24, "Porto Rico (sic) is not forgotten and we mean to have it."[21]

Meanwhile, from Paris, Ramón E. Betances wrote to Julio Henna in early July, to caution against trusting the United States. He predicted, "if the Puerto Ricans don't act fast after the Americans invade, the island will be an American colony forever".[22] A press release from the White House on July 21 confirmed Betances' worst fears. It said in part, "Puerto Rico will be kept... That is settled, and has been the plan from the first. Once taken it will never be released... Its possession will go towards making up the heavy expense of the war to the United States."[23]

The U.S. and Spain at War

The catalyst that drew the United States into the Spanish-Cuban War was said to have been the explosion of the U.S.S Maine at Havana harbor on February 28, 1898. Although many Americans sympathized and collaborated with the Cuban rebels, the U.S. government maintained an official policy of neutrality.

That policy was abandoned shortly after a mysterious explosion destroyed the U.S.S. Maine and killed all the 260 men on board.[24] Although it was suspected even then that the explosion was caused by accidental internal combustion, some newspapers chose to blame the Spaniards in Cuba for the incident. As the phrase "remember the Maine" was whipped into a rallying cry, many Americans began to demand that

Spain be punished for the lost American lives. Spurred by the people's outrage, the U.S. Congress unanimously approved a 50 million dollar appropriation for national defense.[25]

The nation's growing belligerence also catapulted President McKinley into action. On March 25, 1898, he ordered the Madrid government to halt its war against the Cubans, and to allow the United States to mediate the conflict in order to guarantee Cuba's independence.[26] Anxious to keep the United States out of Cuba's affairs, Spain's Prime Minister, Práxedes Mateo Sagasta, responded on April 9 that his government was willing to end the war. He stated also that his government was willing to offer autonomy to Cuba and had thus asked the Pope to mediate their peace negotiations.[27]

Not satisfied with Spain's reply, and viewing this as an opportunity to force Spain out of the Caribbean, President McKinley asked Congress on April 11 for authorization to declare war against Spain. The Congress honored his request and eight days later authorized the nation's armed forces to enter the Spanish-Cuban War, ostensibly to help Cuba achieve its independence.[28]

According to the Teller Amendment, a measure approved by Congress on April 20, 1898, the United States was barred from annexing Cuba. The text of the amendment promised that the United States had "no intention to exercise sovereignty, jurisdiction, or control over [Cuba]" . It also stated that "once pacification of the island [had] been accomplished, [the U.S. would] leave the government and control of the Island to its people."[29] History, however, would show how many ways that promise was subverted.

The arrival of American troops, naval transports, and war matériel did in fact help the Cubans to evict the Spanish rulers from their shores. With the support of American ground forces the Cuban troops were able to liquidate the remaining pockets of Spanish resistance. The U.S. Navy, for its part, encircled and destroyed the Spanish fleet at Santiago Bay on July 3rd. The destruction of its fleet led Spain to sue for peace two weeks later, and to promise to evacuate its troops from Cuban soil by mid-August.[30]

The Teller Amendment, which sought to keep the United States from annexing Cuba, made no mention of Puerto Rico. But to take Puerto Rico, however, the U.S. had to act quickly, before Spain set down the terms of the armistice. The war, as Roosevelt had reminded Lodge, should not end until Puerto Rico was taken. In search of that goal, some of the American forces in Cuba were diverted to Puerto Rico toward the third week of July 1898. It was believed that unless a U.S. military presence was established there, Spain could not be forced to relinquish the island. The commander of the Puerto Rico expedition was General Nelson A. Miles.

The Invasion of Puerto Rico

Prior to the July invasion, another naval fleet, commanded by Rear Admiral William T. Sampson, had already sought to test the island's military readiness. On May 12, 1898, he led a fleet of eleven warships into the San Juan Bay and ordered it to open fire on the city's fortifications, without provocation or prior warning. A witness of that day's events recounted that, while the shells did "little damage to the forts, they hit the city, and caused a number of casualties and widespread panic among the residents."[31]

This attack, and the persistent rumors that the Americans intended to invade Puerto Rico, kept the residents of San Juan in a great state of anxiety. Rumors that the invaders were planning to land at Fajardo, a port on the eastern shore, and from there march on to capture the capital, led the governor to deploy the bulk of his forces along the northeastern coastal areas.

General Miles, who had intended to land his troops at Fajardo, changed course, and sailed directly into the southern Bay of Guánica, where fewer than a dozen soldiers had been left to patrol the area.[32] Miles' change of course was later attributed to the advice of Captain Henry H. Whitney, an American spy on his staff, who had spent May of 1898 exploring Puerto Rico. During his travels, Whitney had noted that the southern region was inadequately protected, and that many of its inhabitants were eager to be rid of Spain, and might cooperate with the Americans.[33]

Reassured by such news, the gunboat Gloucester sailed directly into the Bay of Guánica, and after a brief skirmish in which four Spaniards were killed, landed thirty of its troops, to raise the American flag. The initial group was soon followed by another 3,400 troops from the Massachusetts, the Columbia and the other war and transport ships.[34]

Among those who descended from one of the invading ships was twen-

Spanish shore battery at Fort San Cristobal, Old San Juan,
at the time of the U.S. Invasion in 1898

ty-year old Carl Sandburg, the famed poet and Lincoln biographer, who, recalling the experience years later, said, "...We were rowed to a shallow beach where we dropped into water above our hips. Holding rifles above our heads, we waded ashore. We were in Guánica, a one-street town with palm and coconut trees...."[35]

As Whitney had anticipated, the invading troops had little difficulty securing help from the southern inhabitants. Local scouts and interpreters led the invaders to the neighboring town of Yauco on July 27, where they were received warmly by its mayor, Francisco Mejía. Obviously pleased with the invasion, Mejía referred to it as a "miraculous intervention of a just God, who has sought to return us to the bosom of our mother America."[36] The next day Ponce, too, offered the troops a warm welcome. Sandburg recalled that their initial apprehensions upon landing had vanished, as they began to be "greeted by barefooted men and women smiling and calling to us 'Puerto Rico Americano'."[37]

The combined effects of the scant Spanish resistance and the active cooperation of the region's inhabitants enabled the invaders to take control of the surrounding municipalities within a few days. Between July 28–30 the invading troops were divided and dispatched to Coamo, Juana

Díaz, and Sábana Grande, where armed groups of Creoles, known as "cuadrillas", welcomed them. In Sábana Grande, for instance, a cuadrilla calling itself the "Porto Rican Scouts", had already removed the Spaniards from power before the Americans arrived. The leader of that cuadrilla was Eduardo Lugo-Viña, a well-known American collaborator.

From Sábana Grande, Lugo-Viña led a seventy-man cavalry to neighboring San Germán, where they freed the "political prisoners", and replaced the mayor with one of their choice. The rest of the municipal staff was left in place, ostensibly to help the Americans reorganize the government. The collaboration of the "Porto Rican Scouts", the "Porto Rican Guard" and other similar groups, has been considered in recent years to be a major factor in the invasion's success. It has been suggested that in evicting the Spaniards, the cuadrillas in fact delivered the southern municipalities unencumbered to the Americans.[38]

Such assistance did not go unrewarded by the Americans. Many of the cuadrilla leaders were assigned some of the top municipal jobs vacated by the Spaniards. For example, Mateo Fajardo, a wealthy hacendado from Mayagüez, one of Lugo-Viña's scouts, was appointed mayor of his city. Maximino Luzunaris, a businessman and resident of New York until 1896, was given the directorship of Ponce's Prisons. Rodulfo Figueroa, jailed by the Spaniards in 1887 for his political views, became Chief of the Ponce Police force. Figueroa was rewarded for carrying the American flag through several southern municipalities, before it was finally raised over Ponce's city hall on July 28. By his own account, Figueroa also led a group of fifty men in the attack that deposed the Spanish government from Ciales in mid-August.[39]

Meanwhile, General Miles, still held up in Ponce, issued the first of his proclamations on July 28, to explain the reason for the invasion and to convey his government's intentions with regards Puerto Rico. He described the island's invasion as "a consequence of the war which necessitated action by the United States against Spain, in defense of Liberty, Justice, and Humanity".[40] He said that his mission, as well as that of his government, was to "bring you the armed support of a free nation, whose great power rests in justice and humanity for all who live under her protection..." He was careful to point out, however, that such benefits required that the Puerto Ricans "accept with joy the system of

Raising the flag over San Juan, October 18, 1898

Government of the United States."[41] While local leaders were left to pon-
der the meaning of Miles' message, the General reinforced his forces with
an additional 8,000 troops that had just landed at Arroyo. He dispatched
part of the fresh recruits to neighboring Guayama and Cayey, and others
to Adjuntas and Utuado. The troops sent to Cayey were temporarily halt-
ed by Spanish fire, but those bound for Adjuntas and Utuado found no
such obstacles and captured both towns between July 28 and August 3rd.[42]

Upon capturing a town, the Americans issued notices to the inhabitants
that no harm would come to them as long as they accepted their military
ordinances. They then replaced most of the municipal employees, except

for the court judges who were permitted to remain in their posts and encouraged to carry on their work as they had done before.[43] Thus, civil law remained in effect alongside military rule for nearly two years.

Motives for Collaboration

Lack of evidence makes it difficult to ascertain with any degree of precision how many Puerto Ricans did in fact collaborate with the American invasion. According to Antonio Mattei-Lluveras, a member of the New York-based PRS, and one of that group's members who accompanied Miles' expedition aboard the cruiser St. Louis, there were "over 2,000 armed men" waiting to help the Americans along the southwestern coast of Puerto Rico when they landed. These, he said, had been recruited a few months earlier by "a secret organization whose branches extended to nearly every town and village of the southern region."[44]

Recalling later why these individuals collaborated with the invaders, Mattei-Lluveras offered several explanations. Some, he said, had volunteered their help because they were "firmly convinced" that once the Spanish were evicted from power "the United States would grant them 'independence to some extent'". Others, he said, collaborated because they believed the United States would annex the island and thus grant it "the same home-rule which is accorded every State of the Union". In his view, neither group expected the United States "to take control of the island's affairs, or to place Americans at the head of its government" once the Spaniards were removed.[45]

If Mattei-Lluveras is correct, there were at least two very different groups of allies fighting alongside the Americans, each of which expected to be called upon to rule the island when the war ended. If that was in fact the case, it is possible to suppose that both groups were intent not only on removing the Spaniards from government, but more importantly, the Puerto Rican Autonomists, who had risen to power the previous March through local elections. Both the legislature and the executive council to the governor were in the hands of the Autonomists. Thus, it is also possible to view the allies' collaboration as an extension of the old rivalries that since the 1880s had split the local elite into opposing political factions. The struggles between these factions, as I have discussed elsewhere, had more than once threatened social stability. Unfortunately,

"Are we so soon forgotten"
Chicago Tribune *after the Maine explosion*

"Knocking at the door"
Chicago Tribune

Political Cartoons of 1898

Mattei-Lluveras sheds no light on this issue.

In recent years, it has been suggested that economic considerations may have also motivated some Puerto Ricans to side with Spain's enemy as a way to bring an end to the American blockade against Spanish shipping, in effect since April 29, 1898, which threatened to strangle Puerto Rico's economy. The war's disruption of the island's trade had created severe shortages of essential imports, seriously reduced its export sales, and deprived it of needed revenues. The inability to export crops had pushed producers to cut back production and to lay off many of their workers. Jobless, and often landless, the poorer classes were exposed to untold suffering, as food shortages were accompanied by price gouging.[46]

Thus, for those hurt by the blockade, Spain's defeat might have been considered not only as a way out of the shortages, but as a means to remove the routine trade obstacles Spain imposed. For the sugar growers in particular, the end of Spain's control represented a long-awaited opportunity to engage in tariff-free trade with the United States. The fact that shortly after the U.S. invaded Puerto Rico President McKinley ordered his military commanders to reopen the island's ports, and to facilitate its trade, probably led to the expectation that the local economy would improve if the island linked its fate to that of the United States.

For the southwestern food growers and merchants, the presence of the invading troops brought an immediate economic boost, as the army's demands for foodstuffs and imported goods led to brisk sales in the region.[47] The fact that the soldiers paid for their purchases in cash was probably an added incentive to befriend them.

Although these and other economic arguments help in part to explain why some Puerto Ricans may have collaborated with the Americans, they shed very little light on the question: why the majority of the islanders stood idly by during the invasion. Nor do the available accounts of this period adequately deal with why the Autonomists in power, who stood to lose all they had gained if Spain lost control, did nothing to resist the invaders. Were they, as one contemporary historian suggests, frozen into inaction by their own "idyllic vision of the United States"? Were they, as he also states, blind to the "long history of U.S. aggression"?[48] Or were they under some illusion that they might obtain greater benefits from a future association with the United States than they had wrested from Spain?

Lack of evidence makes it difficult to answer any of these questions. The best that can be said at this point is that their inaction helped to make the war in Puerto Rico a short and relatively bloodless event. According to official sources, the armed conflict in Puerto Rico lasted seventeen days and resulted in 157 casualties, of which 105 were Spaniards and fifty-two were Americans. Of these, twenty-four (seventeen Spaniards and seven Americans) died from combat wounds.[49]

From the victors' viewpoint, such a small price in human lives, and the minimal damage inflicted on the island's properties, was cause enough for celebration. Claiming these to be the result of their own restraint, the commanding officers made sure to congratulate themselves in the reports they issued.[50] Yet their congratulatory mood was soon spoiled by the repeated waves of violence that struck the Puerto Rican countryside beginning in mid-August.

The Armistice and Its Aftermath

After its defeat in the Philippines and Cuba, Spain made some attempts to keep Puerto Rico out of the scheduled peace negotiations, by insisting that it had never been part of the conflict that led to the Spanish-American war. President McKinley threatened to keep the war going and Spain capitulated.[51] Upon achieving his goal of having Puerto Rico included in the peace negotiations, President McKinley signed the pending armistice with Spain on August 12, 1898.

In signing the armistice, Spain agreed to evacuate its troops from Puerto Rico by October, two months before it was to cede the island officially to the United States. For the residents of the island, the concessions made by Spain meant that between mid-August and December they were to be ambiguously ruled by two separate governments. In the western and southwestern regions, where the occupation forces were effectively in control, the inhabitants were unequivocally subjected to American military rule. But in the still unconquered northern and eastern regions, the residents remained under the jurisdiction of the civil, Autonomist government, which had risen to power the previous March. Yet neither the existence of that government nor the fact that Puerto Rico had been declared autonomous by Spain in 1897 was considered by either the Spanish or the American negotiators. Consequently, neither the Puerto Ricans in power, nor the people they represented, were ever consulted regarding the future of their homeland.[52]

It seems that the island's future status had already been decided by some in the United States, for in late August President McKinley stated publicly that, Puerto Rico was to "become a territory of the United States" and its "people dependencies of the United States". That decided, he sought to insure the "future of the territory and its people", by instructing his commanding officers on the island "to maintain law and order", and to encourage trade and other "peaceful economic pursuits".[53]

Yet maintaining law and order proved to be a difficult task for the troops, when part of the island's rural population exploded into violence shortly after the armistice was signed. One recent study suggests that the evacuation of the Spanish troops was in part responsible for unleashing the pent-up violence which had been kept in check by the Spanish troops.[54]

According to the official reports, armed groups of men, ranging from 40 to 200, known collectively as "partidas", descended upon the haciendas and commercial establishments of Spaniards and other proprietors.

They killed or wounded those in charge, and looted and set fire to the properties. The violence, which began in mid-August on the estates of the southern flatlands, spread northward into the neighboring highlands, and from there into the western region. On August 29, for example, a report from hacienda Santa Cruz in Castañer, Lares, described how a group of thirty to forty armed men had looted and destroyed the place, and left the overseer nearly dead. The Lares report also stated that the local authorities were hard pressed to identify the attackers because these had either covered their faces, or darkened them with charcoal.[55]

As many as seventy similar attacks were reported two months later by the authorities of Mayagüez. During the next few months Añasco, Las Marías, and other municipalities of the western highlands reported similar incidents.

The task of insuring social stability belonged to the civilian authorities, but since these were either poorly equipped, or dependent on the occupying forces, the job of squashing the partidas was left to the American troops. As the guarantor of law and order, the invading army was thus placed in the ironic position of having to protect its previous enemies, the Spaniards.

The motives for the social violence that rocked Puerto Rico between 1898 and 1899 are still being investigated. Yet few today would accept the facile official explanation that the partidas' attacks were merely "the criminal acts of bandits and outlaws".[55] Two recent studies of those events offer different and provocative interpretations of the attackers' motives. Extrapolating from the fact that the majority of the rural inhabitants of Puerto Rico were landless, poor, and hungry, one of the scholars concludes that the attacks were probably motivated by a desire to "settle old scores."[57] That point was driven home by his discovery that the partidas destroyed not only the haciendas and commercial establishments of their targets, but also the accounts ledgers they used to record their debts.

The other author contends that the motives of the partidas were political and revolutionary. He explains that the purpose of the attackers was to liberate Puerto Rico from the Americans once Spain had been defeated. Arguing from that vantage point, he presents the August 13 attack on Ciales as a cry for Puerto Rico's independence, and describes the subsequent outbursts in other parts of the island as part of the nationalist struggle.[58]

That thesis has been recently challenged by another scholar, who claims that the men who took part part in the attack of Ciales were far from revolutionary. He argues instead that many of these men were well-known American collaborators, and that their goal was to annex Puerto Rico to the United States. Thus, he concludes that what occurred at Ciales in mid-August was another act of collaboration in which local groups deposed the Spaniards before delivering the towns to the Americans.[59] Lack of evidence makes it difficult to reject or corroborate either thesis.

In any case, the violence unleashed by the partidas had other effects. Ill-equipped to handle social unrest, the Autonomous government left the job of restoring order to the occupying forces. The revelation of its weakness to keep peace among the inhabitants helped to accelerate its own demise as well as to improve the image of the invaders.

By the time the American troops received the assignment to suppress the partidas, problems had also been brewing within the military camps. Without a war to fight, the troops had been left with little to do so, many of them spent their idle time drinking and picking fights at the local bars. Once drunk, they cursed and insulted the local residents and harassed any woman who crossed their paths. These actions were increasingly being denounced by the local press and swiftly punished by the victim's relatives. In some instances the offending parties were badly beaten or seriously wounded.[60]

The growing clashes between the military and the townspeople led in some instances to civil disobedience. In these cases the inhabitants refused to obey the military ordinances, to pay local taxes, or to cooperate with the troops' investigation of civil or criminal cases. On several occasions, the judges themselves refused to try the defendants brought before them, claiming that to do so might lead the person's relatives to retaliate against them.[61]

Thus the assignment to protect the countryside was an opportune task, which gave the troops something to do, and its officers a chance to reorganize them. Some of the troublesome men were sent to the United States while the others were deployed to the countryside, to patrol the roads and protect the properties of the southern and western residents.[62]

Despite the increased vigilance, the violence continued for more than a year, in part because the partidas, which had made their raids in the daytime, began to attack at night, to escape capture by the military. Though in time the army also revised its patroling schedule, it never had enough manpower to protect all the affected areas. As a result, the wealthier merchants and landowners were forced to hire their own guards.[63]

The Surrender of San Juan

In the meantime, on October 18, 1898, the capital itself was officially surrendered to the American forces at the Santa Catalina palace. By most accounts, the transfer of power that day was a solemn affair, devoid of the type of rejoicing the Americans had witnessed in Ponce and other southwestern towns. A reporter for *The Washington Post* witnessing the event remarked that, except for the fact that the American flag "shone over the grim walls of El Morro", where the Spanish had flown, "there was little to mark the occasion".[64] Noting also the absence of the Spanish flag, a local witness lamented that the official publication, *La Gaceta*, had displayed the American eagle, rather than the Spanish coat of arms, on the front cover of that afternoon's edition.[65]

As the U.S. Congress had adjourned without making provisions for the occupied territory, President McKinley resolved the problem by placing the island under military rule. He indicated, however, that military rule was a temporary arrangement, until the Congress decided what form of government it wanted for Puerto Rico.

Three days later, he also appointed a presidential commission, to study the island's laws, customs, and economic conditions. The commissioners were also instructed to issue recommendations as to what form of government they thought best for Puerto Rico.[66]

In reaction to the President's plans for the island, Eugenio María de Hostos, a well-known Puerto Rican separatist, founded a League of Patriots. The group's purpose was twofold: to pressure the U.S. to end the military government; to let the Puerto Rican people decide in a plebiscite between independence and annexation to the U.S. If independence was chosen, the Patriots were prepared to accept a twenty-year protectorate by the U.S. They felt that U.S. help was necessary to launch the island politically and economically.[67] The Patriots' demands were ignored by Washington and Hostos left for the Dominican Republic, where he died in 1903.[68]

The Rule of the Generals

Between October 18, 1898 and May 12, 1900, the island was ruled by three American generals. The first, General John R. Brooke, ruled less than two months, but in that time made a number of substantive changes in the island's government.[69] As a military man, he saw no need for elected officials and so abolished the local assembly and the Provincial Deputation. He reassigned some of the assembly's functions to the Autonomist Council, which he kept, to help his government during the transition. He left in place the municipal assemblies for the same reason.

He divided the administrative offices of the island into two civil and military jurisdictions, with headquarters in Ponce and San Juan. The Ponce office he assigned to General Guy V. Henry and San Juan headquarters to General Frederick D. Grant. In addition to the task of governing these regions he instructed Henry and Grant to enforce strict observance of sanitary regulations.

On October 26, he had the spelling of the island's name changed from "Puerto" to "Porto" Rico and declared English the official language of government. Next, he ordered the normal (teacher-training) schools reopened, and imposed English as part of the public school curriculum.

Between October 26 and December 2, he established a new Supreme Court for Puerto Rico and authorized it to take charge of all the pending appeals cases, including those under review at the Spanish Supreme Court. The latter were to be "claimed through diplomatic channels" and transferred to the Puerto Rico court, for a final decision. Convinced that the lower courts took too long to render their verdicts, he set up a military commission to handle the major cases, such as those involving the partidas. The military legal system, he reported to the adjutant general, was infinitely more effective in handling such cases swiftly and impartially. It was due to the military's good work, he added rather prematurely, that the rural violence was under control.

In the area of the economy, Brooke made very few changes, in part because he felt that was beyond his field of competence. Faced with an empty treasury and a trading system in disarray, he abolished some minor taxes, such as those paid for contracts and the transfers of titles, and urged that the rest be paid on time. Apparently, his success in this sector was limited, for the day he left his post he urged his superiors in Washington to pay closer attention to the economic conditions of the island.

In the end, Brooke's attempts to work with the members of the Autonomist Council did not spare him from criticism. Resentful of the military's usurpation of power, many in the Autonomist circles, vented their anger and frustrations with his programs in the local press. Luis Muñoz-Rivera, for example, a leading figure of the Autonomist government and editor of *La Democracia*, criticized General Brooke for "sending troops into the hill country to check for bandits", instead of "telling the people how his government intended to do justice".[70]

On December 3, a contributor to *La Democracia* wrote to complain about the "cloud of adventurers" who had descended upon Puerto Rico, thinking it was "open for conquest." Another used the same newspaper to criticize the founders of the *San Juan News* (an American-owned newspaper) for its support of the military regime, and the gratuitous remark that those unhappy with the new system "could go to Spain." Still others wrote to criticize the extreme leniency of the military court in dealing with the soldiers and sailors convicted of criminal acts against the locals.

The mounting charges against the military government provoked some in the Ortodoxos faction (also known as "Puros")—previously a wing of the Autonomist party—to rise in defense of the U.S. and its institutions. Eager for an opportunity to lambast their political opponents, they used their own newspaper, *La Nueva Era*, to accuse the leading Autonomists (also known as Liberals) of being diehard Hispanophiles, incapable of comprehending the spirit of the American Constitution.[71] The accused responded in kind, calling the Ortodoxos "turncoats" who until the invasion had been loyal to Spain and referred to the Americans as "hucksters."

With the departure of Brooke on December 6, General Guy V. Henry was assigned to take his place as the island's next military governor. Four days later the Madrid government signed the Paris Peace Treaty, by which it recognized Cuba's independence and ceded Guam, the Philippines, and Puerto Rico to the United States. In the case of Puerto Rico specifically, the Paris Treaty stipulated that the rights of the island-born were to be determined by the U.S. Congress. Those of the Spanish nationals who chose to remain on the island, however, were protected by their Spanish citizenship.[72]

The arrival of General Henry led the members of the Autonomist

Council to present their resignations.[73] Henry refused to accept them, insisting that the councilmen remain as part of his administration. But he then proceeded to reorganize the government and to strip them of most of their functions and powers. Eager to establish his control over every area of government, he divided and reassigned the major agencies. The office of the secretary of state, for instance, whose power also extended over the departments of justice, finance, and interior was divided into four areas. Three of the new posts were then assigned to members of the Autonomist Council willing to accept them. Francisco de Paula Acuña was offered the much smaller job of secretary of state, Herminio Díaz-Navarro that of secretary of justice, and Federico Degetau was named secretary of interior.

Accustomed to arguing and debating every issue, the councilmen were appalled by Henry's overbearing style, which "admitted [neither] discussion, nor that anyone contradict him."[74] Henry, meanwhile, reported to the adjutant general that he was "trying to educate them to the idea that they must help to govern themselves..." and that he was "giving [them] kindergarten instruction in controlling themselves without allowing them too much liberty...."[75]

Unhappy with their loss of power, and angry about Henry's authoritarian manner, some of the councilmen resigned in protest. Henry responded to the challenge by abolishing the Council altogether on February 6, 1899. Having removed the last remaining vestige of the Autonomist government, he proceeded to appoint several Americans, civilians as well as military men, as heads of key departments and agencies. The post of Chief of Police, for example, was assigned to the civilian Frank Techter, while the directorship of the Department of Agriculture and Public Works was given to Commander Josiah Pierse.

Since one of the military's goals was to "Americanize" the islanders, Henry authorized the newly-appointed head of the Education Department, General John Eaton, to bring in American teachers, to speed the instruction of English. The teachers were to be paid salaries of fifty dollars per month from the local treasury. Eaton was also instructed to compile a school code, implement co-educational instruction, and separate the schools from the teachers residences.

Convinced that the ongoing violence in rural Puerto Rico was the result of the courts "indifference to bringing the [culprits] to trial or punishment," Henry created two regiments of the U.S. cavalry, established several military commissions, and placed all criminal cases under military authority.[76]

In need of revenues to finance his projects, General Henry lowered the pre-war tariff rates and duties and authorized the island to trade with friendly foreign nations as well as with the United States. The decision to permit free trade between Puerto Rico and the United States would not be made by Congress until 1901.

Henry's trade adjustments, however, were not enough to compensate for the loss of the Cuban and Spanish markets, which at the end of the war erected high tariff walls against the island's coffee exports. Puerto Rico's coffee was also generally barred from the United States market by the public's preference for the milder Brazilian variety. Sugar and tobacco exports, in demand in the American market, did not benefit as had been expected because the lack of access to free trade and the high cost of the U.S. tariff kept the sales small.

Unable to resolve the free trade question, Henry addressed a number of other issues. He implanted the American system of currency and exchanged the local peso at U.S. sixty cents. The exchange rate was a disappointment to the islanders, who months before the invasion had seen the local peso oscillate between seventy and eighty U.S. cents.

Another area addressed by Henry was the tax system. The tax loads were revised and new rates were devised for the properties in proportion to their assessed value and levels of production. In addition, absentee landholders were more heavily taxed than resident owners. In order to lighten the burden of the poorer classes, Henry abolished the consumer tax on bread and fresh meat and suspended the lottery. But, claiming that he wished to discourage "vice-inducing practices," he prohibited cockfights and levied a high tax on alcohol and tobacco.[77]

Despite his economic measures, the island slipped into financial crisis and many municipalities soon reported that they could not pay their employees's salaries. They blamed their predicament in part on the planters' problems. They explained that many of the producers were no longer able to pay taxes because they were losing their estates to their creditors for lack of payments of their mortages.[78]

Hoping to ease their plight, General Henry declared a one-year moratorium on debts. His measure, however, compounded the problem, as it led the creditors to shut off credit lines, leaving many producers and minor merchants without the capital needed to operate their haciendas and commercial establishments.[79]

Unable to improve the economy, General Henry turned to other areas, imposing his wishes by decree. Determined to bring about the separation of state and church, he abolished the state's subsidy to the clergy, and ruled that Catholic cemeteries were "only for the burial of those of that faith." He ordered also that the state assume the functions previously held by the church in the areas of education, health, and civil services. He sought also to regulate immigration by applying U.S. rules and regulations.[80]

The changes introduced by Henry, like those of his predecesor, were also criticized by the staff of *La Democracia* and *La Metralla*, a Ponce newspaper. Arguing that General Henry had destroyed representative democracy in Puerto Rico, the new editor of *La Democracia*, Mariano Abril, made the point that it was time the U.S. ended its military rule and allow the island to be governed by Puerto Ricans.[81]

Not willing to tolerate criticism, General Henry forbade the press from making any reference to the activities of the army or his government "without conclusive proof". They persisted, and on February 13 he had the editor of *La Democracia* brought to court. Eleven days later *La Metralla* was forced to suspend publication and its editor tried on the charge of "publishing an article derogatory to a public official."[82]

Not easily intimidated, Mariano Abril increased the attacks on Henry's government, and when in April the General had all the newspapers placed under the direction of the military, Abril went to Washington to request his removal.[83] Some of Henry's supporters sought to defend him by charging that Mariano Abril and the Liberals could not be believed because they were against the U.S. government.

By then, however, the General was also in trouble with the U.S. press, which had begun to report rumors that Henry's actions had provoked Muñoz-Rivera and others to plot a revolt against the U.S. Although these rumors proved to be unfounded, Henry's superiors must have felt that it was time to remove him because at the end of April they accepted his resignation.[84] On May 9 they sent the more affable Brigadier General George W. Davis to take his place.

Following Henry's departure Muñoz-Rivera wrote a letter to *La Democracia* (May 13, 1899) taking partial credit for his removal through his intervention with General Brooke and the Minister of War. He claimed that he wished Henry "no evil", but that he had to be removed because "he was transforming my country into a madhouse." He illustrated the point by saying that Henry had suppressed and threatened the press, threatened the City Council of San Juan, freed a number of criminals from the jail of Guayama without consulting the mayor or the judge, and forced the Chief Justice of Ponce to abandon the court while it was in full session, to answer the General's call to assist him as notary.

Yet, except for his lack of tact, one could argue that Henry did the job he was appointed to do. The bitterness the Liberals felt was not so much against Henry as against the United States for having failed to live up to its great democratic tradition. Henry had merely exacerbated the problem by his arrogance and ignorance of local politics. He had failed to see that, although critical of his government, the Liberals or former Autonomists, like the Ortodoxos, favored union with the U.S. The difference between these two political groups was very subtle. He failed to understand that once the Liberals had tasted power it was difficult for them to relinquish the gains they had made under Spain without a fight. Although they wanted the incorporation of Puerto Rico into the American Union, they wished it to be as an autonomous state so that they could continue to rule the island's destiny. Thus, they, unlike the Ortodoxos or the Patriots led by Hostos, did not favor the proposal of a twenty-year apprenticeship period before being granted self-government.[85]

The Ortodoxos, on the other hand, having missed their chance to rise to power in 1897, when they split the Autonomist party, found the U.S. takeover and military protection to their advantage. Henry's acts of dismantling the old and organizing a new government were necessary if they were ever to be called to rule the island. Thus, they protected him from the attacks of the Liberals and became eager friends of the United States. By the time Henry left Puerto Rico in May 1899, he had helped to solidify the pro-annexationist Republican faction and to widen the gulf between them and the Liberals.

His replacement, General Davis, arrived on May 9 and stayed on for nearly a year, until Congress approved a civilian government for Puerto Rico in 1900. Feeling somewhat vindicated by the removal of Henry, Muñoz-Rivera and others in his camp were accepting of General Davis. The new ruler, they had heard, was not "a West Pointer", but rather a scholarly type, a tactful man who presumably had much sympathy for the Puerto Rican people.[86]

Once in office, General Davis continued the centralization policy initiated by Henry, but he apparently did so more diplomatically and without ignoring altogether the wishes of the Liberals. For example, he sought to keep the peace between the two political factions by choosing his advisors from both camps, although he claimed that his choices were based "strictly on merit."[87]

He explained via a circular on August 15 that his main task was to prepare the island for territorial government. In light of that mission he began to reform the judicial system in May, to end the courts' customary delays. To make the system more compatible with that of the United States, he reorganized the judiciary into five districts. Each of these was staffed by five justices, four of whom were to act as associates and one as chief justice. He established also a "provisional U.S. court", with the same jurisdiction as the U.S. district courts, and introduced the writ of *habeas corpus*.[88]

He removed all criminal cases from the military commissions and returned these to the civil courts. It was up to the courts to choose whether they wished or not to adopt the jury system. He also freed the courts from their dependence on the department of justice and placed them under the jurisdiction of a judicial board, composed of five (unpaid) lawyers. The board, in turn, was placed under the authority of the Solicitor General.[89]

In terms of the economy, General Davis campaigned for temporary lower tariffs and duties, but suggested to his superiors that Congress ought to grant the island free trade status. The economy, already shaken by the effects of the war, suffered another major blow on August 8, 1899, as hurricane San Ciriaco swept through the island. The strong winds and torrential rains destroyed most of the crops, flooded much of the territory, killed 3,000 persons, and left another 250,000 (a quarter of the population) homeless.[90]

The coffee industry, in particular, experienced a huge setback as the hurricane uprooted the coffee trees, destroying a crop whose estimated value was seven million dollars. The hurricane also decimated many of the sugar fields, drowned thousands of animals, and left thousands of mountain dwellers stranded as the roads and bridges connecting the interior to the coast were washed away.[91]

Without resources to deal with the effects of this disaster, General Davis set up a Charity Board to coordinate local donations, and appealed to Washington for help. He then notified the mayors of the affected towns that he was also establishing a Board of Health, to arrest the spread of diseases. Among the tasks assigned to the health board were to supply vaccines and insure that the mayors complied with the vaccination program, to enforce strict sanitary laws and educate the populace about the importance of vaccination and hygiene, and to gather vital statistics.[92]

The larger task of rebuilding the economy and repairing the damaged infrastructure required greater sums than were available locally. General Davis appealed to Washington, to authorize the island to borrow 10 million dollars, at an interest rate of no more than 5 percent annually. He explained that such a sum could be repaid in ten years through the sale of government bonds, in denominations of 1.00 to 100 dollars.[93]

Washington did not approve the loan, and conditions in Puerto Rico grew desperate. The new Secretary of War, Elihu Root, sent relief supplies, including food, clothing and medicine. But these often failed to reach many of the people in need, in some cases because roads and bridges were missing and other times because the supplies ran out before the relief workers could reach them. Before long, starvation began taking its toll among the poorer classes.[94]

The aid sent by Washington, estimated at one million dollars, was much less than what the island needed. Unable to hide his frustration, Davis reported to Elihu Root the following February that the reason the island's children were not able to attend school was not for lack of classrooms, but because they were "anemic, half-starved and often naked..." What advantage, he asked, would come... to the pupils from schooling it they were then "to return to their homes of squalor and filth..."[95]

Despite his doubts, Davis did what he could to keep the practices of his predecessor in place, preserving the nine-month school calendar, and recommending that public education be free of religious teachings. He established a Board of Education and replaced the traditional "bachelor's" degree with a secondary school certificate.

To continue with the task of preparing the people for eventual territorial government, he revised the electoral laws in time for the next municipal elections. Arguing that permitting the "ignorant masses to vote" would merely serve the interests of the political bosses, who would seek to manipulate them, he limited the right to vote to literate, taxpaying males, over twenty-one years of age. Eligible voters were also required to have resided in Puerto Rico a minimum of two years, and six months in the municipality where they expected to vote. Unlike the island-wide elections of the Autonomist government, these were to be strictly limited to the municipal level.

The electoral reforms also required the political parties to submit their lists of candidates to the Electoral Board at least twenty days prior to elections. Both the registration and the voting booths in these municipal elections were supervised by military personnel. Voting places were limited to 300 voters, so voters were encouraged to arrive early. Once the polls closed, the military officers counted the ballots and delivered the results to the Army Headquarters in San Juan.[96]

As the last military governor, Davis was consulted about the sort of government he deemed best for Puerto Rico. He expressed the view to Washington that the Puerto Ricans were at the moment "unfit for self-government", in part because the "absence of a middle class made political reforms and honest electoral results impossible."[97] He argued that until the leaders of opposing political parties learned to cooperate with one another they were not ready to form part of an insular legislature. In his view, a period of "tutelage" was necessary.

His ideas coincided closely with those of Secretary of War Root, one of the persons most responsible for shaping Puerto Rico's colonial policy. According to Root, the people in the newly-conquered territories had "no legal right to assert against the United States." What they had, he insisted, was "a moral right to be treated by the United States in accordance with the underlying principles of justice and freedom which we have declared in our Constitution."[98] That moral right, he explained, entitled the Puerto Ricans not to be deprived of life, liberty, or property without due process of law, but not to demand the form of government they wanted.[99]

Like Davis, Root believed the Puerto Ricans were politically inexperienced and needed to be taught "slowly" before they could be entrusted with their own government. Lessons in government, Root explained, were not "a matter of intellectual apprehension, but of character and of acquired habits of thought". He feared, he said, that they would "inevitably fail without a course of tuition under a strong guiding hand." He expressed hope, however, that well guided they would develop their "natural capacity" and in time learn to be a self-governing people.[100]

The fact that such arguments found echo among the majority in Congress insured against the possibility of self-government. Thus, in May 1900, nearly two years after the invasion, the Congress declared Puerto Rico a territorial possession of the U.S., entitled only to a colonial form of government with minimal local representation. The government applied to Puerto Rico was in part based on the Crown colony model which had been utilized by England in Trinidad since 1797.[101] The essential characteristics of that model included an appointed governor, a partly appointed executive council, and a unicameral legislature.[102]

In sum, by mid-1900, the inhabitants of Puerto Rico had reverted to the colonial past they had fought to overcome for more than a century. Like the Tainos before them, the Puerto Ricans found that conquest was once again justified by the imperialists' desire to spread their own form of civilization. In the fifteenth century the Spaniards had invoked religion to justify their expansion, claiming that their mission was to save the savages' souls from eternal damnation.

Since the outbreak of the French Revolution, when the Catholic church was dethroned along with divine rule, such arguments had lost credibility. At the end of the nineteenth century the United States also promised salvation, but of a more mundane nature. No longer able to offer heaven, the new imperialists promised freedom from political bondage and poverty. In that spirit, General Miles explained to the inhabitants of Puerto Rico that the American troops were there "not only to overthrow the armed authority of Spain, but to bring you protection,... to promote your prosperity, and to bestow upon you the immunities and blessings of the liberal institutions of our government."[103]

Suggested Readings

Alger, R.A. (Secretary of War), *The Spanish-American War, March 5, 1897-August 1, 1899* (New York: Harper & Brothers, 1901).

Berbusse, Edward, *The United States in Puerto Rico, 1898-1900* (Chapel Hill: The University of North Carolina Press, 1966).

Blanco, Tomás, *Prontuario Histórico de Puerto Rico* (San Juan: Instituto de Cultura Puertorriqueña, 1973).

Chiles, Paul Nelson, "The Puerto Rican Press Reaction to the United States, 1888-1898," Doctoral Dissertation, University of Pennsylvania, Philadelphia, 1944.

Coll y Toste, Cayetano, *Boletín Histórico de Puerto Rico*. 14 vols. (San Juan: Tip. Cantero Fernández & Co., 1914).

Cruz-Monclova, Lidio. *Historia de Puerto Rico (Siglo XIX)*, 6 vols. (Río Piedras: Editorial Universidad de Puerto Rico, 1970), Tomo III, Tercera Parte.

Dallek, Robert, *1898: McKinley's Decision: The U.S. Declares War on Spain*(New York: Chelsea House Publishers, 1969).

Delgado, Juan Manuel, "Las Partidas Sediciosas", *La Toga*, Vol. 10, Num. 1 (abril 1978).

————, "Frontón y el Levantamiento de Ciales", in: Juan A. Corretjer, editor, *Origen y Desarrollo del Independentismo Cialeño en el Siglo XX* (Ciales, Puerto Rico: Sociedad Ciales Histórico, 1980).

De Hostos, Eugenio M., "Madre Isla," *Obras Completas*. vol. 5. (La Habana, Cuba: Cultural S.A., 1939).

"Diary of the War," *Harper's Weekly*, Aug. 13, 1898.

La Correspondencia, Aug. 19, 30, 1898.

La Democracia, Dec. 3, 6, 8, 15, 1898; Feb. 22, 1899.

La Gaceta, May 14, Oct. 18, 1898.

Lodge, Henry Cabot, "Our Blundering Foreign Policy," *Forum*, March, 1895.

————, *The War With Spain* (New York: Harpers and Brothers, 1899).

Luque de Sánchez, María Dolores, *La Ocupación norteamericana y la ley Foraker* (Río Piedras, Puerto Rico: Editorial Universitaria, 1980).

Mahan, Alfred T., "The U.S. Looking Outward," *Atlantic Monthly* December, 1890.

Miles, Nelson A., *Serving the Republic* (New York: Harper and Brothers,

1911).

Millis, Walter, *The Martial Spirit: A Study of Our War With Spain* (New York: Houghton and Mifflin, 1931).

Morales Carrión, Arturo, *Puerto Rico: A Political and Cultural History* (New York: W.W. Norton, 1983).

Morison, Samuel Eliot, et. al., *The Growth of the American Republic*. vol. 2, 7th Edition (New York: Oxford U. Press, 1980).

Musick, John R., *History of the War With Spain* (New York: J. Ogilvie Pub. Co., 1898).

Negrón de Montilla, Aida. *Americanization in Puerto Rico and the Public School System, 1900–1930* (Río Piedras, Puerto Rico: Editorial Edil, Inc., 1971).

Negrón Portillo, Mariano. *Cuadrillas Anexionistas y Revueltas Campesinas en Puerto Rico, 1898–1900* (Río Piedras: Universidad de Puerto Rico, Centro de Investigaciones Sociales, 1987).

New York Journal of Commerce, May 11, 1898.

New York Times, July 4, 11, Aug. 5, 1898.

Picó, Fernando, *1898: La Guerra Después de la Guerra* (Río: Piedras: Ediciones Huracán, 1987).

Ribes-Tovar, Federico, *100 Outstanding Puerto Ricans* (New York: Plus Ultra, 1976).

Rivero, Angel. *Crónica de la Guerra Hispanoamericana en Puerto Rico* (Madrid, España: Suc. de Rivadeneyra, 1922).

Rosario Natal, Carmelo. *Puerto Rico y la crisis de la Guerra Hispanoamericana* (Hato Rey, Puerto Rico: Ramallo Brothers Printing Co., 1975).

Rogozinski, Jan, *A Brief History of the Caribbean* (New York: Meridian Books, 1992).

Root, Elihu, "The Principles of Colonial Policy," in *The Military and Colonial Policy of the United States: Addresses and Reports* (Cambridge, Mass., 1916).

Sandburg, Carl, "Soldier," in *Always the Young Strangers* (New York: Harcourt, Brace, 1953).

Salivia, Luis A., *Historia de los Temporales de Puerto Rico, 1508-1949)* (San Juan, 1950).

Scarano, Francisco, *Puerto Rico: Cinco Siglos de Historia* (Mexico:

McGraw Hill Interamericana, 1993).

Selections from the Correspondence of Theodore Roosevelt and H.C. Lodge, 1884–1918. 2 vols. (New York: Charles Scribner's Sons, 1925).

Silvestrini, Blanca and Luque de Sánchez, María Dolores, *Historia de Puerto Rico: Trayectoria de un pueblo* (San Juan: Cultural Puertorriqueña, Inc., 1987).

Sparks, Edwin Erle, *The Expansion of the American People* (Chicago: Scott, Foresman and Co., 1900).

The Washington Post, April 20, 1898.

Todd, Roberto H., *Desfile de Gobernadores de Puerto Rico*. 2da. Edición (Madrid: Ediciones Iberoamericanas, S.A., 1966).

———, *José Julio Henna, 1848–1924* (San Juan, 1930).

Toro, Fernando Bayron. *Elecciones y partidos políticos de Puerto Rico (1809–1976)* (Mayagüez, Puerto Rico: Editorial Isla, Inc., 1977).

U.S. War Department, Adjutant-General's Office, *Military Government of Puerto Rico* (Washington, D. C.,: Government Printing Office, 1902).

Wagenheim, Kal and Olga Jiménez de Wagenheim, *The Puerto Ricans: A Documentary History* (Princeton: Markus Wiener Publishers, 1993).

Wells, Henry, *The Modernization of Puerto Rico: A Political Study of Changing Values and Institutions* (Cambridge, Mass.: Harvard U. Press, 1969).

White, Trumbull, *Our New Possessions* (Copyrighted by T. White, 1898).

The remains of Ponce de León being moved in 1913 to San Juan Cathedral, where they now lie beneath a marble slab

CHAPTER TEN

Portrait of the Society

During the nineteenth century Puerto Rico underwent enormous change. In addition to rapid population growth and economic transformation, the local intelligentsia began a search for self-definition, which in time led to a conscious awareness of the island's uniqueness and worth. As the value of that discovery became accepted by the leading circles of the society, the old feelings of inferiority, nurtured by centuries of imperial neglect, were transformed into feelings of pride and purpose. These feelings were manifested through the establishment of educational institutions, a flowering of literary and artistic activities, and the quest by women and workers for rights and recognition of their roles.

Life in San Juan

Until the first decade of the nineteenth century, San Juan, the capital of Puerto Rico, was divided into four barrios, wards of unpaved streets and few important constructions. Its barrios were generally identified by prominent landmarks in the area, such as a convent, a church, a lavish mansion, or commercial establishment. Thus, the northwest quadrant of the city was known as barrio Santo Domingo, after the Dominican Convent there. The northeast, the area reserved for free blacks and mulattoes, was known as Santa Bárbara (patron saint of many blacks), while the southeast was named San Francisco, after the Franciscan convent in the area. The southwest was called barrio San Juan, or Fortaleza in honor of the governor's residence. Barrio Fortaleza, however, housed a few other important landmarks, such as the "ayuntamiento" (present-day City Hall), the Military Plaza ("Plaza de Armas"), and several commercial establishments.[1]

As the population grew during the first half of the century, the city expanded southward into the bay-front marshlands of La Puntilla. During the 1820s the marshlands were filled in to accommodate the growing population and its demands for public spaces and commerce. The filled in area became the city's fifth ward, known as La Marina. City plots previously used for farming disappeared, as farmers were pushed eastward into Puerta de Tierra, a stretch of land between fort San Cristóbal and the San Antonio bridge. Due to its short distance from the walled city, Puerta de Tierra was placed under the jurisdiction of barrio San Francisco.[2] Farther east, past the San Antonio bridge, lay Cangrejos (present-day Santurce), a settlement of free blacks, many of them descendants of fugitive slaves from other Caribbean islands, who since 1664 had been welcomed by local authorities.

Some of the vacated city plots were used to erect public buildings, and to create plazas and "paseos" (walkways) for its dwellers. Among the new constructions were the Intendencia, the San Juan Theater (later renamed Tapia Theater after a local playwright), the Seminary, and the Casa de Beneficencia (House of Charity). The best known paseos in the area were the Covadonga, in Puerta de Tierra and the Princesa in La Marina. The most popular plazas included San José, in barrio Santo Domingo, Colón at the entrance of the city, in barrio San Francisco, and Plaza de Armas in barrio Fortaleza.[3]

The typical homes in the city in the early 1800s were single-story houses, rectangular in shape, with high ceilings, divided into long, narrow rooms. The houses were typically made of wood, or brick-and-mortar, and had either porches or long windows, framed by cast iron rails or louvered wooden panes. The floors of such houses were commonly covered with bricks or tiles. Water for daily use was collected in "aljibes" (cisterns) or in wells dug in the interior patios. Furnishings in the wealthier homes were either imported, or made locally from mahogany and other hard woods. The living room furniture in these homes commonly included a settee, two or more rocking chairs and an equal number of straight-back chairs. The wooden frames of these pieces often displayed elaborate carvings, while the backrests and seats were made of woven cane. Bedroom furniture in such homes typically included a four-poster bed, with a cotton cushion or mattress. In most bedrooms there was a trunk or two for linen and clothing, a table, and a paraffin lamp. The dishes, glass-es, silverware, and most of the kitchen utensils used by these families were imported since these were not made on the island.[4]

As demand for housing within the walled city expanded, single story-houses, with their traditional interior patios and enclosed gardens, gave way to taller buildings. Deprived of the patios and gardens, the newer buildings often compensated by decorating the entrances and stairwells with colorful tiles. Each building provided a common well for its residents.

The lower floors of the tall buildings tended to be occupied by modest shops that opened onto the street. The spaces within these establishments were usually divided by long wooden counters, upon which the shops' goods were displayed. The shops also provided rustic benches as resting places for their customers.[5]

The major stores in the city, generally owned by Spaniards, were known as "pulperías" and "pulperías mixtas". The first were strictly food shops which specialized in imported items such as rice, grains, oils, dried fish, fruit preserves, nuts, wines and special foods. The second were general stores which, in addition to food, sold dishes, kitchenware, and hardware goods. Both types of stores purchased their goods from larger distributors in neighboring Saint Thomas.

Besides the larger establishments, there were a series of smaller shops, kiosks known as "ventorrillos". These, usually owned by Puerto Ricans, sold primarily locally grown fruits and vegetables. Occasionally they also carried imported items.[6]

The arrival of ships from Saint Thomas, according to a city resident, was an eagerly awaited distraction from the daily routine. On such days, he said, the larger shops became centers of attraction, as "the women went from store to store, to examine the goods, and the men [who accompanied them] turned the day's event into lengthy discussions."[7]

The World Beyond San Juan

Beyond the capital, the inhabitants continued to live in scattered fashion throughout the countryside, despite the increase in population and the formation of new urban settlements. The arrival of newcomers, and the tendency of older families from the northeast to move to the interior in search of land, led to the establishment of such municipalities as Ciales

Morovis, and Corozal. A similar movement from the northwest into the interior highlands was responsible for the creation of the municipalities of Lares and Utuado.[8]

Authorization to incorporate a town was granted by the governor when petioners demonstrated that they had sufficent residents in the area to finance the construction of a church and other municipal institutions. In the case of Lares, the petioners (originally under the jurisdiciton of neighboring San Sebastián del Pepino) received authorization to incorporate the town in 1827, three years after they requested it. The leader of the group, as was customary, was appointed overseer of the project.[9]

The frenzy of town-founding groups sometimes resulted in the establishment of minuscule municipalities in certain regions. Two such examples are the neighboring towns of Camuy and Hatillo in the northern coastal district of Arecibo. In other instances, the redistricting of towns was initiated by the government. A case in point is the present-day Las Marías, south of San Sebastián, separated from the district of Mayagüez in 1871. The incorporation of this town was ostensibly authorized because the area's residents contributed substantially to the colonial treasury.[10]

Although less populated than the northeast, the southern flatlands also experienced migratory movements during the century. In this case part of the movement inland by many older families was motivated by changing ecological conditions. Apparently, the recurrent droughts experienced by the coastal area led these families to move inland in search of water, grazing lands, and more fertile soil. Some of the families, for instance, moved to the outskirts of Juana Díaz, where they eventually founded the municipality of Villalba. Others moved further inland into the much cooler highlands of present-day Adjuntas, while some moved north into Barranquitas, or east into Cayey and Hato Grande (present-day San Lorenzo).[11]

Each municipality followed the traditional Spanish grid, which stipulated that it have an urban settlement, a central plaza, a church, and ayuntamiento (city hall), which in the smallest towns also served as the militia headquarters. The church and city hall occupied two sides of the plaza while the other two were left for businesses and residences of the wealthier residents. The majority of the smaller towns, however, were no more

View of San Juan, 1870

than somnolent villages of one or two unpaved streets and a few inhabitants. The poorer people, many of whom worked for the town's residents, lived on the outskirts, in what was known as the "barrio del pueblo".

The majority of the island's inhabitants lived in the countryside and had little or no contact with those in the urban areas. Typically, rural dwellers went into town three times in their entire lives: to register and baptize their children, to marry, and to be buried at the church's cemetery. The wealthier rural residents, such as the hacendados and cattle ranchers, might visit the town occasionally, to conduct business or to attend mass on Sundays and high holidays, but they rarely built their homes in the town.

They preferred to live on their estates, in spacious houses made of weather resistant hard woods, often roofed with red tiles. The houses were built on stilts, to create lower levels which were later used as places to store crops or as shelters for the horses. The houses also had broad verandahs shaded by fruit or flowering trees (the flamboyán, with its orange flowers was the most common). The verandahs were commonly furnished with hammocks and rocking chairs. Living rooms in these homes were lightly furnished with rockers, settees, and chairs made locally of hard woods and woven cane.[12]

If the hacendado owned slaves, he built sleeping quarters for them behind the main house. In some cases, he built separate quarters for the married slaves. Such quarters, as discussed elsewhere, were primarily used during the evenings and were thus equipped with a few hammocks. The kitchen utensils used in these quarters were fashioned from gourds and coconut shells by the slaves themselves.

The houses of the peasants and jornaleros (free laborers) were generally small huts they built themselves. Their houses were usually frames of poles with thatches and walls of wattle. Free laborers generally lived at a distance from the plantation, on plots they did not own. In some cases they squatted on public lands and other times they lived on plots set aside by the hacendado for whom they worked. Faithful retainers in the estates were sometimes permitted to plant subsistence crops or to raise pigs and chickens.[13]

Government disregard for the poor helped to widen the social and economic gaps among the groups. The Spanish rulers tended to agree with the planters that poverty was the result of laziness and lack of thrift by the poor. To eliminate poverty, they prescribed work, casually ignoring the fact that employment on the haciendas was seasonal, and that the wages they paid—50 to 63 centavos daily during the late 1890s—barely guaranteed the workers' subsistence. Yet these sorts of arguments prevailed until the last quarter of the nineteenth century, when some members of the Creole intelligentsia suggested that education might be a faster road out of ignorance and poverty. Education, however, like all other avenues of upward mobility, was dependent not only on the whims of the colonial rulers, but on the willingness of local taxpayers to support the schools.

Education: An Uphill Battle

In nineteenth century Puerto Rico education still remained the responsibility of the church and a few private institutions. Catholic schools were often annexes to existing churches, while private lay schools usually operated out of the teacher's homes, since few municipalities built separate educational facilities.[14] The majority of the teaching institutions were limited to the elementary grades until the 1870s, and their curriculum focused on the three R's and lessons in catechism. Lessons for girls usually included sewing and embroidery. Boys and girls were taught separately by teachers of their same sex.[15]

In theory, all children were entitled to an education. Those too poor to pay the cost of attending school were to be admitted free of charge, or could petition the city council to subsidize them. In the latter cases, the city council was expected to pay the schools a small sum, to cover the cost of tuition and books of each child and part of the teacher's yearly salary.[16]

Teachers generally were poorly paid, and those who depended on the city councils for the bulk of their income were either paid late or not at all. This was certainly the case of the three women teachers hired by the city council of San Juan in 1799, at a promised salary of fifty pesos annually. Five years later all three were still trying to collect salaries that had gone unpaid for several years.[17]

In 1866, a Caguas taxpayer reported that the typical salary of a teacher in his town was 180 pesos per year. That amount was less than one half of the wages paid to the state executioner, who worked only a few days a year.[18] Female instructors were paid one third less than was paid to the male teachers. The difference in pay scale often forced the women teachers to take on additional pupils, or to do sewing or embroidery work to supplement their income.

Despite the lack of incentives, education on the island made some headway during the latter part of the century, in part due to the devotion of a few selfless individuals. San Juan, for example, benefited greatly from the work of the Cordero-Molina family, free blacks, who for more than fifty years taught the poor children of the city free of charge.[19]

Although the best known member of that family is Rafael, it is now known that he was merely following in the footsteps of his his parents, Lucas Cordero and Rita Molina, who in addition to their own children taught the three R's and the basics of Catholicism to the poor children of San Juan. In 1814, his sister Celestina also opened a school for the poor girls of the city.

Rafael, a cigar-maker by trade, is believed to have started his first school in San Germán, where he lived temporarily during 1810. Four years later, he was back in San Juan, operating a school out of his home on Luna Street. At first, he taught the poor blacks, but as his reputation grew, he also attracted white pupils. Two of the latter, Román Baldorioty de Castro (1822–1889) and Jose Julián Acosta (1825–1889) went on to become prominent educators and abolitionists.

Cordero's contribution to the community was eventually recognized by the "Sociedad Económica Amigos del País", which in 1858 awarded him a prize of one hundred pesos. A modest man, Cordero divided the prize money among his poorest pupils and the beggars of the city. His gesture led the abolitionist Julio Vizcarrondo to pressure the Sociedad to grant Cordero a monthly pension of fifteen pesos.[20]

There were no secondary schools in San Juan until 1832, when a group of clergymen established the Seminario Conciliar. Originally conceived as a school to train priests, the Seminario expanded its curriculum to meet the growing demands of lay students. It added courses in physics, chemistry, geology and mathematics to those generally offered in the liberal arts.

Among the individuals most responsible for establishing the Seminario were the bishops Alejo de Arizmendi, Juan B. Zengotita, and Pedro Gutiérrez de Cos, who conceived the project and contributed land and materials. The others were the Creole patron Miguel Xiorro, who financed the construction of the building, and the Spanish priest Rufo Manuel Fernández, who developed and taught the physics and chemistry courses.[21]

Before he relocated to Puerto Rico in 1823, Father Fernández (known locally as Padre Rufo) had taught philosophy and theology at the University of Santiago de Compostela. After a few years at the Seminario, Padre Rufo presented a plan for a university to the Sociedad Económica Amigos del País. The Sociedad was enthusiastic, but was unable to raise the 30,000 pesos required to establish the university.[22]

Determined to have his students receive university training, Padre Rufo solicited scholarships from several European universities. In 1846, he succeeded in sending four of his brightest students to the Universidad Central in Madrid. Two of them died upon reaching Madrid, but José Julián Acosta and Román Baldorioty de Castro went on to receive degrees in the natural sciences. They returned home in 1853 and were hired by the Seminario to teach physics, mathematics, and botany.

Outside San Juan, few municipalities had more than one or two schools. Having a school, however, was no guarantee that classes would be held. Lack of funds or lack of qualified instructors often kept the schools closed. An example of the latter problem was reported by the councilmen of Lares in the late 1850s. They said that the town's two-year search for a teacher had been in vain, even though two candidates had applied for the position. These, they explained, were unsuitable for the job: one because of "his politics" and the other on account of his "immoral behavior". The first was known to be critical of the government, and the other lived out of wedlock with a woman.

In this case, the councilmen resolved to appoint the local priest to the position "until the unmarried bachelor settled his affairs." What they meant by this phrase was not explained.[23] But the fact that this candidate was hired soon after he abandoned the woman in question suggests that in 19th century Puerto Rico "immoral behavior" was more easily forgiven than political dissidence.

Despite such obstacles, official figures reveal that in 1864 Puerto Rico had 122 public schools, 74 for boys and 48 for girls. It had also some 24 private schools, 16 of which were attended by boys and nine by girls. The majority of the pupils—54.8 percent (1,315) of the boys and 63.6 percent (695) of the girls—were subsidized by the city councils throughout the island.[24]

The same figures indicate that 142 teachers were employed in 1864, four less than were needed if we consider that there were 146 schools in Puerto Rico that year. Of those employed, 61.9 percent (88) were males and 38.1 percent (54) were females.[25] The fact that male teachers dominated the field is not surprising if we keep in mind that females in Puerto Rico were less likely than the males to be sent to school, and that teaching was one of the first paid careers available to women. The fact also that women held more than one-third of the teaching jobs in the 1860s could be interpreted as an indication that social attitudes were changing and that some women insisted on attaining a degree of economic independence.

From time to time, colonial officials reviewed the state of the island's education and offered blueprints or suggestions of how it could be improved. In 1865, for instance, Governor Felix María Messina devised an extensive educational plan and sent it to the cabildos to implement it. One of the features of his plan was to require at least one child in every household to be sent to school.[26] Compliance with that requirement in a society where more than half of the students had to be subsidized was an expense few municipalities could afford on their own. Since the governor did not provide funds, the plan was shelved.

The result of the limited support received by the educational system was reflected in the official figures issued in 1866, which indicate that only 51,250 adults in Puerto Rico were literate in a population that numbered well over 600,000. The literate adults were represented by 52.6 percent white males, 34.5 percent white females, and 12.9 percent free persons of mixed African ancestry.[27]

The struggle to educate the population, especially beyond the primary level, gained momentum after the 1860s. Again, private sponsors and educators took the initiative by founding a number of secondary schools in the island's major cities. In 1873, a group in San Juan established the Instituto Civil de Segunda Enseñanza (the Civil Institute for Secondary Education). The group's plans, however, were aborted the following year when the governor closed the Instituto over some disagreement with the group. It took them another eight years of petioning Madrid before the school was reopened.[28]

Other colegios and institutos established during that period in Santurce, Ponce, and Mayagüez were more fortunate. Ponce, the island's largest southern city, founded the "Colegio Central"; Mayagüez, the major western city, established a "Liceo", while Santurce, an extension of San Juan, built the "Colegio de Escolapios" and the "Colegio de Jesuitas". Since none of these accepted women, in 1880 a group of clergymen established the Academia del Sagrado Corazón (Academy of the Sacred Heart) as a secondary school for women. Located in Santurce, the Academia, later known as "Colegio de las Madres", soon became an important school for the daughters of the island's upper classes.[29]

In 1882, the Instituto was finally reopened, under the directorship of José Julián Acosta. Under his leadership the Instituto took the lead among the island's secondary institutions, by insisting that all the schools teach a uniform curriculum and that they measure the students' progress through standardized tests, which it provided. To help the schools comply with the Instituto's requirements, Acosta organized an examining board and assigned it to make periodic visits to the schools.[30]

Between the 1860s and 1890s the number of schools on the island quintupled. Thus, by 1897, the island had 551 schools and 27,938 pupils attending them. The schools were divided into 510 public and 41 private institutions. Nearly three-quarters of the schools (403) were attended by boys and the remaining (148) were used to teach girls. Boys comprised 68.2 percent of the student population and girls 31.8 percent. Approximately 5,000 of all the students received subsidies from the city councils. The public budget devoted to education that year was 332,367 pesos.

Despite the increasing number of schools, there were not enough facilities to meet the needs of 125,000 school-age children (65,365 boys and 60,330 girls) who were not in school.[31] Also at the end of the century the dream of establishing a university was still unrealized. As a result, those who wished to specialize in a given field were forced to go abroad. Law and medicine, for instance, were best studied in Europe, since U.S. degrees in these disciplines were not accepted in Puerto Rico. The degrees more likely to be accepted from American universities were in engineering and the technical sciences.

Cultural Institutions

During the 1870s some members of the island's intelligentsia began to establish cultural centers. San Juan, as usual, led the way with the "Ateneo Puertorriqueño" (Puerto Rican Atheneum). Established in 1876, the Ateneo was the prized project of Manuel de Elzaburu (1851–1892) a lawyer with a great passion for French poetry. It was widely supported, however, by such figures as José Julián Acosta and Román Baldorioty de Castro, and the scientist Agustín Stahl (1842–1917) among others.[32]

Through its conferences, literary gatherings, and prizes for excellence in literature and the arts, the Atheneum became an important forum where local cultural creativity was stimulated. The Atheneum also offered an eclectic list of courses, ranging from philosophy, to music theory, to shorthand and language lessons in French and German.

Outside San Juan, educated individuals also struggled to create institutions for recreation and learning. In Cabo Rojo, for example, historian Salvador Brau founded a theater, while others in Mayagüez founded a Casino, a public library, and the Cervantes theater. Men of similar spirit formed "círculos literarios" in Arecibo and Barranquitas.[33]

Cultural Expressions

Despite the slow progress of education, numerous literary works, paintings, and musical compositions were produced after the 1820s. Introduction of the printing press in 1806 made it possible for the islanders to disseminate their views through newspapers, magazines, and pamphlets. The oldest publications on the island were *La Gaceta*, the government's newspaper, the *Diario Económico de Puerto Rico*, founded originally by Intendant Ramírez, but later published by the Sociedad Económica Amigos del País, and the *Boletín Mercantil*, one of the longest running business publications.[34]

Privately owned publications had enormous difficulties satisfying the censors, and rarely lasted a year. Nonetheless, they served as an important medium for budding poets and writers. Among the first poetic works to be published in Puerto Rico during the 1820s was Miguel Cabrera's "Peasant Couplets". Through his verses, Cabrera sought to convey the language, customs, dreams, and longings of the Creole peasantry. [35]

Twelve years later María Bibiana Benítez (1783–1873), the first Puerto Rican woman to have her poetry published in Spain, continued Cabrera's practice of focusing on local topics for her creativity. She wrote an ode to her homeland titled "the Nymph of Puerto Rico".[36]

Nostalgia for the homeland led a group of Puerto Rican students in Madrid to publish three anthologies of prose and poetry titled *Aguinaldo de Puerto Rico* (1843), *Album de Puerto Rico* (1844), and *Canciones de Boriquén* (1846). Eager to convey their nationalist sentiments, they stated in the preface of the first book that theirs was an "entirely indigenous publication." These books were not only popular during the nineteeth century, but are still considered important sources for anyone wishing to study the customs, forms of speech, and national traits of the Puerto Rican rural society.

Hoping to contain the spread of nationalist sentiments, local authorities attempted to block the dissemination of the first book (*Aguinaldo de Puerto Rico*) on grounds that it contained revolutionary ideas. In reality, there was nothing very revolutionary about any of the books, except for the authors' praise of the island and its rural population. Yet, in the stifling world of nineteenth century Puerto Rico, any reaffirmation of one's culture was interpreted by the colonial rulers as an unacceptable challenge to Spain's power over the island.

In 1849, Manuel A. Alonso (1822–1889), one of the authors of the earlier anthologies, continued to praise the beauty of the island and the virtues of its people in *El Gíbaro*. This book created such a sensation that by the early 1850s the term "jíbaro" (peasant, or mountain dweller) had been adopted by many writers and journalists to represent "the embodiment of the true Puerto Rican." In later years, the term was also employed by dissidents seeking political emancipation.[37]

In literary circles, the publication of *El Gíbaro* gave way to a trend known locally as "criollismo." The term generally refers to the way Creoles used the themes of love, nature, and beauty to convey their own interpretation of reality. Influenced by the romantic movement, many of the criollista writers rescued the Indian past, and wove tales around persons and events that rarely were substantiated by historical fact. Attributing heroic deeds to figures of the distant past was a strategy the writers used to disguise their nationalist sentiments. That certainly was the way Daniel

Lola Rodríguez de Tió

Rivera was permitted, in 1854, to publish part of his poem "Agüeybana el Bravo". In the poem, Rivera lets the Indian rebel voice the author's desire of seeing the island free of its oppressors.[38]

Two other well-known romantic poets were José Gautier Benítez (1851–1880) and Lola Rodríguez de Tió (1843–1924). In his poem "Puerto Rico" (1879), Gautier Benítez depicts the island as a "serene landscape, inhabited by gentle people." Rodríguez de Tió, also known for her revolutionary ideals, was exiled from Puerto Rico in the mid-1870s, accused of collaborating with the Lares conspirators.[39]

Others to distinguish themselves during this period were: Alejandro Tapia y Rivera (1826–1882), Eugenio María de Hostos (1839–1903), Salvador Brau (1842–1912), José Julián Acosta (1825–1889), and Cayetano Coll y Toste (1850–1930).

Tapia, considered the father of the Puerto Rican theater, was also the island's first novelist and historian. Strongly influenced by the romantic movement, Tapia's writings reflect a great love for the homeland. In his work, *La palma del cacique*, he bypasses the Spanish cultural legacy by tracing the island's roots to the distant Indian past. Tapia, however, stood apart from many of his contemporaries in his denunciations of slavery. His play, *La Cuarterona* (the Quadroon, 1847), was the first work of fiction written by a Puerto Rican to address the issue of racial discrimination.[40]

In addition to his literary contribution, Tapia donated a large collection of historical documents to the island that he and several of his compatriots collected at the Spanish archives. He edited and published these in 1854 as part of the *Biblioteca Histórica de Puerto Rico*.

Hostos, best known as an educator and "thinker", was also a prolific, versatile writer. In 1863, Hostos wrote a political novel titled, *La Peregrinación de Bayoán* (Bayoan's Pilgrimage). His essays on the social and moral issues of his day were, and still are, used by students and scholars throughout Spanish America and the Caribbean.

Eugenio María de Hostos

A patriot who defended the island's right to determine its own destiny, he nonetheless insisted on promoting the idea of a Pan-Caribbean federation. For Hostos, the Caribbean constituted a separate cultural entity, with a unique personality and identity, shaped by the area's history, geographic location, and ethnic composition. He believed that the area was a necessary buffer between the two American continents, and an ideal place for the people of the region to come together to free themselves from the shackles that kept them bound to Europe.[41]

A voluntary exile most of his adult life, Hostos lived in Chile, Venezuela, and the Dominican Republic. He was well-known for his political activism, as well as for his philosophical writings and the idea that women should be educated as well as men. That conviction led him to establish a normal school for women in the Dominican Republic in 1880 and to propose a similar school for women in Chile eight years later.[42]

Acosta, a respected teacher of physics and mathematics at the Seminario Conciliar in San Juan, ventured into other fields. He is thus known as a journalist, writer, abolitionist, and advocate of political autonomy. The best known of Acosta's writings is "Notas" (1866), a revised, annotated version of the history of Puerto Rico, written by Fray Iñigo Abbad y Lasierra nearly a century earlier. His "Notas" provide important corrections and additions to Abbad's text. In 1868 he was accused of taking part in the conspiracy that led to the Lares uprising.[43]

Coll y Toste, a physician, also became a writer and an accomplished historian. Best known for his multi-volume encyclopedic work, *El Boletín Histórico de Puerto Rico* (published between 1914 and 1930), Coll y Toste also wrote chronicles of his native Arecibo (1891), a study of slavery in Puerto Rico, and ninety legends and traditions. In his *Leyendas y Tradiciones Puertorriqueñas*, Coll y Toste recreates personalities and events of the island's past. The best known of his legends are: "Guanina", a story about the Taino princess placed in encomienda in 1511; "Becerrillo", a brave dog used by the Spaniards during the conquest of Puerto Rico; and "The Pirate Cofresí," a recounting of the capture and execution of the feared Puerto Rican pirate.[44]

Salvador Brau, essayist, poet, historian, is best remembered for his historical treatises on Puerto Rico and his insightful essays on women and the laboring classes. His books, *Ensayos: Disquisiciones Sociológicas* (written between the 1880s and 1890s), *Historia de Puerto Rico* (published in New York, 1903) and *La Colonización de Puerto Rico* (1930) are part of the classic literature. Until quite recently these books were used as primary texts in the schools of Puerto Rico.[45]

The love of homeland so evident among the historians and poets is also reflected in the novels of the physician Manuel Zeno Gandía (1855–1930), a native of Arecibo. Although he also published some works on philosophy and drama in Spain between 1873–1876, it was in Puerto Rico where he found the material for four novels he published between the 1890s and 1920s, under the heading "Chronicles of a Sick World." Influenced by the naturalist movement and the writings of Emile Zola, Zeno Gandía ended the romantic trend of the earlier writers with his novels, *La Charca* (The Pond, 1894), *Garduña* (1896), *El Negocio* (The Business, 1922), and *Redentores* (The Saviors, 1925).

La Charca portrays the painful existence of Puerto Rico's peasantry during the 1860s. The stagnant waters of "The Pond" are a metaphor for the never-ending cycle of poverty, sickness, and decay that characterized the lives of the rural poor. The novel ends with the tragic death of the heroine Silvina, who casts herself down a ravine towards the Río Grande of Arecibo. The ending, like the stagnant lives of the other characters, was a far cry from the idealized vision of rural life portrayed by the romantic writers.[46]

Music, Dance, and the Oral Tradition

In addition to the literary movement, Puerto Rico also had an older, rich oral tradition that dated back to the beginning of the colonial period. The mixing of the Indian, Spanish and African cultures generated an abundant crop of stories, proverbs, songs, dances, and expressions which has been kept alive over the centuries. In the rural areas, in particular, anonymous popular poets recreated the oral tradition through improvised "décimas" (ten stanza couplets), "coplas" (ballads), "villancicos" and "aguinaldos" (Christmas carols).[47]

Although essentially Spanish in origin, these verses were adapted by local singers to fit the occasion they were celebrating. The décima seemed to provide the best format for the rural men and women to improvise songs about their daily lives, to express their hopes, dreams, joys, and pains.[48]

The "aguinaldo" and "villancico", also Spanish in origin, are two forms of Christmas carols that were adapted by the Puerto Rican people to reflect the distinct life styles. The villancico, which praises the birth of Christ and other religious figures, generally became associated with the people of the city, while the aguinaldo, more versatile in format, was adopted by the people of the countryside. Another distinction between the two is that the villancico does not require musical accompaniment, as does the aguinaldo. The most common musical instruments used to accompany an aguinaldo song are the Spanish guitar, the "güiro", (a hollowed out gourd) and the "cuatro" (a ten-string Puerto Rican guitar).[49]

Local talents were also evidenced in the tunes and music of the "seis", the typical dance of the interior, and of the "bomba", the dance of the blacks of the coastal regions. Both of these are dances as well as untitled songs that can be adapted to different occasions. The "seis", however, has several dance variations, the most common of which are the "seis chorreao" and the "seis bombeao". In the first, the dancers focus their attention on the steps; while in the second, the emphasis is on the verses that each couple must recite every time the music stops. Both require the dancers to be in top form, since the pace of the dance is quite fast and the songs very long. The "seis" is considered the soul music of the jíbaros and the instruments used to accompany them are the guitar, the cuatro, and the güiro.[50]

The "bomba", the dance of the slaves on the plantations of the coastal region, is also a song, which is accompanied by drums, "maracas" (rattles, an inheritance of the Tainos) and "palillos" or sticks. In this dance, the music also stops at intervals, to allow the dancers to talk to the others through a brief, rhymed song. At first, the bomba was only danced by the slaves, but by the late nineteenth century, it had been adopted by the popular classes of the interior.[51] Since the 1950s, it has been redefined, together with "la plena" and other more recent creations, as a national Puerto Rican dance.

In the nineteenth century, each social group danced its particular dances. While the jíbaros stepped to the seis, and the slaves danced the bomba, the upper classes of San Juan and other cities tended to look to Europe for their music and dance. At least until the 1840s, the island's dances were divided into two types: one known as the "bailes de sociedad", or high society dances, which consisted of adaptations of polkas, waltzes, and other European dances, and the "bailes de garabato" (a reference to the movements and contorsions of the dancers), the popular dances just described.[52]

The first break with the music of Europe among the upper classes of Puerto Rico came in 1842, when the "danza", created in Havana, Cuba (but today considered Puerto Rico's national dance) was introduced in the dance halls of San Juan. Witnesses of this event claimed that the new dance became so popular that the governor tried to outlaw it.[53] The objection, apparently was, that the dance enabled the dancers to get too close.

While dancing was the most widespread form of entertainment in the rural area, the wealthier urban classes developed other means of recreation, such as theatrical dramas, the opera, and outdoor concerts. By 1823, San Juan already had a Philharmonic Society. The performers in this group were professionals from the Municipal Theater Band, and amateur musicians from the area. The combined interests of the city bands and the wealthier classes in European music enabled the San Juan Foundation to bring foreign entertainers and musicians to the capital.[54]

A few local musicians also excelled as composers during this period. Felipe Gutiérrez Espinosa, a musician in the Granada Regiment band, became music instructor of the Cathedral of San Juan, and composer of several musical genres. Although he composed "zarzuelas" (Spanish operettas), symphonies, and religious music, he is best known for the opera "Guarionex", based on Alejandro Tapia's novel, *La palma del cacique*. In 1857, the elite of San Juan witnessed the first native production of Alejandro Tapia's play, *Bernardo de Palissy*.[55]

Other well-known composers of the nineteenth century were Manuel Tavarez (1843–1883) Julián Andino (1845–1920), Braulio Dueño Colón (1854–1934), Juan Morel Campos (1857–1896), and José I. Quintón (1881–1925). The most popular composer was Morel Campos, whose "danzas" were (and continue to be) played throughout the island. A native of Ponce, Morel Campos studied music with Manuel G. Tavarez, when the old master moved to Ponce in 1871.

In 1877 Morel Campos founded the "Lira Ponceña" orchestra for which he composed numerous danzas, waltzes, and symphonies. A versatile musician, Morel Campos played for other groups, especially for zarzuela and opera companies visiting the island. Yet, he is best remembered for his danzas, which in addition to capturing the creole spirit, combined the best of the Spanish musical legacy with the popular rythms of the island.[56]

No other danza reflects the popularity of the genre more vividly than "La Borinqueña", a variation of an 1867 composition titled "Bellísima Trigueña". Originally intended as a tribute to the Creole woman, its lyrics were transformed into a revolutionary anthem in 1868 by Lola Rodríguez de Tió. The present-day version of La Borinqueña which became Puerto Rico's national anthem in 1952, was written by Manuel Fernández Juncos, with music by Ramón Collado.[57]

Another form of entertainment for the professionals and the literary elite throughout the island was the "tertulia", social gatherings where they discussed important events or held musical recitals. Tertulias were open to men as well as women. More informal discussions also took place at the town's drugstore, the barber shop, and other places where men congregated. One of the most popular tertulia centers in Mayagüez during the late 1860s was the home of Lola Rodríguez de Tió. Tertulias were feared by the colonial authorities, and many a governor sought to ban them after the Latin American Wars of Independence deprived Spain of almost all her colonies.[58]

In rural Puerto Rico, the most common meeting grounds for men were the cockpits and the "ventorillos", kiosks that sold liquor. Cockfights were (and still are) an extremely popular sport for Puerto Rican men of all social classes. Rural women, for their part, exchanged their views, village secrets, and information on childrearing, and health remedies at the river and water wells, or during the occasional visits they paid one another.[59]

A common form of recreation for the rural families, in addition to the dances, was story-telling. On special evenings, children and adults gathered around an elder and listened to stories about dead persons whose souls were believed to roam the earth after sundown. Such souls, the story teller explained, returned to protect treasures they had hidden in secret places, while they were still alive, or to repay some moral debt they had incurred with someone in the neighborhood. While the ghosts of the mountainous interior could be found roaming along river beds and caves near the mountains, those of the coastal area floated right into town. If the spirits in question were of pirates who had left behind treasure chests, they were likely to be heard at night along the beaches, dragging and fastening their heavy chains. Upon hearing such stories, no child, and few adults, dared to venture far from home after dark.

Two very popular characters of other oral tales were "Juan Bobo" (Juan, the Fool), and "Juan sin Miedo" (Fearless Juan). The stories of Juan the Fool were generally funny accounts, while those of Fearless Juan recounted how courage and valor had pulled Juan out of difficult straits. The purpose of the story teller was to convey lessons of morality and good citizenship while entertaining the children.[60] Remnants of this folklore are still evident in rural Puerto Rico.

Although chronicles of the early colonization claim that the Tainos believed that their dead roamed the earth at night, scholars of folklore have not found evidence to connect any part of the island's oral tradition to the Indian world. Their search, however, identified dozens of Taino words that are still used in Puerto Rico at present, and pressed the government to collect and display Taino objects and artistic works in local museums. Part of their effort to trace the Taino legacy led also to the restoration of the Caguana park, the major Taino ceremonial center in Utuado. No such efforts, to my knowledge, have been made to trace the island's African legacy.

The Visual Arts

Many of the earliest works created by nineteenth century Puerto Rican artists used religious and historical themes and figures as their source of inspiration. Some of the best known painters of the first decades of the century were Joaquín Goyena, Ramón Atila Pérez (a student of José Campeche), Juan Cleto Noa and his daughters Amalia, Asunción, and Magdalena.

The works of Joaquín Goyena, whose production spanned from the late eighteenth to the early nineteenth century, include the portraits of the canon José Gutiérrez del Arroyo, and a military official. Atila Pérez was best known for his portrait of the intendant Alejandro Ramírez, while the Cleto Noa sisters and their father won several awards for religious works. The Cleto Noa family were also art teachers.[61]

Art critics agree, however, that the best Puerto Rican painter of this period was Francisco Oller (1833–1917). Born in Bayamón, Oller studied with the Cleto Noa family for a few years. At age fifteem, he was commissioned to paint the church of Río Grande. Three years later, he went to the Royal Academy of San Fernando in Madrid. In 1858, he went to Paris, to study with the realist Gustave Courbet.

In Paris, Oller joined the Impressionists, whose style he would later take back to Madrid. Although Oller spent many years in Europe, he devoted many of his canvases to depicting the reality and tropical beauty of Puerto Rico. Oller was "a painter of the modernist tradition, who used Impressionism as well as Realism to show his disapproval of slavery, injustice and ignorance."[62] Among his better known paintings of this tradition are "El velorio" (the Wake), "El almuerzo del rico" (the Rich Man's Lunch), "El almuerzo del pobre" (The Poor Man's Lunch), "Un mendigo" (a Pauper). These paintings, together with his "La escuela del maestro Rafael" (the School of Teacher Rafael) became well known outside Puerto Rico. His most famous painting, "the Student" hangs in the Louvre Museum. In 1872, he was appointed Painter of the Royal Court of Madrid, a post he held for many years before returning to Puerto Rico.

Oller, like his predecessors, also did religious paintings for the church and portraits of important figures of his time. Most notable among his portraits are those of his compatriots, José Julián Acosta and Román Baldorioty de Castro.

Oller believed that artists, like writers, had social responsibilities. He was quoted as saying: "the artist, like the writer, must be of his time...[and] has the obligation to be useful. His painting must be a book that teaches, that serves to improve the human condition, that punishes evil, that exalts virtue."[63]

In addition to the painters, the island had excellent smiths and craftsmen, whose skills were in demand by churches and the gold and silver shops in San Juan and other major cities. Tinsmiths were generally in demand in the plantations and the smaller towns. Samples of their works are still seen in island churches and museums.

Sculpture in nineteenth century Puerto Rico was limited to the wood carvings of religious figures, locally known as "santos", saints. These were usually made to order, as local churches and families became devoted to specific saints. Rural families kept one or more of these religious icons in their homes. The "santero", saint carver, usually made a replica of the saint ordered and painted it according to the characteristics the saint was supposed to represent. The most popular saints in the rural homes were reproductions of the Virgin, with and without the baby Jesus, and "Los tres reyes magos", the three wise men.[64] Although nearly every municipality had at least one santero, none surpassed the dexterity and devotion of the Cabán family, which kept alive this artistic tradition until the middle part of this century. Numerous samples of saints are still found in museums in Puerto Rico and the United States.

Women and the Society

In nearly every census of the nineteenth century women were reported to represent half or more of the island's population. Yet, so little research has been done on these women's lives that it is nearly impossible to reconstruct their history. For the most part, the evidence about them is fragmented and weighted in favor of biographical sketches of figures who excelled in some field, or who suffered jail or exile for daring to challenge the colonial system. This reality, in turn, has led most historians to ignore the roles women played and the contributions they made. My own sense is that we should report the information we have, no matter how fragmentary.

For example, official records make it possible to assert that women in nineteenth century Puerto Rico were as harshly treated as men when they conspired against the colonial government. As noted elsewhere, at least five creole women were jailed and/or exiled during the century for their political beliefs in independence. The first of these, María Mercedes Barbudo, was exiled to Cuba during the 1820s for allegedly distributing revolutionary propaganda in San Juan. Four others, who were accused of taking part in the conspiracy of Lares (1868), experienced different fates. Eduviges Beauchamp was confined to house arrest, Lola Rodríguez de Tió was exiled, while Mariana Bracetti and Francisca Brignoni were jailed for a few months, until a general amnesty freed all the prisoners linked to the Lares uprising.[65]

The imperial strategy, as noted elsewhere, was to keep the islanders ignorant and dependent on the metropolis. As a result, the policies the rulers implemented deprived most women of educational and employment opportunities. Although lack of freedom, poor education, and poverty affected many sectors of the population, women were additionally burdened by their own subjugation to the male-dominated society. Their lives were shaped by values that stemmed from the old European legacies of patriarchy, Christianity and slavery. Their movements were thus circumscribed not only by the external forces of colonialism and economic dependence, but by social customs which took for granted that men were superior to women and thus entitled to rule them.

The fact that well-paying jobs were scarce in nineteenth century Puerto Rico made it relatively easy for middle and upper class men to exert their alleged superiority by denying their wives and daughters permission to work outside the home. Male economic control was reinforced by a discriminatory legal system that declared women minors before the law. Properties and family assets, including those brought to the marriage by women as dowries or inheritances, were traditionally administered by the adult males in the family. Women—especially widows and single, adult females—were permitted to engage in commercial and legal transactions, but they had to be accompanied by male witnesses and surrogates to represent them.[66]

As mentioned elsewhere, one of the first professional jobs occupied by Puerto Rico's women was teaching. In the agrarian, export economy of Puerto Rico the jobs available to women were either in the fields or in the domestic sector. In 1846, for example, working women (1,339) in San Juan represented approximately 8 percent of the city's total population, and most of them worked as servants (449), seamstresses (442), laundresses (355), and cooks (84) according to Felix Matos.[67] Hence, the income earned by the majority (1,101) of the working women Matos studied, came from washing, ironing, and cooking meals for families in the capital. Only a small group among them earned their living peddling food and other items door-to-door in the streets of San Juan. Matos' data also indicate that many of the working women were single heads of household whose families could not have survived without their income.[68]

Scattered data on the rural society, gleaned from notarial archives, suggest that, except for the wives of wealthy landowners, the majority of the rural women also worked outside the home. Women in peasant families, for instance, were called upon by their male relations to perform a variety of tasks, from planting to harvesting crops, to ensure holding on to the family farms.[69]

Women without land or property contributed to the family's survival by harvesting crops in neighboring haciendas, or by taking jobs in the hacendados' homes as washers, maids, and cooks. Yet the myth that rural women did not participate in the economy prevails, in part because they were not paid directly for their work (usually payment went to the males in their families) and partly because their work was often accepted in lieu of payment for the subsistence plots their families occupied on the hacendado's estates.[70]

If women were in fact a visible presence in the economy, why was their participation dismissed or ignored? Perhaps because the recognition of women's value (economic or otherwise) was viewed by society as a threat to the traditional patriarchal system which assigned the males the role of provider. The fact that women were capable of supporting themselves was merely another reminder of the eroding power of the males, who already had to contend with the indignities of colonial political repression, and economic dependence.

Resentful about their perceived loss of authority, municipal guards and other males often harassed the working women they encountered in public places. Laundresses, forced to perform their work at public springs and wells, were commonly subjected to "verbal, physical and sexual abuses", according to Matos. The very act of venturing out in public, Matos explains, deprived these women of "much of the protection" they would have enjoyed had they remained within the confines of their homes.[71]

Unwilling to concede that women's roles needed changing, some sectors within the society insisted that they remain obedient daughters, dutiful wives, and devoted mothers. Although most women conformed to these roles, a few refused to abide by the rules and fled their homes, as an 1824 decree suggests. In an effort to discourage that practice, the authorities threatened to fine and/or imprison anyone who "assisted runaway slaves, minors, and women... to make a life for themselves in cities or in the island's interior."[72] Women's resistance, and the growing acceptance of modern values by some sectors of the society after the 1850s led a few individuals to denounce the "deplorable state of ignorance" in which the women were kept, and to suggest improving their education .

Among the first to espouse the cause of educating the island's women was the Spanish journalist Ignacio Guasp, who in 1856 founded a magazine "entirely devoted to the fairer sex" for the expressed purpose of helping the island's women "become intellectually attuned to the times." Through his journal, the *Guirnalda Puertorriqueña*, Guasp promised to expose them to "pleasant literature" and the latest fashions in Europe and the United States.

The reason for his mission, Guasp admitted, was self-serving, since he, as well as his male colleagues, preferred the company of pleasant, educated females. Thus, for Guasp and other males of his generation the purpose of female education, says María Barceló Miller, was to make them more attractive to the opposite sex, and to help them become better wives and mothers.[73] Ironically, the well-known Mayagüez poet Alejandrina Benítez agreed in part with Guasp's notion in her 1856 article, "Sobre la educación de las mujeres" ("Women's Education"). Benítez, explains Barceló Miller, supported the idea of educating women so that they could better "fulfill their divine mission." To keep the young women from deviating from this mission, Benítez cautioned against exposing them to the dangers of the frivolous, romantic literature arriving from Europe. In her view, these books were likely "to contaminate the[ir] souls" with ridiculous tales of "delirious love affairs." In their place, she recommended the sober works of well-known Christian authors. Benítez, like many men of her generation, not only did not question the traditional roles of women, but failed to see the value of educating women for their own sake.[74]

Although others also wrote in support of women's education, the line of argument did not vary significantly until the 1870s, when both the "discourse and the goal" of some writers became "feminist", according to Barceló Miller. Their "feminist writings", she explains, differed from the earlier "feminine" treatises in that they questioned the traditional roles assigned to women, and argued that their ignorance was the result of their subjugation and the confined conditions in which they lived. The feminist writings differed also from earlier writings in that they demanded immediate and equal social rights for women.[75]

One of the first authors to promote such feminist views was the well-known playwright, and editor of *La Azucena*, Alejandro Tapia. In an article titled, "El aprecio a la mujer es barómetro de civilización" ("Esteem for Women is a Barometer of Civilization") (1870), Tapia recounted the numerous contributions women had made throughout history. He warned that societies that had kept their women in servile positions had condemned themselves to barbarism.

In Tapia's view, civilization was dependent on the emergence of the "new woman", one capable of helping to forge a new society, based on equality and justice. Yet, such a woman would not emerge, Tapia explained, until she obtained the same rights as man. Without these rights, he feared, women would continue to be "pariah[s] crowned with flowers." And "wherever pariahs exists", he commented, "there is no true society nor moral progress possible." He concluded that "the greatest problem of the modern era is the lack of citizenship of its women."[76]

Tapia's advocacy on behalf of women's rights led him to publish many articles about the struggles of North American women and their successes in taking jobs in areas traditionally reserved for men. In publishing D. Macre's essay, "Las mujeres norteamericanas" ("The North American Women"), Tapia sought to dispel the commonly held view that women who pursued careers and professions were likely to abandon their traditional roles. That line of argument, Barceló Miller explains, was revisited by the island's feminists two decades later. In 1875, Tapia also published excerpts of the book, *La Mujer del Porvenir* (The Woman of the Future) by the Spanish feminist, Concepción Arenal.[77]

Eugenio María de Hostos, also a well-known defender of women's rights, cautioned his compatriots not to do society a disservice by denying women the right to equal education. Yet, Hostos' vision of "educated womanhood only made sense in terms of reinscribing 'women' within the goal—and 'common good'—of motherhood," according to Gladys Jiménez Muñoz.[78]

During the 1880s other advocates with similar enlightened views singled out the poor and the rural women as groups in need of urgent attention. In 1886, for example, a group of San Juan women, led by Belén Zequeira, founded the "Asociación de Damas para la Instrucción de la Mujer", for the purpose of aiding poor females to obtain teaching degrees.[79] There is no information whether they failed or succeeded in this mission.

One of those who took up the cause of the rural woman was the historian Salvador Brau. In his essay, "La Campesina" ("The Peasant Woman") (1888), Brau not only defended the right of rural women to attend school, but suggested the way this could be accomplished. He explained that 81 percent of the island's population lived in the countryside and that rural women lived "in the most abject state of ignorance." Convinced that education was the way "to lift them from their moral degradation," he suggested using some of the 257 rural schools to educate the rural girls.

For Brau, educating the females even took precedence over the males, for he believed that once "enlightened" this group would not only pass down their knowledge to their children, but would "provide the lever that will guide us toward our intellectual development."[80]

Feminist Press and Organization

Although grateful to the males for their support, some women thought it was time they began to speak for themselves. Thus, in 1893, a group of Puerto Rican women led by the teacher Ana Roqué de Duprey (1853–1933) founded *La Mujer*, a magazine by and for women. Many of the magazine's articles denounced the deplorable state of the women's education and demanded equal access for them in the secondary teaching institutions. As a teacher, Roqué de Duprey was convinced, as were many of her readers, that education was the road to equality between the sexes.

Thus, she used the proceeds from *La Mujer* to create a scholarship fund to help finance poor female students.[81]

One who benefited from Roqué de Duprey's vision was the gifted piano student Ana Otero who was able to study music in Europe with the help of one her scholarships. Many years later, Otero, already an accomplished pianist, toured the United States in an effort to raise funds for Puerto Rico's independence.[82]

La Mujer sought to raise social consciousness by stressing the message that women were equal to men in intelligence and skills. It also advised and encouraged its female readers to take their rightful place in public life. Occasionally, however, some of the writers tempered their message by claiming that, while women were born equal to men, they were still far from being able to compete with them. Dolores Baldoni (1896), one of those who shared that view, explained the basis of the inequality by saying: "...we are equal to men in intelligence and aptitude, with souls just as big [and] similar attributes, but we are weaker [than they are] because of the poor education we have received."[83]

Aware that their struggle to change society would take time, some of the writers conceded now and then that their main goal was "to smooth the road for future generations." Yet, they accomplished a lot more than that. Through their writings and demands the writers of *La Mujer* not only awakened an interest in the women's plight, but mobilized the women themselves to take charge of their own destinies.

During the last decade of the century many more women enrolled in secondary schools while others entered the labor force in greater numbers. In 1898, for instance, twelve women had graduated from the Atheneum's secondary program, 120 were studying at Colegio de las Madres, and fifty were studying to become teachers at the Escuela Normal.[84] Official figures reveal that in 1898 approximately 47,701 women, 9.9 percent of the island's labor force, had jobs that took them outside the home. The majority of them, as had been the case with the San Juan working women in 1846, were predominantely employed in domestic-related jobs such as servants (18,453), laundresses (16,855), and seamstresses (5,785). A smaller group (3,910) worked as laborers.[85]

Within the narrow confines of the island's economy, teaching still remained the preferred paid profession for women. In 1898, women represented 30.4 percent of the teachers islandwide.[86] Out of the schools there gradually emerged a cadre of feminist leaders intent on securing other rights for women, including the right to vote. They succeeded in the latter quest after several decades of struggle.

Workers Begin to Organize

By the late 1890s the island's workers had founded several craft guilds, cooperatives, and mutual aid societies.[87] These, in turn, enabled them to gather together to discuss their problems, to read about the struggles of workers elsewhere, and to examine the socialist and anarcho-syndicalist ideas filtering in from Europe. Their quest for solutions to common problems led them to forge group solidarity and to devise new ways to articulate their demands. Although most of the organizations were supervised and regulated by the government, they were viewed with apprehension by employers and the upper classes.

Even though the majority of the workers were illiterate, workers' publications began circulating in Puerto Rico in the 1870s. *El Artesano*, the first to appear in 1874, was followed by *El Obrero* in 1889, *El Eco Proletario*, in 1892, and the more radical *Ensayo Obrero* in 1897. Read by a select minority, the workers' papers nonetheless served as important vehicles for labor leaders, such as the Creoles Ramón Romero Rosa, José Ferrer y Ferrer, and the charismatic Spanish-born labor activist Santiago Iglesias, to disseminate their views and relay information about issues pertinent to the workers' struggle.[88]

Forced to flee Spain in 1884 and Cuba twelve years later because of his activism, Iglesias arrived in Puerto Rico at an opportune time in 1896. During the next two years he sought to establish linkages between the island's labor groups and the Spanish socialist workers, and helped to establish the *Federación Regional de los Trabajadores* (FRT), an anarchist regional federation of the Workers International Movement, and the FRT's journal, *Ensayo Obrero*. Vowing to continue to struggle "until the complete emancipation of the proletariat is achieved," he joined strikes and agitated on behalf of workers' rights. For these activities and his writings in which he denounced the injustices against the workers, he was sent to jail several times between 1897 and 1898, along with Ramón Romero Rosa, by order of the Autonomic government. Arrested in April

1898, he was still in prison seven months later, when the American military sought his release.[89]

Once out of prison, Iglesias took advantage of the new relatively tolerant attitudes of the Americans and placed himself at the head of the emerging labor movement with the support, and within the guidelines, of the American Federation of Labor (AFL).

Although he preferred the Americans to the Autonomists, he insisted that he was more attached to the brotherhood of the oppressed than to any political ideology, and sought to steer the workers away from party politics.[90] The occupation and new colonization of the island, however, made that position untenable, as those around him began to worry about the economic and political implications of the island's new colonial status.

Thus, in 1899, when local political parties reorganized and made known their positions concerning the island's future status, many of the FRT members joined one or another party. Those who believed that a better future rested with the U.S. threw their support behind the pro-annexationist Republican party and placed the FRT's newspaper *Ensayo Obrero* at the disposal of the party. The acquisition of this publication enabled the Republican leaders to mount a press campaign against their opponents, the followers of the Federal party.[91]

Those who favored autonomy (or independence) for the island joined the Federal party and established a rival newspaper, *El Obrero Liberal*. Through its pages, the Federalistas countered the Republicans' attacks and mounted an attack of their own against their opponents.[92] Still hoping to bridge the gap between the two labor factions, Iglesias and several others abandoned the FRT and founded the *Federación Libre de los Trabajadores*, FLT (Free Federation of Labor), a presumably apolitical group.[93]

The division could not be bridged, to the detriment of the fledgling labor movement. The bickering and split among the leaders robbed the movement of the impetus it had attained before the American invasion and reduced the workers' chances to achieve their goals. The split, caused in part by the leader's changing ideology, was further exacerbated by the economic dislocations that followed the war-trade embargo and the structural and financial changes introduced by the Americans. The devastation of the island by hurricane San Ciriaco in 1899 merely compounded the workers' problems by depriving them of jobs. As unemployment grew, the basis of support for the labor movement weakened significantly. As a result, the workers' struggle had to be rebuilt during the twentieth century, a period outside the scope of this study.

Final Considerations

Puerto Rico's population in 1898 totaled 953,243 persons. Of these, nearly 150,000 were Spanish-born and 14,000 were born in France, Germany, Italy, and England respectively. The 1899 census, taken by the U.S. War Department, divided the island's population as two-thirds white and one-third Negroes or mixed bloods. It described the population density as roughly 250 persons per square mile. Yet the island's major cities still had relatively few inhabitants: Ponce had 40,000; San Juan, 33,000; Mayagüez, between 12,000 and 15,000.[94]

Transportation on the island had improved somewhat during the last quarter of the century as approximately 216 kilometers of railways were added to the dirt roads. The longest and best kept road was the military highway, which crossed the island from north to south, connecting the eastern city of San Juan to the southern city of Ponce. Built across the central Cordillera, the military road, reported an American journalist in 1898, ..."is a work of the highest credit to the engineers who built it." The road was paved with layers of crushed rock and brick and packed earth. Its finished surface was made of ground and polished limestone. The military road, the same journalist recalled, was intercepted at intervals by "substantial buildings", for use by the civil guard, and "solid masonry bridges". Much of the road, he explained, was "shaded by flowering trees" which had been "deliberately planted on both sides" of it.[95]

Travel along that road from Ponce to San Juan, a distance of ninety-seven kilometers, was done in daily coaches, and took nearly twenty hours. The same trip could be made in a relatively shorter time (fifteen to sixteen hours) by those willing to hire a private carriage. In either case horses had to be changed four or five times during the journey.[96]

The railway lines, built by a French company between the 1870s and 1890s, rarely connected with one another. The longest stretch, a distance of one hundred kilometers, ran from San Juan to Camuy, along the north coast. Another line, covering fifty-eight kilometers, ran from the western

Market scene in Ponce, Puerto Rico in 1898

port of Aguadilla through Mayagüez to Hormigueros in the south. The shortest line, approximately twenty-three kilometers long, stretched from San Juan to the eastern city of Carolina. Train service along these lines was slow, at speeds of twelve to twenty kilometers per hour, so that the trip from San Juan to Camuy took a minimum of five hours. The cost of travel by train ranged from five centavos per kilometer for first class, three centavos for second, and two centavos for third.[97]

Changes in usage and land tenure during the last quarter of the century led to gradual mechanization and consolidation of the best plots. As a result, in 1898, more than 76 percent of the productive units occupied 20.7 percent of the cultivated land, while the top 2.2 percent of the units held 35.9 percent. The average size of the smaller holdings (the bottom three quarters) was less than ten cuerdas each, while those of the top 2.2 percent averaged one hundred cuerdas.[98]

The smaller plots survived longest in the interior, in part because the difficulty of the terrain delayed the encroachment of the expanding haciendas, and partly because peasant farmers fended off the larger holders by planting cash crops (generally coffee) alongside subsistence crops. Those able to supplement the family income through this process were better able to hold on to the family farm than those who planted only subsistence crops.

As the population expanded and the farms were lost or subdivided into tiny plots, the peasants' access to land declined rapidly after the 1870s. Thus, in 1898, nearly 75 percent of the rural families were landless.[99] In San José, a coffee-producing area of the southern highlands, the number of landowning families shrunk by nearly two-thirds, from 1,660 in 1871 to 555 in 1892.[100]

One way the landless had traditionally gained access to subsistence plots had been through the practice of "agrego", which permitted them to gain usufruct rights over certain plots on public lands and private estates. That practice, however, came under attack in 1850, when the government, seeking to regulate the work force, ruled that the landless move their residences to the nearest town, where they were to be assigned municipal plots. The effect of that ruling is exemplified by the case of Lares. By 1870, less than one-third (32.8 percent) of the agregado families had usufruct rights to the land, whereas in 1846 more than 84 percent of such families enjoyed this right.[101]

As the agrego system waned, and the population grew, producers sought to bind the workers to their estates by other means, namely with offers of cash wages. But since their cash reserves were often small, the planters compensated the workers with "vales", vouchers redeemable only at the estate's company store.[102] Others, especially some of the coffee growers, paid their workers in coffee and local foods. In both cases, the lack of cash wages deprived the workers of the flexibility to spend their earnings where they wished, or to save part of what they earned.

Much has been made of the fact that in Puerto Rico 93 percent of the landholders lived on their own farms in 1898, suggesting that absentee ownership was not an important factor.[103] Yet a closer look at the way the land and other properties were held reveals that while the island's economy had grown during the century, and some social sectors had prospered, the majority of the inhabitants had benefited little, if at all. At the end of the nineteenth century more than three-quarters of the island's inhabitants were landless, illiterate, desperately poor, and unemployed. Perhaps it was this reality, along with the conviction that conditions were not likely to change under Spain, that led some sectors of the society to welcome the Americans, or at the very least not resist them.

Suggested Readings

Acosta-Belén, Edna and Hidalgo-Christensen, Elia, Editors. *The Puerto Rican Woman* (New York: Praeger Publishers, 1979).

Babín, María Teresa, *The Puerto Rican's Spirit: Their History, Live and Culture* (New York: Collier Books, 1971).

———— and Stan Steiner, eds. *Borínquen: An Anthology of Puerto Rican Literature* (New York: Vintage, 1974).

Barceló Miller, María de F., "Voto, Colonialismo y Clase: La Lucha por el Sufragio Femenino en Puerto Rico, 1896-1935," Ph.D. dissertation, Departamento de Historia, Universidad de Puerto Rico, 1993.

Benítez, Marimar, "A Glance at the Art of Puerto Rico" in *Puerto Rico: 500 Years of Change and Continuity* (Washington, D.C., Institute for Puerto Rican Affairs, 1991).

Brau, Salvador, "La Campesina," in *Disquisiciones Sociológicas* (San

Juan: Ediciones del Instituto de Cultura, Universidad de Puerto Rico Press, 1956) 217-236.

Cabrera, Francisco M., *Historia de la Literatura Puertorriquena* (Río Piedras, Puerto Rico: Editorial Cultural, Inc., 1982).

Canino-Salgado, Marcelino, *El Cantar Folklórico de Puerto Rico* (Río Piedras: Editorial Universidad de Puerto Rico, 1986).

Cordova, Gonzalo F., *Santiago Iglesias, creador del movimiento obrero de Puerto Rico* (Rio Piedras: Editorial U.P.R, 1980).

De Hostos, Eugenio María, *Obras Completas* (Barcelona: Editorial Planeta, 1960).

Delgado Mercado, Osiris, "Las artes plásticas", in *La Gran Enciclopedia de Puerto Rico* (Madrid: Ediciones "R", 1976).

Dietz, James L., *Economic History of Puerto Rico: Institutional Change and Capitalist Development* (Princeton: Princeton University Press, 1986).

Fernández Méndez, Eugenio, *Historia Cultural de Puerto Rico, 1498-1968* (San Juan: Ediciones El Cemí, 1970).

Foster, George M., *Culture and Conquest, America's Spanish Heritage* (New York: Wener G. Foundation, 1960).

Gómez Acevedo, Labor, *Organización y Reglamentación en el Trabajo del Siglo XIX (Propietarios y Jornaleros)* (San Juan: Instituto de Cultura Puertorriqueña, 1970).

Jiménez Muñoz, Gladys M., "A Storm Dressed in Skirts: Ambivalence in the Debate on Women's Suffrage in Puerto Rico, 1927-1929" Ph.D. dissertation, History, SUNY-Binghamton, 1993.

Jiménez de Wagenheim, Olga, "The Puerto Rican Woman in the 19th Century: An Agenda for Research" Revista/Review Interamericana, Vol. XI, No. 2 (Summer 1981).

Matos Rodríguez, Félix V., "Street Vendors, Peddlers, Shop Owners and Domestics: Some Aspects of Women's Economic Roles in Nineteenth Century San Juan, Puerto Rico (1820-1870)," Unpublished paper.

Matos Rodríguez, Félix V., "Lavanderas y domésticas en San Juan en el Siglo XIX: Control Socioeconómico y Espacio Urbano en las Décadas Previas a la Abolición de la Esclavitud," paper presented at the Latin American Sudies Association (LASA) Conference, Atlanta, Georgia, March 1994.

Meléndez, Edgardo, *Puerto Rico's Statehood Movement* (Westport, CT: Greenwood Press, 1988).

Miles, Galvin, *The Organized Labor Movement in Puerto Rico* (Madison, NJ: Fairleigh Dickinson University Press, 1979).

Negrón-Muñoz, Ángela, *Mujeres de Puerto Rico: desde el período de colonización hasta el primer tercio del siglo XX* (San Juan: Imprenta Venezuela, 1935).

Picó, Fernando, "Mitos y Realidades en la Historia de la Familia Puertorriqueña en la Zona Cafetalera en el Siglo 19," *Homines*, Vol. 7, nums., 1 & 2 (feb.-dic. 1983) 223-26.

Rivera de Álvarez, Josefina, *Literatura puertorriqueña: Su proceso en el tiempo*, Tomo 1 (Madrid: Ed. Partenon, 1983).

Rodríguez de Laguna, Asela, "Puerto Rican Literary Heritage" in Puerto Rico: *500 Years of Change and Continuity* (Washington, D.C., Institute for Puerto Rican Affairs, 1991).

Tapia, Alejandro, *Mis Memorias* Reprint. (San Juan: Editorial Edil, 1971).

Vecchini, Haydee, "Filosofía educativa de tres ordenes religiosas femeninas en Puerto Rico," unpublished paper, presented at Sagrado Corazon's Second Encounter of Church Historians, April 1986.

Zeno-Gandía, Manuel, *La Charca* (Maplewood, NJ: Waterfront Press, 1982).

Notes

Chapter One, pp. 1–18

The author has used the terms "Amerindians" and "Indians" throughout the book, rather than "Native Americans" or "First Nations," because the former are commonly used in Puerto Rico and reflect the historical development described in the book.

1. References to India and the Great Khan appear in John Cummins, *The Voyage of Christopher Columbus: Columbus's Own Journal of Discovery Newly Restored and Translated* (U.S. Edition, 1992).
2. Jan Rogozinski, *A Brief History of the Caribbean: From the Arawak and the Caribe to the Present* (New York, 1992), pp. 5–6.
3. Discussions of the Caribbean Sea and islands are generally found in accounts of the British West Indies. One useful source is: David Watts, *The West Indies: Patterns of Development, Culture and Environmental Change since 1492* (New York, 1987), ch. 1.
4. Kal Wagenheim, *Puerto Rico: A Profile.* 2nd ed.(New York, 1975) 13–14.
5. Ibid.
6. Rafael Picó, *Nueva Geografía de Puerto Rico* (Río Piedras, Puerto Rico, 1975), ch. 1.
7. Ibid, chs. 2 & 3.
8. Jalil Sued-Badillo, *La mujer indígena y su sociedad* (Río Piedras, 1979), pp. 25–26.
9. Picó, op. cit.; Luis A. Salivia, *Historia de los Temporales de Puerto Rico, 1508–1949* (San Juan, 1950), p. 16.
10. Picó, op. cit., p. 79.
11. Ibid, ch. 8.
12. Ibid, ch. 5; Virgilio Biaggi, *Las Aves de Puerto Rico* (Río Piedras, 1970), pp. 61–62; Elbert L. Little, Jr., Frank H. Wadsworth and José Marrero, *Árboles Comunes de Puerto Rico y las Islas Virgénes* (Río Piedras, 1967), pp. 671–672, 239.
13. Sol Luis Descartes, *Puerto Rico: Trasfondo de su Economía* (Hato Rey, Puerto Rico, 1973); Kal Wagenheim, "Copper: The Billion-Dollar Secret." *San Juan Review* (January 1965).
14. Ibid.
15. Information on the pre-Taino cultures was compiled from several sources, including: Ricardo Alegría, "El juego de pelota entre los aborígenes antillanos", *Revista Mexicana de Estudios Antropológicos*, vol. 12 (1951), pp. 313–315; Alegría, "La

población aborigen antillana y su relación con otras areas de America", in Aida Caro-Costas, *Antología de lecturas de historia de Puerto Rico* (San Juan, 1971), pp. 47–63; Labor Gómez y Manuel Ballesteros, *Culturas indígenas de Puerto Rico* (Río Piedras, Puerto Rico, 1978), pp. 17–72; Fred Olsen, *On the Trail of the Arawaks* Reprint of 1891 edition (Oklahoma, 1974), pp. 195–96, 230–32, 252–53, 279–86.

16. Ibid.

17. Ibid.

18. Ibid.

19. Ibid.

20. Ibid; For details about the Ostionoids, see Arturo Morales-Carrión, *Puerto Rico: A Political and Cultural History* (New York, 1983), pp. 4–6.

21. Ibid.

22. Ibid; Material for the section on the Tainos was selected from: Ricardo Alegría, "Apuntes para el estudio de los caciques de Puerto Rico", Separata de la *Revista del Instituto de Cultura Puertorriqueña*, No. 85 (December 1979); Alegría, *Discovery,Conquest and Colonization of Puerto Rico, 1493–1599* (San Juan, 1971); Gómez y Ballesteros, op. cit.; Walter J. Fewkes, *The Aborigines of Porto Rico and Neighboring Islands* (25th Annual Report of the Bureau of American Ethnology, 1903–04)(Washington, D.C.,1970); Ramón Pané, "The Indian Way of Life", [the Spanish version of this appears in Eugenio Fernández Méndez, editor, *Crónicas de Puerto Rico: 1493–1797*, vol. I (San Juan, 1957); for a reproduction of the English version, see Kal Wagenheim and Olga Jiménez de Wagenheim, eds., *The Puerto Ricans: A Documentary History* (NY, 1973); Sued-Badillo, *La mujer indígena*, op. cit.; Antonio Stevens-Arroyo, *Cave of the Jagua: The Mythological World of the Tainos* (New Mexico, 1988).

23. Ibid; Pané, op. cit.

24. Pané, op. cit.; Stevens-Arroyo, op. cit.

25. Sued-Badillo, op. cit.

26. Alegría, op. cit.; Pané, op. cit.

27. Ibid.

29. Ibid.

30. Sued-Badillo, op. cit., pp. 33–37.

31. Alegría, op. cit.; References to the Carib appear in Olsen, op. cit. pp. 33–38; Jalil Sued-Badillo, *Los caribes: realidad o fábula: ensayo de rectificación histórica* (Rio Piedras: 1978).

Chapter Two, pp. 19–34

1. For details about Spain and Europe, see S. Sobrequés Vidal, *Hispania: Síntesis de Historia de España*. 9th ed. (Barcelona, 1979), ch. 28.

2. For details on Ancient Spain, Sobrequés Vidal, pp. 1–54; For similar details about Portugal, see Charles E. Nowell, *Portugal: The Modern Nation in Historical Perspective* (Englewood Cliffs, NJ, 1973), ch.2.

3. Ibid, pp. 58–62; For a good introduction to Muslim Spain, see Louis Bertrand and Sir

Charles Petrie, *The History of Spain* (New York, 1971), chs. 1 & 2; also Nowell, op. cit.

4. For a detailed account of the Reconquest, see Lyle N. McAlister, *Spain and Portugal in the New World, 1492–1700* (Minnesota, 1984), chs. 1 & 2; also Bertrand and Petri, op. cit., ch. 5.

5. Caetano Beirao, *A Short History of Portugal* (Lisbon, 1960), pp. 41–55; Nowell, op. cit., pp.42–45.

6. Nowell, Ibid, p. 49.

7. McAlister, op. cit.; Sobrequés Vidal, op. cit., pp. 63–84.

8. Ibid.

9. McAlister, op. cit., pp. 17–18.

10. A very good discussion about the strengths and weaknesses of Castile and Aragón is provided by J.H. Elliott, *Imperial Spain, 1469–1716* (New York, 1963), pp. 17–43.

11. Ibid.

12. McAlister, op. cit., p. 69.

13. The government of Spain is best described by Elliott, op. cit., pp. 75–96.

14. For information on the power and functions of the Spanish Catholic church, see also Elliott, op. cit., pp. 97–108.

15. Ibid.

16. Ibid.

17. Ibid.

18. Elliott, op. cit., pp. 108–127. For information on the society, family, patriarchy and women's roles in Iberia and colonial America, see Francesca Miller, "Precursoras" in *Latin American Women and the Search for Social Justice*, edited by Francesca Miller (Hanover, NH, 1991); A.J.R. Russell-Wood, "Female and Family in the Economy and Society of Brazil" in *Latin American Women: Historical Perspectives*, edited by Asunción Lavrin (Westwood, Conn.: 1978); Asunción Lavrin, ed., *Sexuality and Marriage in Colonial Latin America* (Lincoln, Nebraska: 1989); James Lockhart, "Spanish Women of the Second Generation in Peru", in *Spanish Peru*, 1532–1560 by James Lockhart (Madison, Wisconsin: 1968); Rosa Santiago Marazzi, "La Immigración de mujeres españolas a Puerto Rico en el período colonial español" in *Homines*, Vol. 10, No. 2 (1986–87).

19. Ibid.

20. A discussion on Africa before the slave trade began appears in Basil Davidson, *The African Slave Trade: Pre-Colonial History 1450–1850* (Boston, 1961), ch. 1; Gary B. Nash, *Red, White, and Black* (Englewood Cliffs, NJ, 1974), ch. 3.

21. Ibid.

22. Davidson, op. cit., ch. 2; Philip Curtin, "Measuring the Atlantic Slave Trade," in *Race and Slavery in the Western Hemisphere: Quantitative Studies*. Edited by Stanley Engerman and Eugene D. Genovese (Princeton, 1975.

23. Rolando Mellafe, *A Brief History of Negro Slavery in Latin America* (Berkeley, 1975), ch. 1; Leslie Rout, Jr., *The African Experience in Spanish America, 1502 to the present day* (Mass: 1976), ch. 1.

24. Curtin, op. cit.

25. Details about slavery in Puerto Rico will be provided throughout this work.

Chapter Three, pp. 35–58

1. Samuel Eliot Morison. *Admiral of the Ocean Sea: A Life of Christopher Columbus* (Boston, 1942) pp. 64–68; for a daily account of the first two voyages, see "Columbus's Journal." in John Cummins, The Voyage of Christopher Columbus, op., cit.
2. For a discussion of the Pope's role as mediator between Spain and Portugal, see Frances Gardiner Davenport, editor. *European Treaties bearing on the History of the United States and its Dependencies to 1648* (Washington, D.C., 1917), I, pp. 11-12; Silvio Zavala, *Ensayos sobre la colonización española en América* (Buenos Aires, 1944), ch. 2.
3. Ibid.
4. Frank Moya Pons, *Manual de Historia Dominicana* (Santiago, República Dominicana, 1980), ch. 3.
5. Ibid.
6. Ibid.
7. Ibid. For a partial transcription of the 1503-1504 edicts, see Salvador Brau, *La Colonización de Puerto Rico* (San Juan, 1969), pp. 89–90; Moya Pons, op. cit., pp. 24–25.
8. Ibid.
9. Transcript of the "Ordenanzas para el tratamiento de los indios." (January 1513) appears in Aida R. Caro-Costas, editor, *Antología de Lecturas de Historia de Puerto Rico (Siglos XV- XVIII)* (San Juan: n.p., 1989), 107–112.
10. The texts of the sermons of Montesinos appear in: Lewis Hanke and Jane M. Rausch, editors, *People and Issues in Latin American History: The Colonial Experience* (Princeton, 1993), pp. 87–89.
11. Ibid.
12. Ibid.
13. For details about Bartolomé de las Casas, see Lewis Hanke, The Spanish Struggle for Justice in the Conquest of America (Boston, 1965), pp. 17–18.
14. References to Palacios Rubios' comments and a copy of the text of the Requirement are found in Hanke and Rausch, op. cit., pp. 89–91.
15. Information of Ponce de León's activities was gathered from various sources, including his own report: "Relación hecha por Ponce de León", transcribed and included in: Caro-Costas, op. cit., 97–100 and Brau, op. cit., ch. 4.
16. Ibid; Gonzalo Fernández de Oviedo, *Historia General y Natural de las Indias* (1535), Libro XVI, Cápitulos 1–18, Reproduced by Alejandro Tapia, editor, *Biblioteca Histórica de Puerto Rico* (San Juan: Instituto de Literatura, 1945), 26-100.
17. Ibid; "Memoria y Descripción de la Isla de Puerto Rico." Ordered by King Philip II in 1582. Reproduced by Cayetano Coll y Toste, editor, Boletín Histórico de Puerto Rico (14 Tomos) (San Juan, 1914), Tomo I, 75–91.
18. "Memoria y Descripción," (1582) op. cit.; Brau, op. cit., chs. 5–6.
19. Ibid.
20. Ibid.
21. Ibid.

22. Ibid; Brau, op. cit., ch. 7
23. "Memoria y Descripción," (1582), op. cit.
24. Ibid.
25. According to a report sent by Governor Manuel de Lando to his king in 1530 (hereafter cited as Lando's Report). Cited in Brau, op. cit., ch. 16.
26. Ibid.
27. Morales-Carrión. *Puerto Rico and the Non-Hispanic Caribbean* (San Juan, 1974), p. 5.
28. For much of the information on the first settlers and first towns in Puerto Rico, see Brau, op. cit., 364–372.
29. Sivestrini and Luque, op. cit., ch. 4.
30. Details about San Germán are found in Fernando Picó, *Historia General de Puerto Rico* (Río Piedras, 1986), pp. 53–54.
31. Aida R. Caro Costas, "The Outpost of Empire." In: Arturo Morales-Carrión, editor, *Puerto Rico: A Political and Cultural History* (New York: W.W. Norton & Co., 1983); Brau, op. cit., pp. 9–24.
32. Cristina Campo Lacasa, *Historia de la Iglesia en Puerto Rico* (San Juan, 1977), pp. 27–37.
33. Regarding the religious institutions erected in 16th century Puerto Rico, see, Campo Lacasa, op. cit., ch. 7.
34. For details about the first Spanish economic ventures in Puerto Rico, see Brau, op. cit., pp. 455–460; Gonzalo Fernández de Oviedo, "Fragmentos de la Historia General y Natural de las Indias." (1535). See book 16 and several chapters from other books which appear in Eugenio Fernández Méndez, *Crónicas de Puerto Rico, 1493–1797* (San Juan, 1957), pp. 100–106.
35. Ibid.
36. Brau, op. cit., pp. 455-460; Silvestrini and Luque, ch. 4.

Chapter Four, pp. 59–76

1. "Sinopsis del primer ataque inglés," by Juan Manuel Zapatero, Excerpt from his book, *La Guerra del Caribe en el Siglo XVIII* which appears in *Antología de Lecturas de Puerto Rico: Siglos XV–XVIII*. Compiled by Aida R. Caro-Costas (San Juan, 1989), 287–290; Caro-Costas, "The Outpost of Empire", in Arturo Morales-Carrión. Editor. *Puerto Rico: A Political and Cultural History* (New York, 1983) (hereafter cited as A Political History), pp. 9–24.
2. Zapatero, op. cit., "Sinopsis del segundo ataque inglés", in Caro-Costas, *Antología,* pp. 291–294; "Relación del viaje a Puerto Rico de George Clifford, 1598", in Eugenio Fernández-Méndez, Editor. *Crónicas de Puerto Rico* (1493–1797) (San Juan, 1957), pp. 137–156.
3. Ibid.
4. Ibid.
5. Ibid.
6. Ibid.

7. "Sinopsis del ataque holandés", in Caro-Costas, *Antología*, pp. 429–432; Zapatero, op. cit., "Breve noticia del proceso de evolución de las fortificaciones de San Juan durante el siglo xvii", in Caro-Costas, *Antología*, pp. 423–427; Caro-Costas, "The Outpost of Empire", op. cit.

8. Ibid.

9. Ibid.

10. Arturo Morales-Carrión, *Puerto Rico and the Non-Hispanic Caribbean* (Río Piedras, 1974) (hereafter cited as The Non- Hispanic), p. 63.

11. For details about the European designs on Vieques, see Morales-Carrión, *The Non-Hispanic*, ch. 4.

12. Aida Caro-Costas, "The Organization of an Instutional and Social Life", in Morales-Carrión, *A Political History*, pp. 25–40; Sebastián González-García, "Notas Sobre el Gobierno y los Gobernadores en Puerto Rico en el Siglo XVII", in Caro-Costas, *Antología*, pp. 381–397.

13. Ibid.

14. Ibid.

15. Ibid.

16. Cayetano Coll y Toste, "La Propiedad Territorial en Puerto Rico, Su Desenvolvimiento Histórico", B.H.P.R., I, 253–254; "Memoria Melgarejo", B.H.P.R., I, 85-86; Diego de Torres Vargas, "Descripción de la Isla y Ciudad de Puerto Rico..., 1647", in Caro-Costas, *Antología*, pp. 319-368.

17. Ibid.

18. Ibid.

19. Ibid.

20. Ibid.

21. Ibid.

22. Ibid.

23. J.H. Elliott, *Imperial Spain*, op. cit., pp. 182–183.

24. Ibid.

25. Coll y Toste, "La propiedad territorial en Puerto Rico," op. cit., pp. 253–254.

26. Ibid.

27. Angel López Cantos, *Historia de Puerto Rico, 1650–1700* (Sevilla, 1975) p. 274; Salvador Perea, *Historia de Puerto Rico, 1537-1700* (San Juan, 1972).

28. Ibid.

29. Morales-Carrión, *The Non-Hispanic*, op. cit., p. 70. 27. "Documentos Sobre el Corsario Puertorriqueño Miguel Henríquez", *La Revista del Centro de Estudios Avanzados de Puerto Rico y el Caribe*, Num. 1 (julio-diciembre 1985), 151–167.

30. Ibid.

31. Silvestrini and Luque, op. cit., pp. 102–105.

32. Salvador Brau, "Fundación de Pueblos en Puerto Rico: Apuntes de un Cronista", *Boletín Histórico de Puerto Rico*, vol. 7, pp. 87–88.

33. For details about Padilla, see Campo Lacasa, *Historia de la Iglesia en Puerto Rico*, op. cit, pp. 92–93.

34. Diego de Torres Vargas,"Descripción de la Isla y Ciudad de Puerto Rico..." (1647) in Caro-Costa, *Antología*, pp. 319–368.

35. Details about Ayerra and Ramírez appear in Manrique Cabrera, op. cit., pp. 40–42.

36. Ibid.

Chapter Five, pp. 77–104

1. Jan Rogozinski. *A Brief History of the Caribbean* (New York, 1994), pp. 100–101; Benjamin Keen. *A History of Latin America* (Boston, 1996), vol. I, pp. 135–36.
2. Salvador Brau. Historia de Puerto Rico. Reprint of 1904 Edition (San Juan: Editorial Coqui' 1966), pp.161, 163.
3. Arturo Morales-Carrión. *Puerto Rico and the Non-Hispanic Caribbean* (Río Piedras, 1974), 62–67; Keen, op. cit., 135–137.
4. George H. Nelson, "Contraband Trade Under the Asiento, 1730–1739", in *American Historica Review,* LI (1945); Morales-Carrión, *Puerto Rico and the Non-Hispanic Caribbean,* op. cit., pp. 76–79.
5. Luis González-Vales, "The Eighteen Century Society", in Morales-Carrión, *Puerto Rico: A Political and Cultural History,* op. cit., 41–50.
6. For a general discussion of the Bourbon reforms in Latin America, see Keen, op. cit., Ch. 7; For the Bourbon reforms in Puerto Rico, see Arturo Santana. "Puerto Rico in a Revolutionary World", in Morales-Carrión. *Puerto Rico: A Political and Cultural History* op. cit., pp. 51–78.
7. Bibiano Torres Ramírez. *La Isla de Puerto Rico, 1765–1800* (San Juan, 1968), ch. 4.
8. Alejandro O'Reilly. "Memoria Sobre la Isla de Puerto Rico, 1765", in Eugenio Fernández-Méndez, Crónicas, op. cit. 239–69.
9. Torres-Ramírez, op. cit. Ibid.
10. Hector R. Feliciano, "El Comercio de Contrabando en la Costa Sur de Puerto Rico, 1750–1778", in *Revista/Review Interamericana,* XIV (Winter-Spring 1984), pp. 80–89.
11. Torres-Ramírez, op. cit., ch. 5.
12. R. F. Nichols. "Trade Relations and the Establishment of the United States Consulate in Spanish America, 1779–1809", in *Hispanic American Historical Review,* XIII (1933), p, 291.
13. Several documents with respect to the land reform appear in Caro-Costas, *Antología,* op. cit., 495–519; Torres-Ramírez, op. cit., ch. 2; Eugenio Fernández Méndez. *Historia Cultural de Puerto Rico* (San Juan, 1970), pp. 171–175.
14. Ibid; Altagracia Ortiz, *Eighteenth-Century Reforms in the Caribbean: Miguel de Muesas, Governor of Puerto Rico, 1769–76* (Rutherford, NJ, 1983), pp. 69–70, 76–78.
15. Ibid.
16. Ibid.
17. Abbad y Lasierra, Iñigo. *Historia Geográfica, Civil y Natural de la Isla de San Juan Bautista de Puerto Rico* (Río Piedras, 1970), Chs. XXI-XXIV; Fernando Picó. *Historia General de Puerto Rico* (Río Piedras, 1986), pp. 106–108; Fernández-Méndez, *Historia Cultural,* p. 160.
18. Picó, *Historia,* p.108; Silvestrini and Luque, op. cit., pp. 107-109.
19. Torres-Ramírez, op. cit., ch. 3; Ortiz, op. cit., p. 69.
20. Silvestrini and Luque, op. cit., pp. 107, 109.
21. Francisco Scarano, *Puerto Rico: Cinco Siglos de Historia* (Mexico: McGraw-Hill, 1993), 285-286.

22. Picó,op. cit., p. 138.
23. Picó, op. cit, pp. 142-143.
24. Andre Pierre Ledru. *Viaje a la Isla de Puerto Rieo en 1797*. Translated by Julio L. Vizcarrondo. Reprint of 1863 Edition (San Juan, 1971), pp, 88-90, 96-97, 102-103.
25. Scarano, op. cit., pp. 363-366.
26. Picó, op. cit. p. 139-142; Pilar Gonzalbo. "Perspectiva de la historia de la familia en America Latina", *OP.CIT. Boletín del Centro de Investigaciones Históricas*, num. 6 (1991), pp. 65-87; Fernández-Méndez, *Historia Cultural*, p. 191.
27. Ledru, op. cit., ch. 7.
28. Ibid.
29. The roles of men and women in the Spanish family in colonial America are discussed by Francesca Miller, "Precursoras", op. cit.; Details about the Spanish women in Puerto Rico are offered by Santiago-Marazzi, La immigración de mujeres españolas a Puerto Rico...", op. cit.
30. Details about the economic roles women played are found in the notarial records of each municipality.
31. The case of María Verdugo Segarra appears in Francisco LLuch Mora. *La Rebelión de San Germán* (Mayagüez, 1981), pp. 34, 37, 46.
32. For a discussion of the compadrazgo system, see Eugenio Fernández Méndez, editor. *Portrait of a Society* (Río Piedras, 1972), pp. 23–24, 37, 89–90, 123, 126, 160.
33. Ortiz, op. cit., pp. 198–199.
34. Picó, op. cit., 160–165.
35. Ibid.
36. Muesas' plan is included in Alfonso López-Yustos. *Historia Documental de la Educación en Puerto Rico, 1503-1970* (San Juan, 1985), pp. 46–46; Ortiz, op. cit., pp. 205–206.
37. A biographical sketch of José Campeche is included in Juan A. Gaya-Nuño, "La Pintura en Puerto Rico durante el Siglo XVIII", *Revista del Museo de Antropología, Historia y Arte*, 2 (enero-junio, 1980), pp. 15–26.
38. A biographical sketch of Tiburcio Espada is found in Federico Ribes-Tovar, *100 Oustanding Puerto Ricans* (New York, 1976), pp. 47–49.
39. Copies of O'Reilly's report are found in numerous sources. An English version (the one used here) appears in Loida Figueroa, *History of Puerto Rico* (New York, 1974), pp. 433–439.
40. Information on the military reforms after the 1770s is found in Torres-Ramírez, op. cit., chs. 8 and 9; José Rigau-Pérez, "On his Majesty's Secret Service: Un espía inglés en San Juan en 1779", *Revista de Historia*, num. 3 (Jan–June, 1986), pp. 169–179.
41. Ibid; Ortiz, op. cit., 81–88.
42. Ibid, ch. 10; José Rigau-Pérez, "Astonished at their Bravery: El relato de un invasor inglés en Puerto Rico en 1797", *Revista de Historia*, num. 7 (enero-diciembre, 1988), pp. 81–94. 43. 44. Ibid.
43. Ibid.
44. Ibid.

Chapter Six, pp. 105–136

1. Morales-Carrión. *The Non-Hispanic*, op. cit; Luis E. González-Vales. "Towards a Plantation Society", in Morales-Carrión, *A Political and Cultural History* op. cit., 79–107.
2. Ibid.
3. Salvador Brau. *Historia de Puerto Rico*. Reprint of 1904 edition (Río Piedras: Editorial Edil, 1974), pp. 215-21.
4. Lidio Cruz Monclova. *Historia de Puerto Rico: Siglo XIX*, Vol. 1 (1800–1868) (Río Piedras, 1970), Ch. 1; González-Vales, "Towards a Plantation Society", op. cit.
5. Ibid.
6. Ibid.
7. Ibid.
8. Aida Caro de Delgado. *Ramón Power y Giralt (Compilación de Documentos)* (Barcelona, Spain: Imprenta Manuel Pareja, 1969); Rafael Ramírez de Arellano, Editor. *Instrucciones al Diputado Don Ramón Power y Giralt* (Río Piedras: Editorial Universitaria, 1936) 46–61; A short biography of Power appears in Ribes-Tovar, op. cit, pp. 51–53.
9. Caro de Delgado, *Ramón Power, Documentos*; Ramírez de Arellano, *Instrucciones*.
10. Cruz-Monclova, Ibid.
11. Caro de Delgado, *Ramón Power*, op. cit.; Ramírez de Arellano, *Instrucciones*.
12. Loida Figuera. *History of Puerto Rico* (New York: Anaya Book Company, 1974), ch. 7 (Part 2); Cruz Monclova, Ibid.
13. Ibid.
14. Ibid.
15. Ibid.
16. Luis E. González Vales. *Alejandro Ramírez y su Tiempo* (Río Piedras, 1978), pp. 9–41.
17. Ibid.
18. Figueroa, op. cit; Cruz Monclova, op. cit.
19. Ibid.
20. Arturo Santana. "Puerto Rico in a Revolutionary World", in Morales-Carrión. *A Political History*, op. cit., 51–78.
21. Luis González-Vales, "Towards a Plantation Society" op. cit.; Copy of the Text of the Cédula de Gracias appears in Cayetano Coll y Toste. *Boletín Histórico de Puerto Rico*. 14 vols. (San Juan: Tipografía Cantero Fernández, 1914–1927), vol. I, 297–307. Cited hereafter as Coll y Toste, B.H.P.R..
22. González-Vales, *Alejandro Ramírez*, op, cit, pp. 9–41.
23. Cruz Monclova, op. cit.; Brau, op. cit.
24. Ibid.
25. Ibid.
26. Ibid.
27. Jesús R. Navarro-García. "Fuentes documentales españolas para el estudio del gobierno de Miguel De La Torre (Conde de Torrepando) en Puerto Rico: de la desintegración colonial a la revolución liberal (1822-1837)", in *Revista de Historia*, Nums. 5 y 6 (enero-diciembre 1987), pp. 44–62.
28. For details about England's efforts to abolish the slave trade in the Caribbean, see

Rogozinski, op. cit., pp. 178–180.

29. Ibid; Guillermo Baralt. *Esclavos Rebeldes: conspiraciones y sublevaciones de esclavos en Puerto Rico, 1795–1873* (Río Piedras, 1981), ch. 1; Benjamín Nistal-Moret. *Esclavos Prófugos y Cimarrones: Puerto Rico, 1770–1870* (Río Piedras, 1984), p. 11.
30. Baralt, op. cit., ch. 2.
31. Ibid, pp. 33-42.
32. Ibid, pp. 67-72; Nistal-Moret, op. cit., p. 15.
33. Ibid.
34. Ibid.
35. Cruz Monclova, op. cit., pp. 37-38.
36. Santana, "Puerto Rico in a Revolutionary World", op. cit.
37. A discussion of the 1822 conspiracy and Ducoudray's role in it appears in òrsula Acosta. "Ducoudray y Holstein: Hombre al margen de la historia", in *Revista de Historia,* Num. 2 (julio-diciembre 1985), pp. 63–85; Brau, *Historia,* op. cit., 235–36.
38. Santana, "Puerto Rico in a Revolutionary World", op. cit.,; Cruz-Monclova, op. cit., pp. 151-52.
39. Cruz-Monclova, op. cit., pp. 155, 180, 184.
40. Ibid.
41. Ivette Pérez-Vega. "El apresamiento de barcos norteamericanos por corsarios españoles en Puerto Rico, en 1816-1830", in *Homines,* vol. 12, nums. 1 y 2 (marzo 1988–enero 1989), 56–63.
42. Alberto Cibes Viadé. "Antonio Valero, soldado libertador", in *Homines,* vol. 8, num. 1 (enero–junio 1984) 31–42.
43. Ibid; Pérez-Vega, op. cit.; A. Santana, op. cit.
44. Ibid.
45. Arthur P. Whitaker. *The United States and the Independence of Latin America, 1800–1830* (Baltimore, 1941), pp. 16–20; Cruz- Monclova, op. cit., pp. 185.
46. A Spanish translation of Secretary Clay's message appears in Cruz-Monclova, op. cit., pp. 207–08.
47. Navarro-García, "Fuentes Documentales", op. cit.; Cruz- Monclova, op. cit., p. 192
48. Ibid.
49. James L. Dietz. *Economic History of Puerto Rico: Institutional Change and Capitalist Development* (Princeton, 1986), 16–19.
50. George D. Flinter. *An Account of the Present State of Puerto Rico* (London, 1834), Cited in Francisco Scarano, *Sugar and Slavery The Plantation Economy of Ponce, 1800–1850* (Wisconsin, 1984), pp. 26-29.
51. Laird W. Bergad. *Coffee and the Growth of Agrarian Capitalism in Nineteenth-Century Puerto Rico* (Princeton, 1983), pp. 9–10.
52. Scarano, op. cit., p. 7; Bergad, op. cit., p. 16.
53. Bergad, Ibid, p. 60.
54. Scarano, Ibid.
55. Cited by Scarano, Ibid, p. 14.
56. Scarano, op. cit., p, 74.
57. Ibid (see Table 4.1), p. 82.
58. Ricardo Camuñas. *Hacendados y Comerciantes en Puerto Rico en Torno a la Década Revolucionaria de 1860* 2nd. edition (Mayagüez, 1994), pp. 105–117.

Chapter Seven, pp. 137–162

1. James Dietz, *Economic History of Puerto Rico* (Princeton, 1986), pp. 16–24; Darío Ormachea, "Memoria acerca de la agricultura, el comercio, y las rentas internas de la isla de Puerto Rico" (1847) in Eugenio Fernández Méndez, *Crónicas de Puerto Rico, 1809–1955* (San Juan, 1957), vol. 2, pp. 57–59.

2. Ibid.

3. Dietz, Ibid.

4. Francisco Scarano, *Sugar and Slavery in Puerto Rico: The Plantation Economy of Ponce, 1800–1850* (Wisconsin, 1984), 3-25; Dietz, op. cit., 16–24.

5. Ibid.

6. Ibid.

7. Ibid.

8. Ibid.

9. Luis Díaz Soler, *Historia de la Esclavitud Negra en Puerto Rico.* 3d ed. (Río Piedras, 1970); Scarano, op. cit., 25-34.

10. George D. Flinter. *Examen del estado actual de los esclavos de la isla de Puerto Rico bajo el gobierno español.* Reprint of 1832 ed. (San Juan: Instituto de Cultura Puertorriqueña, 1976), pp. 16, 22, 24-25.

11. Victor Schoelcher. *Colonies etrangeres et Haiti, resultats de Líemancipation anglaise.* 2 vols. Paris: Pagnerre, 1843. Cited in Scarano, op. cit., 29–30.

12. Ibid.

13. The slaves' practice of fleeing the haciendas in Puerto Rico was first addressed by Governor Muesas in 1770 and remained a source of worry for the planters until 1873, when slavery was abolished on the island. For details about the slaves forms of resistance, see Benjamín Nistal Moret, *Esclavos Prófugos y Cimarrones: Puerto Rico 1770–1870* (Río Piedras, 1984), pp. 22–24, 36–41.

14. See any of the conspiracies discussed by Guillermo Baralt, *Esclavos rebeldes: conspiraciones y sublevaciones de esclavos en Puerto Rico, 1795–1873.* (Río Piedras, 1982), pp. 50–56 (La conspiración de Guayama, 1822), 91–100 (La conspiración de esclavos en Ponce, 1841).

15. Scarano, op. cit., p. 28; Andrés Ramos-Mattei. *La Hacienda Azucarera: su crecimiento y crisis en Puerto Rico (Siglo XIX).* San Juan: CEREP, 1981), pp. 96–98; José A. Curet. "De la esclavitud a la abolición: transiciones económicas en las haciendas azucareras de Ponce, 1845–1873" in Andrés Ramos-Mattei, Editor. *Azucar y Esclavitud.* (San Juan, 1982), pp. 52–86.

16. Ibid.

17. Ibid.

18. Nistal, op. cit.; Baralt, op. cit.

19. Labor Gómez Acevedo. *Organización y Reglamentación del Trabajo en el Puerto Rico del siglo XIX: Propietarios y Jornaleros.* (San Juan: Instituto de Cultura Puertorriqueña, 1970), ch.1.; Fernando Picó. *Registro General de Jornaleros: Utuado Puerto Rico, 1849–50.* (Río Piedras, 1976), pp. 9–13.

20. Ibid.

21. Ibid.

22. Ibid.

23. Ricardo Camuñas. *Hacendados y Comerciantes en Puerto Rico en Torno a la Década Revolucionaria de 1860.* 2nd. Edition. (Mayagüez, Puerto Rico, 1994), p. 82.
24. The comments of the planters was cited in Labor Gómez-Acevedo, op. cit. Letters in Appendix II,III and IV, pp. 455–475.
25. Ibid.
26. The prices quoted here in effect in Lares, see "Diario Económico de la Casa Marquez, No. 4", Colección Emiliano Pol, AGPR, Lares 1864–1871; Fernando Picó. "Deshumanización del trabajo, cosificación del café en el Utuado del siglo XIX," Francisco Scarano, Editor. **Inmigración y clases sociales en el Puerto Rico del siglo xix** (Río Piedras, 1981) 187–206.
27. Olga Jiménez de Wagenheim. *Puerto Rico's Revolt for Independence: El Grito de Lares* (Princeton, 1993), ch. 1.
28. Ibid.
29. Estela Cifre de Loubriel. *La Formación del Pueblo Puertorriqueño: La Contribución de los Catalanes, Baleáricos y Valencianos* (San Juan, 1975). 9–25.
30. Laird Bergad. "Towards Puerto Rico' Grito de Lares: Coffee, Social Stratification, and Class Conflicts, 1828-1868," in *Hispanic American Historical Review* 60, no. 4 (Nov. 1980) 617–642. 31. Andres Ramos-Mattei."La importación de trabajadores contratados para la industria azucarera puertorriqueña: 1860–1880," in Scarano, *Inmigración y clases sociales,* 125–141.
32. Bergad, "Towards Puerto Rico's Grito de Lares", op. cit.
33. Jiménez de Wagenheim, op. cit.
34. Julio L. Vizcarrondo. *Elementos de Historia y Geografía de la Isla de Puerto Rico* (San Juan, 1863), p. 38.
35. Census figures cited in José Pérez Moris, *Historia de la Insurrección de Lares.* 2nd Ed. (Río Piedras, 1975), pp. 280–281.
36. Jesús Lalinde Abadía. *La administración española el el siglo xix puertorriqueño* (Sevilla, 1980), pp. 125–171.
37. Ibid.
38. Ibid.
39. Ibid; Cruz Monclova, *Historia,* op. cit., p. 234.
40. Ibid.
41. Fernando Bayron Toro, *Elecciones y Partidos Políticos de Puerto Rico, 1809–1976* (Mayagüez, 1977), p. 42, 45–47.
42. Baralt, op. cit., 129–131.
43. Ibid.
44. Tapia describes the reasons for his exile by order of Governor Pezuela in *Mis Memorias,* op cit., pp. 138–143, 162.
45. Tapia, op. cit., p. 152.
46. Manrique Cabrera, op. cit., p. 112; Cruz Monclova, *Historia,* op. cit. 299–300.
47. For details about the abolitionist work and exile of Julio Vizcarrondo, see Cruz-Monclova, Ibid, p. 291, 357, 375, 427.
48. Ibid; a short biography of Julio L. Vizcarrondo appears in Federico Ribes-Tovar. *100 Outstanding Puerto Ricans* (New York, 1976) 96–98.
49. The details of U.S. expansion into Texas and present-day American southwest can be found in any text of the American nation's history. The most brazen offer to purchase

Cuba was the "Ostend Manifesto" (1853), during the administration of Franklin Pierce.

50. Cruz Monclova, op. cit. 377–380.
51. Ibid, 388–392.
52. Ibid, 392–394.
53. Ibid.
54. The arguments presented by the Puerto Rican abolitionists were published as "Proyecto para la abolición de la esclavitud en Puerto Rico" (San Juan, 1959); excerpts of it can be read in Cruz-Monclova, op. cit., pp. 390–91.

Chapter Eight, pp. 163–194

1. Cruz-Monclova, *Historia,* op. cit., pp. 430–31.
2. Ibid.
3. Ibid.
4. Ibid, pp. 433-34.
5. For details, see Jiménez de Wagenheim, op. cit., pp. 14–15.
6. Ibid.
7. Ibid.
8. Ibid.
9. Proclamation of July 16, 1867.
10. Letter from Manuel María Mangual to the Intendant of Puerto Rico, December 2, 1867, in Municipal Archives of Mayagüez (AMM) (Bound Documents), 1867, vol. 2.
11. Brau, op. cit., pp. 249-50.
12. Protocolos Notariales, Lares, 1846, at the Archivo General de Puerto Rico (AGPR), caja 1430, f. 24.
13. AGPR, "Libro de Inventario de la Casa Marquez y Co.," Coleccion Emiliano Pol, Lares 1864–71.
14. Judgment based on the transactions of this firm which appear in the Notarial Records of Lares, 1840s–60s.
15. Ibid.
16. Ibid.
17. For an account of Rojas' purchases and debts, see Jiménez de Wagenheim, op. cit., pp. 48–49.
18. Ibid.
19. Ibid.
20. Details about the racist attitudes of Mayor Coca in Jiménez de Wagenheim, op. cit., p. 52.
21. Ibid.
22. Ibid. Bernabé Pol was also barred from a government job because he was a mulatto.
23. Cruz-Monclova, *Historia,* op. cit., pp. 440–46.
24. Ibid.
25. Letter from Ramón E. Betances to Father Merino, January 24, 1868. The letter is found in Luis Bonafoux, *Betances* (San Juan, 1970), pp. 95–97.

26. The Gamir Plan can be found in Coll y Toste, BHPR, op. cit., vol.2, pp. 276–283.

27. See letters from Betances to other rebels in Puerto Rico, in Bonafoux, op. cit., pp. 3, 4–5, 12, 77, 83.

28. Details of the arrest of Manuel María González are found in the report sent by Colonel Manuel de Iturriaga, the military commander of Arecibo, to Governor Julián Juan Pavía (Dec. 19, 1868), in AGPR, FGEPR, "La Revolución de Lares 1868", caja 180, pieza 43, f. 75.

29. Testimony of Frutos Caloca to Judge Navascués, Lares, October 19, 1868, in AGPR, Ibid. 30. For details about the social composition of the rebels, see Jiménez de Wagenheim, op. cit., pp. 29–38.

31. Ibid, p. 84.

32. Ibid, pp. 86–92; Testimony of the Spaniard Manuel Bernal, who organized the defense of Pepino, in *Boletín de Historia Puertorriqueña*, vo. II, no. 5 (abril 1950), pp. 131–32.

33. Ibid.

34. Ibid.

35. Ibid.

36. The capture of the Lares rebels was reported by numerous officials. See excerpts of these in José Pérez Moris, *Historia de la Insurrección de Lares* Reprint of 1872 edition (Río Piedras, 1975), pp. 177–78, 180, 183–84, 190–192; also a report from Captain Prats to Governor Pavía in *La Gaceta*, October 24, 1868.

37. Ibid.

38. Ibid.

39. Ibid.

40. Melchor Fernández Almagro, *Historia Política de la España Contemporanea,* 3 vols. (Madrid, 1969), vol. 1, p. 7–17.

41. Fernando Bayron Toro, *Elecciones y Partidos Politicos de Puerto Rico, 1809–1976* (Mayagüez, 1977), pp. 45–49.

42. Details about the islanders' petitions appear in "Interpelación del brigadier don Luis Padial", diputado por Puerto Rico a las cortes de 1869 (Fragmento) reprinted in Coll y Toste, BHPR, op cit., vol. 4, pp. 33–35 .

43. María A. García-Ochoa, *La política española en Puerto Rico durante el siglo xix* (Río Piedras, 1982), pp. 154–161; Cruz-Monclova, op. cit., Tomo II, Primera Parte, pp. 13–15.

44. Ibid.

45. Cruz-Monclova, op. cit., pp. 48–53.

46. Fernández Almagro, op. cit., pp. 77–81.

47. Picó, *Historia,* op. cit., 206–07.

48. Cruz-Monclova, op. cit., pp. 54–55; García-Ochoa, op. cit. pp. 164–168, 178–80.

49. Ibid, p. 182.

50. Details about the 1871 elections are found in Bayron Toro, op. cit., pp. 51–55; those of 1879, in pp. 75–78.

51. For details about the impact of Sanz, see Labor Gómez Acevedo, Sanz: Promotor de la Conciencia Separatista en Puerto Rico (Río Piedras, 1974), pp. 132–167; 219–292.

52. See details about Baldorioty de Castro in the biographical sketch offered by Rives-Tovar, op. cit., pp. 76–80; Germán Delgado-Pasapera, *Puerto Rico: sus luchas eman-*

cipadoras (Río Piedras, 1984), pp. 370–71.

53. The discussion about Baldorioty's plan is based on information from several sources, including: Cruz Monclova, *Historia,* op. cit., Tomo II (Segunda Parte), pp. 532–41; Bayron Toro, op. cit. pp. 79–108; García-Ochoa, op. cit., pp. 191–206.
54. Ibid.
55. Delgado-Pasapera, op. cit., pp. 370–384.
56. Ibid, pp. 384–99.
57. Ibid.
58. Ibid.
59. Ibid, pp. 399–403.
60. The increasing political factionalism is discussed by Pilar Barbosa de Rosario, *De Baldorioty a Barbosa: Historia del Autonomismo Puertorriqueño* (San Juan, 1974), pp. 167–71; 195–202; 208–11.
61. Ibid, pp. 316–22.
62. Morales-Carrión, *A Political History*, op. cit., pp. 118–25.
63. Laird Bergad, *Coffee and the Growth of Agrarian Capitalism,* op. cit., p. 68.
64. Ibid.
65. The roles played by Spanish and foreign merchants in the development of Puerto Rico's coffee industry are discussed in Carlos Buitrago-Ortiz, *Haciendas Cafetaleras y Clases Terratenientes en el Puerto Rico Décimonónico* (Río Piedras, 1882), in particular, see, ch. 7; Bergad, op. cit., pp. 18–26, 73–89.
66. The notarial records of Lares, Camuy, and other municipalities list the obligations of hacendados and jornaleros with respect to the public works.
67. Buitrago Ortiz, op. cit., p. 135.
68. Bergad, op. cit., p. 73.
69. Ibid, p. 145.
70. Scarano, *Cinco Siglos,* op. cit., p. 466; Bergad, ch. 3.
71. *Informe Sobre el Censo de Puerto Rico* (1899) (Wash., D.C., 1900), pp. 132–33, 144–45.
72. Trumbull White, *Our New Possessions* (New York, 1898), p. 348.
73. Galvin Miles, *The Organized Labor Movement in Puerto Rico* (Madison, NJ, 1979), ch. 1.

Chapter Nine, pp. 195 – 226

1. Lidio Cruz-Monclova, *Historia de Puerto Rico* (Siglo XIX), 6 vols. (Río Piedras, 1970), Tomo III, Tercera Parte, p. 223.
2. Edwin E. Sparkes, *The Expansion of the American People* (Chicago, 1900), pp. 439–450.
3. Alfred T. Mahan, "The U.S. Looking Outward." *Atlantic Monthly*, December, 1890.
4. Walter Millis, *The Martial Spirit: A Study of Our War With Spain* (New York, 1931), pp. 224–226.
5. *New York Times*, July 4, 1898, p. 4
6. Ibid.

7. *The Washington Post,* April 20, 1898.

8. Henry Cabot Lodge, "Our Blundering Foreign Policy." *Forum,* March, 1895.

9. Quoted in Kal Wagenheim and Olga Jiménez de Wagenheim, *The Puerto Ricans: A Documentary History* (Princeton, N.J.,1994), p. 78.

10. *New York Journal of Commerce,* May 11, 1898.

11. *New York Times,* July 11, 1898.

12. Carmelo Rosario-Natal, *Puerto Rico y la Crisis de la Guerra Hispanomericana, 1895–1898* (San Juan, 1975), pp. 79–115.

13. Ibid

14. Ibid.

15. Ibid.

16. Ibid.

17. Angel Rivero, *Crónica de la Guerra Hispanoamericana en Puerto Rico* (Madrid, 1922) p. 18.

18. The activities of Henna and Todd are described in *Memoria de los Trabajos Realizados por la Sección Puerto Rico del Partido Revolucionario Cubano, 1895–1898* (New York, 1898); Roberto H. Todd, *José Julio Henna, 1848–1924* (San Juan, 1930), pp. 18–21.

19. Morison, J. M. Blum and J.J. Buckley, Editors. *The Letters of Theodore Roosevelt* (Cambridge, Mass., 1951) 1: p. 607.

20. Selections from the *Correspondence of Theodore Roosevelt and H.C. Lodge, 1184–1918* (New York, 1925) Vol. 1, pp. 299–300.

21. H. C. Lodge, *The War With Spain* (New York, 1899),pp. 168–169.

22. Quoted in Rivero, *Crónica de la Guerra,* p. 19

23. *New York Times,* July 30, 1898, p.1; *Harper's Weekly,* August 13, 1898.

24. John R. Musick, *History of the War With Spain* (New York, 1898), pp. 98, 104.

25. Musick, op. cit., p. 107.

26. Robert Dallek, *1898: McKinley's Decision: The U.S. Declares War on Spain* (New York, 1969) 203–212; Musick, op. cit., pp. 346–364.

27. Ibid.

28. Ibid.

29. The Teller Amendment was a Congressional Act of April 20, 1898. It was included in the U.S. declaration of war against Spain. The text of it appears in Musick, op. cit., pp 108–109.

30. Millis, op. cit., pp. 224–226; Musick, op. cit., Ibid.

31. Rivero, op. cit., p. 69; *La Gaceta,* May 14, 1898.

32. Nelson A. Miles, *Serving the Republic* (New York, 1911), pp. 296–305.

33. Miles gives credit to Whitney for the success of the invasion. Miles, *Serving the Republic,* p. 298; Rivero, *Crónica de la Guerra,* p. 501; R.A. Alger (Secretary of War), *The Spanish- American War, March 5, 1897-August 1, 1899* (New York, 1901), pp. 298–317.

34. Miles confirms he had planned to land at Fajardo. Miles, *Serving the Republic,* pp. 296–97.

35. Carl Sandburg, "Soldier." Originally published in *Always the Young Strangers* (New York, 1953), pp. 403–24; Rpr. in Wagenheim, and Jiménez de Wagenheim, op. cit., p. 96–98.

36. Rosario-Natal, op. cit., p. 225; A reproduction of Mejia's proclamation appears in Rivero, *Crónica de la Guerra*, p. 218; Musick, op. cit., pp. 404–405.

37. Sandburg, Ibid.

38. Mariano Negrón-Portillo, *Cuadrillas Anexionistas y Revueltas Campesinas en Puerto Rico, 1898–1899* (Río Piedras, 1987), pp. 9–11, 15–18.

39. A reproduction of Rodulfo Figueroa's letter to General Miles appears in Fernando Picó, *1898: La Guerra Después de la Guerra* (Río Piedras, 1987), pp. 92-93; Negrón-Portillo, op. cit., pp. 19–20.

40. Reproduction of Miles' 1st Proclamation (Ponce, July 28, 1898) appears in Rivero, *Crónica de la Guerra*, p. 232.

41. U.S. War Department. *Military Government of Puerto Rico From October 18, 1898 to April 30, 1900* (Washington, D.C., 1902).

42. Picó, op. cit., p. 62; *New York Times*, Aug. 5, 1898, p. 1.

43. U.S. War Department, *Military Government*, op. cit. 44. "Diary of the War." *Harper's Weekly*, August 13, 1898, p. 801

45. Ibid.

46. U.S. blockade against Spanish commerce began on April 29, 1898. A Drawing of the ships blockading the San Juan Bay on June 12, 1898 appear in Rivero, *Crónica de la Guerra*, p. 145.

47. The economic motives for the collaboration appear in Fernando Picó, op. cit., pp. 96–99 and 116–26.

48. Tomás Blanco, *Prontuario Histórico de Puerto Rico* (San Juan, 1973), pp. 104–107.

49. Trumbull White, *Our New Possessions* (Copyrighted by T. White, 1898), p. 258.

50. See reports sent by the American Generals in Puerto Rico to the Adjutant General, July 1898 to December 1898. Washington, MS, NAUS, BIA. Cited in Edward Berbusse, *The United States in Puerto Rico, 1898–1900* (Chapel Hill, 1966), pp. 77–110.

51. "Diary of the War," op. cit.

52. Hostos believed the cession of Puerto Rico was illegal. His view was that the United States should recogize Puerto Rico's legal personality and prepare the island for republican democracy and a plebiscite. For more details, see his diary, "Madre Isla," *Obras Completas*, Vol. 5 (La Habana, 1939).

53. Arturo Morales-Carrión, *Puerto Rico: A Political and Cultural History* (New York, 1983), p. 135.

54. A Spanish reproduction of General Brooke's report on the actions of the partidas appears in Rosario-Natal, op. cit., pp. 333–335; For related information, Picó, op. cit., pp. 116–126.

55. Picó, op. cit., pp. 95–98; Accounts of these attacks appear in *La Correspondencia,* Aug. 19, 1898, p. 1, Aug. 30, 1898, p. 2.

56. Brooke's Report, in Rosario-Natal, op. cit., pp. 333–335.

57. Fernando Picó, op. cit.

58. Juan Manuel Delgado, "Las Partidas Sediciosas," *La Toga*, Vol. 10, Num. 1 (abril 1978); also by Delgado, "Frontón y el Levantamiento de Ciales," in Juan A. Corretjer, editor. *Origen y Desarrollo del Independentismo Cialeño en el Siglo XX* (Ciales, Puerto Rico: Sociedad Ciales Histórico, 1980).

59. Mariano Negrón-Portillo, *Cuadrillas Anexionistas y Revueltas Campesinas en Puerto*

Rico, 1898–1900 (Río Piedras, 1987), pp. 15–19.

60. The drunken brawls and other incidents provoked by the American soldiers were reported in Picó, op. cit., pp. 171–172; also in *La Democracia*, Feb. 22, 1899, p. 2.
61. Picó, op, cit., pp. 84–85.
62. Picó, op. cit., p. 109.
63. Ibid.
64. Cited in Albert G. Robinson, *The Porto Rico of Today* (New York, 1899), p. 222.
65. Reproduction of the front cover of *La Gaceta*, Oct. 18, 1898 appears in Rivero, *Crónica de la Guerra*, p. 414.
66. Morales-Carrión, op. cit., p. 135.
67. Hostos founded the League of Patriots on July 25, 1898. For details on the League's mission, see, "Madre Isla," op. cit.
68. Federico Ribes-Tobar, *100 Outstanding Puerto Ricans* (New York, 1976), p. 103.
69. Berbusse, op. cit., pp. 77–110.
70. *La Democracia*, Dec. 3, 1898; Berbusse, op. cit., p. 85.
71. Ibid.
72. A Spanish translation of the Articles of the Treaty of Paris pertaining to Puerto Rico appears in Rosario-Natal, op. cit., pp. 341–342.
73. Berbusse, op. cit., pp. 88–97.
74. Roberto H. Todd, *Desfiles de Gobernadores de Puerto Rico.* (Madrid, 1966), pp. 6–8.
75. Remarks appear in "Report of General Henry to Adjutant General", Washington, Dec. 8, 1898, MS, NAUS, BIA, 81. Reproduced in Berbusse, op. cit., pp. 88–89.
76. Picó, op. cit., p. 149; Berbusse, op. cit., pp. 88–97.
77. Berbusse, Ibid.
78. Francisco Scarano, *Puerto Rico: Cinco Siglos de Historia.* (Mexico, 1993), p. 565; Berbusse, op. cit., 93–94.
79. Ibid.
80. Berbusse, op. cit., pp. 94–97.
81. *La Democracia*, Dec. 6,8, 15, 1898.
82. For details about the Puerto Rican reactions see, Paul Nelson Chiles, *The Puerto Rican Press Reaction to the United States, 1888–1898* (Phila., 1944). Henry's retaliatory measures are discussed by Morales-Carrión, op. cit., p. 146.
83. Berbusse, op. cit., p. 94.
84. The government of General Davis is discussed by Berbusse, op. cit., pp. 98–110; Morales-Carrión, op. cit., pp. 147–151.
85. Muñoz-Rivera's views on the island's future status are found in Cayetano Coll y Toste, *Boletín Histórico de Puerto Rico* (San Juan, 1926), Vol. 13, pp. 355–358; Hostos, "Madre Isla," op. cit.
86. Henry Wells, *The Modernization of Puerto Rico: A Political Study of Changing Values and Institutions* (Cambridge, Mass., 1969), pp. 76–79.
87. Ibid.
88. Davis' reorganization of the legal system is explained in Berbusse, op. cit., pp. 98–100.
89. Ibid.
90. For details about this hurricane, see, Salivia, Luis A., *Historia de los Temporales de Puerto Rico,1508–1949* (San Juan, 1950), pp. 255–277.

91. Ibid.

92. Ibid.

93. Berbusse, op. cit., p. 104.

94. Berbusse, op. cit., pp. 104–05.

95. Letter from George W. Davis to Elihu Root, Secretary of War, February 26, 1900. Cited in Berbusse, op. cit., p. 105.

96. Davis electoral reforms are discussed in Blanca Silvestrini and María D. Luque de Sánchez, *Historia de Puerto Rico: Trayectoria de un Pueblo* (San Juan, 1987), p. 384; Berbusse, op. cit., pp. 105-06.

97. Ibid, p. 116.

98. Elihu Root, "The Principles of Colonial Policy," in his book, *The Military and Colonial Policy of the United States: Addresses and Reports* (Cambridge, Mass., 1916), pp. 163–165.

99. Ibid.

100. Ibid.

101. The Trinidadian model is discussed in Jan Rogozinski, *A Brief History of the Caribbean* (New York, 1992), pp. 192–193.

102. Ibid.

103. Miles' Proclamation, "To the Inhabitants of Porto Rico," in U.S. War Department, *Military Government of Puerto Rico from October 18, 1898 to April 30, 1900* (Washington, D.C., 1902). Reprint appears in Wagenheim and Jiménez de Wagenheim, *The Puerto Ricans*, p. 94.

Chapter Ten, pp. 227–262

1. Blanca Silvestrini and María Dolores Luque. *Historia de Puerto Rico: Trayectoria de un pueblo* (San Juan, 1987), p. 298.

2. Ibid, p. 299.

3. Ibid, p. 301.

4. Ibid, p. 302.

5. Ibid.

6. Ibid.

7. Alejandro Tapia. *Mis Memorias* (San Juan, 1971), p. 17.

8. The tendency of the Puerto Rican rural population to live in scattered fashion was reported by many Spanish chroniclers and foreign visitors. It was first mentioned by Spanish officials since Alejandro O'Reilly's visit in 1765 and by American journalists in 1898.

9. For a detailed history of Lares, see Generoso Morales Muñoz, *Fundación del Pueblo de Lares* (San Juan, 1946), pp. 157–158.

10. Silvestrini and Luque, op. cit., p. 303.

11. For details about the formation of these and other towns, see Fernando Picó, *Historia General de Puerto Rico* (Río Piedras, Puerto Rico, 1986), pp. 149–150.

12. George Flinter, *Examen del estado actual de la Isla de Puerto Rico* (San Juan, 1970), pp. 41–42.

13. The lives of the Puerto Rican peasantry have been described by many Spanish offi-
    cials and foreign visitors. The most notable of these are: Alejandro O'Reilly (1765),
    Andre P. Ledru (1797), Pedro Tomás de Córdova (1831), George Flinter (1832) and
    Trumbull White (1898). For the jornaleros' own accounts, see references in Jiménez
    de Wagenheim, *Puerto Rico's Revolt for Independence*, op. cit., pp. 20–21; Henry K.
    Carroll, *Report on Porto Rico, with recommendations, 1899* (Treasury Department
    Doc. 2118) (Washington, D.C., 1900), p. 726. 14. Juan José Osuna. *A History of
    Education in Puerto Rico* (Río Piedras, Puerto Rico, 1949), pp, 17–19.
15. Ibid.
16. Ibid.
17. Ibid.
18. Letter from Don Nicolás Aguayo to Governor Marchesi, Caguas, May 31, 1866,
    which appears in Labor Gómez Acevedo, *Organización y Reglamentación en el
    Trabajo del Siglo XIX (Propietarios y Jornaleros)* (San Juan, 1970), pp. 469–475.
19. The work of the Cordero-Molina family is described by Ribes Tovar as part of the bio-
    graphical sketch of Rafael Cordero.
20. Details of Rafael Cordero's life appear in Federico Ribes-Tovar, *100 Outstanding
    Puerto Ricans* (New York, 1976), pp.57–60.
21. Silvestrini and Luque, op. cit., p. 318.
22. The contributions of Padre Rufo are described also in Ribes-Tovar, op. cit., pp. 56–57.
23. The Lares' school system was discussed by Antonio Rivera, "Ubicación de un
    Municipio: Lares," *Historia* vol. 5 no. 1, pp. 39–40.
24. Figures appear in José Julián Acosta, "Notas" to Iñigo Abbad y Lasierra *Historia
    Geográfica Civil y Natural de la Isla de San Juan de Puerto Rico* (San Juan, 1866)
    305; Carroll, Report, p. 200.
25. Silvestrini and Luque, op. cit., p. 320.
26. See, section on "Education" in Rubén del Rosario, et. al., *Breve Enciclopedia de la
    Cultura Puertorriqueña* (San Juan, 1976), pp.162–171.
27. Estimates appear in Acosta, "Notas," p. 305.
28. Rubén del Rosario, et. al., op. cit., pp. 166–68.
29. Ibid.
30. Ibid.
31. Trumbull White, *Our New Possessions* (American Home Reference Library, 1898),
    pp. 353–354.
32. Rubén del Rosario, et. al., op. cit., pp. 42–43.
33. Silvestrini and Luque, op. cit., p. 321.
34. Francisco Manrique Cabrera, *Historia de la literatura puertorriqueña* (Río Piedras,
    1982), p. 66.
35. Cabrera's couplets, first appeared in *El Investigador*, June 22, 1820. A copy of them
    can be read in Josefina Rivera de Àlvarez, *Antología General de la Literatura
    Puertorriqueña* (Prosa-Verso-Teatro), Tomo I (Madrid, 1982), pp. 60–61.
36. Ibid, pp. 66–67.
37. Comments by the literary critic María Teresa Babín in her essay, "A Special Voice:
    The Cultural Expression," in Morales-Carrión, *Puerto Rico*, op. cit, p. 324.
38. Asela Rodríguez de Laguna. "The Puerto Rican Literary Heritage," in *Puerto Rico:
    500 Years of Change and Continuity* (Washington, D.C., 1991), pp. 47–54.

39. Details about Rodríguez de Tió's poetry appear in Manrique Cabrera, op. cit., pp. 212–15; a short biography can be found in Rubén del Rosario, et. al., op. cit., pp. 393–95.

40. One of the best sources for Tapia's writings is Manrique Cabrera, op. cit., pp. 114–26; for a short biography, see Rubén del Rosario, et. al., op. cit., pp. 418–22.

41. Short biographies of Hostos are found in Federico Ribes-Tovar, *100 Outstanding Puerto Ricans* (New York, 1976), pp. 99–103; Rubén del Rosario, et. al., op. cit., pp. 238–240.

42. Eugenio María de Hostos, "Discurso", Leído en la Academia de Bellas Letras de Santiago, Chile (1872), published in Hostos, *Obras Completas* (Barcelona, 1960), Tomo III, pp. 45–55.

43. Information on Acosta appears in numerous sources. Two easily accessible are: Rives-Tovar, op. pp. 82–84; also in Rubén del Rosario, et. al., op. cit., pp. 11–12.

44. Coll y Toste's works are readily available. Biographical details are provided by Ribes-Tovar, op. cit., pp. 167–170; also by Rubén del Rosario, et. al., op. cit., pp. 96–97.

45. Salvador Brau's works are cited throughout this work.

46. See English translation of *La Charca*, published by Waterfront Press (Maplewood, NJ, 1982). Details on Zeno-Gandía's life and work appearn in Ribes-Tovar, op. cit., pp. 134–136.

47. One of the first to describe the folklore and way of life of the Puerto Rican peasants (jíbaros) was Manuel Alonso, in *El Gíbaro* (1849). Details about the "aguinaldo" appear in a recent edition of Alonso's book (Editorial Cultural Puertorriqueña, 1896–1992), pp. 103–09; Marcelino Canino Salgado, *El Cantar Folklórico de Puerto Rico* (Río Piedras, Puerto Rico, 1986), pp. 58, 207–211 and pp. 254–255, 260.

48. Canino Salgado, Ibid, 254–55; see also by the same author, "Música y Baile" (1976) in Rubén del Rosario, et. al,. op. cit., pp. 307–316.

49. Canino Salgado, *Cantar Folklórico* p. 310; "Música y Baile," pp. 314–315; Alonso, op. cit., p. 107.

50. Description of the variety of popular dances appear in Alonso, Ibid, pp. 49–58.

51. Ibid.

52. Alonso, Ibid., pp. 54–55.

53. The information about the origin of the danza was taken from Salvador Brau's essay, " La danza puertorriqueña", which appears as part of his *Ensayos,* op. cit., pp. 77–91 (the specific reference about its birth in Havana is found on p. 83); for other discussions on this topic, see Marisa Rosado, compiler. "Ensayos sobre la danza puertorriqueña" (San Juan, 1977); see also Canino Salgado, "Música y Baile," pp. 310–311.

54. Silvestrini and Luque, op. cit., 334–335.

55. Ibid.

56. Ibid.

57. Ibid; Rubén del Rosario, et. al., op. cit., pp. 301–303.

58. Cruz Monclova, op. cit., vol. 1, pp. 362, 498.

59. Fernando Picó, "Mitos y Realidades en la Historia de la Familia Puertorriqueña en la Zona Cafetalera en el Siglo 19", in Homines, vol. 7, nums. 1 & 2 (Feb.–Dec. 1983), pp. 223–226.

60. Manrique Cabrera, op. cit., pp. 60–62.

61. Osiris Delgado, "Pintura", in Rubén del Rosario et al., op. cit., pp. 349–358; Marimar

Benítez, "A Glance at the Art of Puerto Rico." in *Puerto Rico: 500 Years of Change and Continuity* (Washington, D.C., 1991), pp. 27–35.

62. Ibid.
63. Ibid.
64. Osiris Delgado, "Escultura", in Rubén del Rosario et. al., op. cit., pp. 178–183.
65. Lidio Cruz Monclova, op. cit., Tomo I, pp. 180; Information for the female rebels of Lares is available in the multiple biographical sketches that exist under each of their names.
66. The best examples of this legal reality are found in the notary records of the various municipalities, found at the Archivo General de Puerto Rico in San Juan. Some of the examples used were: Camuy, 1866–69, box 1702; Lares, 1844–1856, box 1430; Mayagüez, "Asuntos Varios" (Bound Documents), vol. 1 & 2 (1866, 1867, 1869).
67. Félix Matos Rodríguez, "Street Vendors, Peddlers, Shop Owners and Domestics: Some Aspects of Women's Economic Roles in Nineteenth Century San Juan, Puerto Rico, 1820–1870." Unpublished paper (excerpt from his Ph.D dissertation), provided by Matos.
68. Ibid.
70. Fernando Picó, "Mitos y realidades...", pp. 223–226.
71. Félix Matos Rodríguez, "Lavanderas y domésticas en San Juan en el Siglo XIX: Control Socioeconómico y Espacio Urbano en las Décadas Previas a la Abolición de la Esclavitud," Paper presented at LASA Conference, Atlanta, Georgia, March 1994.
72. Olga Jiménez de Wagenheim, "The Puerto Rican Woman in the 19th Century: An Agenda for Research," *Revista/Review Interamericana*, vol. XI, No. 2 (Summer 1981), pp. 196–202.
73. Ibid; María de F. Barceló Miller, "Voto, Colonialismo y Clase: La Lucha por el Sufragio Femenino en Puerto Rico, 1896-1935". Ph.D. dissertation (Departamento de Historia, U.P.R., 1993), pp. 27–29.
74. Ibid, pp. 30–31.
75. Ibid, pp. 26–27.
76. Ibid, pp. 34–39.
77. Ibid.
78. Gladys Jiménez Muñoz, "A Storm Dressed in Skirts: Ambivalence in the Debate on Women's Suffrage in Puerto Rico, 1927–1929", Ph.D. dissertation, SUNY-Binghamton, 1993, ch. 2, p. 37.
79. Barceló Miller, op. cit., p. 6.
80. Salvador Brau, "La campesina", in Brau, *Ensayos: Disquisiciones Sociológicas* (Río Piedras: Editorial Edil, 1972), pp. 93–122; see also, Brau, "Las clases jornaleras de Puerto Rico", in Ibid, pp. 26, 32, 36.
81. See Lizabeth Paravisini-Gebert, "Esquema biográfico de Ana Roqué", in *Luz y Sombra* (San Juan, 1991), pp. 151–159; Barcelo-Miller, op. cit., pp. 39–40.
82. Ángela Negrón Muñoz, "Ana Roqué de Duprey", *Mujeres de Puerto Rico: desde el período de colonización hasta el primer tercio del siglo XX* (San Juan, 1935), pp. 104–111.
83. Cited in Barceló Miller, op. cit., p. 40.
84. Trumbull White, op. cit., p. 354; Osuna, op. cit., pp. 98–99.
85. Isabel Picó de Hernández, "The History of Women's Struggle for Equality in Puerto

Rico", in Edna Acosta-Belén and Elia Hidalgo-Christensen, editors. *The Puerto Rican Woman* (New York, 1979), p. 26.

86. Osuna, op. cit.

87. Details about the history of labor organization in Puerto Rico were compiled from several sources, including: Antonio J. González, "Apuntes para la historia del movimiento sindical de Puerto Rico: 1896–1941", *Revista de Ciencias Sociales*, vo. 1, no. 3 (Septiembre, 1957), pp. 499–568; Angel G. Quintero-Rivera, editor. *Lucha Obrera en Puerto Rico* (Documents) (Río Piedras, n.d.), Preface, pp. 5–11.

88. Quintero-Rivera, op. cit., pp. 13–15; Gonzalo F. Córdova, *Santiago Iglesias: Creador del Movimiento Obrero de Puerto Rico* (Río Piedras, 1980), ch. 1.

89. Córdova, Ibid, p. 37; see also a biography of Iglesias in Rives-Tovar, op. cit., pp. 198–202.

90. Galvin, op. cit., ch. 1: Edgardo Meléndez, *Puerto Rico's Statehood Movement* (Westport, Ct, 1988), pp. 25–29, 36–38.

91. Ibid.

92. Ibid.

93. Ibid.

94. USDW, 1899 Census, pp. 41; White, op. cit., pp. 281, 286.

95. Ibid, pp. 293–94.

96. Ibid.

97. Ibid, pp. 288–292.

98. USDW, 1899 Census, pp. 45–46,61, 354, 355, tables 39 & 40. Cited in James Dietz, *Economic History of Puerto Rico: Institutional Change and Capitalist Development* (Princeton, 1986), p. 67.

99. Ibid.

100. Wolf, "San José", cited in Dietz, op. cit., p. 65.

101. Bergad, *Coffee and the Growth of Agrarian Capitalism*, op. cit., pp. 64–65.

102. Dietz, op cit., p. 48.

103. An example of this point is found in Morales-Carrión, *A Political History*, op. cit., p. 137.

Index